A Unique Flight

Published in Australia in 2008 by
This edition published in 2009
New Holland Publishers (Australia) Pty Ltd
Sydney • Auckland • London • Cape Town
1/66 Gibbes St Chatswood NSW 2067 Australia
218 Lake Road Northcote Auckland 0627 New Zealand
86 Edgware Road London W2 2EA United Kingdom
80 McKenzie Street Cape Town 8001 South Africa

10 9 8 7 6 5 4 3 2

National Library of Australia cataloguing in publication data

A unique flight : the historic aircraft collection of the Australian War Memorial / Michael Nelmes

Nelmes, Michael V, 1964-
352 p. : ill. (some col.), ports. ; 29 cm.
ISBN   9781741107685
Notes
Includes Glossary of terms; Appendices; Selected sources, Notes, and Index.
Subjects   Australia. - Royal Australian Air Force - History - World War, 1939-1945. | Australian War Memorial. | World War, 1939-1945 - Pacific Area - Aerial operations, Australia. | Airplanes, Military - Australia - History. | Vietnam War, 1961-1975 - Aerial operations, Australia. | Korean War, 1950-1953 - Aerial operations, Australia. | Australia - History, Military.

4533251

ISBN: 9781741107685

Publisher: Fiona Schultz
Publishing Manager: Lliane Clarke
Designer: Barbara Cowan
Cover Design: Tania Gomes
Production Manager: Olga Dementiev
Printer: SNP/Leefung Printing Co., Ltd (China)

A Unique Flight

THE HISTORIC AIRCRAFT COLLECTION OF
THE AUSTRALIAN WAR MEMORIAL

Michael Nelmes

NEW
HOLLAND

CONTENTS

Foreword

Through war and peace, Qantas has served Australia for 87 years—and our history is synonymous with the development of Australian civil aviation.

Qantas is proud to partner with the Australian War Memorial and sponsor this important aircraft collection, which will enable the preservation and restoration of Australian wartime aviation history. We know it will serve as a permanent reminder of the skill and courage of all those Australians who served their country in aviation through times of war.

The aircraft collection holds particular significance for Qantas: the airline was founded in 1920 by three First World War veterans—Wilmot Hudson Fysh and Paul McGinness, both aviators, and Arthur Baird, who had served as a flight mechanic.

Through the years Qantas has played a significant auxiliary role in Australia's military endeavours, keeping open vital air links, transporting Australian troops and supplies, providing evacuation and rescue missions, and maintaining aircraft. Qantas Defence Services still provides aviation maintenance services for current and future Australian Defence Force programs.

The Memorial's collection illustrates the historic advances in aviation technology, from the first fragile biplanes to the birth of the jet engine. This book showcases 29 complete aircraft, including the Lancaster bomber 'G for George', a rare 1913 monoplane, and an Iroquois helicopter used in the Vietnam War.

The Qantas Group is proud to make a significant contribution to the restoration and conservation of so many unique aircraft, many of which have played their role in the Qantas story.

And we are pleased to play our role in reminding all Australians of the vital and enduring partnership between Australian civil aviation and our nation's security.

Alan Joyce
Chief Executive Officer, Qantas

Director's foreword

The Australian War Memorial is one of the great commemorative institutions in the world. Its museum galleries support its commemorative role and have been continually developed and reinvigorated over the years. The Memorial's broad and diverse collection is fundamental to this.

The Qantas aircraft collection is a significant part of the overall collection: for me as an engineer, it is one of my favourite parts. Aircraft and the stories of those who flew and serviced them have always captured the public imagination, and the collection has continued to draw many interested visitors over the years. Some aircraft are famous in their own right: the Lancaster bomber 'G for George', the best known aircraft flown by Australians during the Second World War, survived some 90 operations over occupied Europe. Australian air aces have found a place in Australia's history: the stories of Harry Cobby, Clive Caldwell and Keith Truscott have an important place in the galleries, as do some famous aces of former enemy forces, such as Manfred von Richthofen, the 'Red Baron'.

The extensive scope of the aircraft collection is in itself a major attraction. Our First World War aircraft have always been popular, and highlight the bravery of those who flew what were often barely tested machines and relatively fragile airframes. For those interested in the technology of flight, the collection illustrates remarkable advances, from the biplanes of the First World War to the more advanced aircraft of the Second World War, and on into the age of the jet engine, which first appears in our collection with the German Me262 and the MiG-15 and Meteor flown in the Korean War. Of course, the story does not end there, and the Memorial continues to enhance its collection whenever possible.

As a museum we must do much more than simply house a collection. We have a responsibility to conserve it, to display it and, using modern methods, to engage the public's interest. The Memorial has over many years put a great deal of effort into conserving its aircraft. The three-year $1 million conservation project for 'G for George' was a major undertaking that involved the work of many staff and volunteers. The bomber's 'object theatre' exhibition, titled *Striking by night*, brings the aircraft to life and continues to be one of our most engaging and thought-provoking presentations.

Currently the Memorial is undertaking a major restoration project on five of its First World War aircraft. Such aircraft in well-preserved condition are becoming quite rare, as are the technical skills required to work on them. This venture has provided a rare opportunity for cooperation with international experts in the field.

It has been very satisfying to see this book brought to fruition. Its author, Mike Nelmes, is to be congratulated for the skill and dedication he delivered to the project, and I should thank Mike's branch head, Nola Anderson, and his colleagues, Mike Cecil, John White and Rebecca Britt, for their encouragement and assistance. Finally, special thanks are due to our sponsors, Qantas, who have generously supported the Memorial and its aircraft collection.

Steve Gower AO AO (Mil)
Director, Australian War Memorial

Australian War Memorial
Australian Tourism Awards
Major Tourist Attraction
HALL OF FAME

Acknowledgements

The original research and draft work from which this book evolved was funded by the Australian War Memorial's Major Research Program. Its final steps towards publication are due to the initiative and foresight of the Australian War Memorial, and I would like to especially acknowledge its Director, Steve Gower, in this regard. The guidance of Mike Cecil, Head of Military Heraldry and Technology and the support of Nola Anderson, Assistant Director, National Collection, have also been greatly appreciated. Memorial editors Robert Nichols and Andrew McDonald have contributed greatly to the final form of the book. Ashley Ekins (Head, Military History), Nigel Steel, Karl James and others reviewed the text and made many useful suggestions. The Memorial's production managers for the project, Rebecca Britt and Linda Byrne, carried it through its final stages. I am indebted to all for helping to turn this project into reality.

Research into the Memorial's aircraft collection has been the ongoing work of many people since the early 1980s. John White (Senior Curator of Military Technology) has, over that period, conducted a great deal of the research drawn upon here; he has also offered useful insights, improvements and corrections to the draft. Foundation work was begun in the 1970s by Peter Burness (at the time, Curator of Relics), and expanded in the 1980s when the Memorial first engaged specialist curators, Jim Heaton and Mark Clayton, for its military technology collection. David Crotty and Chris Goddard subsequently researched several of the aircraft. Not only curatorial but physical conservation work has brought to light many historical insights, and the Memorial's conservation staff at the Treloar Technology Centre, Mitchell, ACT, have conducted or overseen much of this work.

Other staff of the Memorial to whom recognition is due include those of the Research Centre, Document Control Centre, Photographs Film and Sound Section, and Multimedia Services. The latter section, led by Hans Reppin and including Fiona Silsby, Roland Henderson and Adam Kropinski-Myers, were responsible for the high quality display and interior images.

Memorial volunteers have also contributed many years of work to the research drawn upon in these pages: these include former RAAF navigator Alan Storr, in particular, who produced a good deal of material used in the book; former RAAF engine fitter Derek Fowler and former army pilot and Memorial historian Colonel David Chinn (who died while the book was being written), who interviewed surviving aircrew of the Beaufort and Canberra aircraft.

Bob Piper, David Wilson and staff of the RAAF Historical Section (now the Office of Air Force History), Department of Defence, arranged access to relevant records and were of invaluable assistance to the Memorial's curatorial staff and volunteer researchers from the early 1980s onwards. Research by aviation historians including Colin Owers (1914–18 aircraft), Ken Merrick (*Luftwaffe* aircraft), Bob Waugh (1914–18 German aircraft) and David Vincent (RAAF aircraft) has also been used.

Numerous publications (see Sources) have proven invaluable in contributing relevant contextual background to the aircraft types. For the aircraft flown by the Australian armed forces, the *In Australian service* series of books written by Stewart Wilson and published by Aerospace Publications were particularly useful.

The efforts of innumerable military and government personnel, over nearly a century, in securing the aircraft for the Memorial's collection in the first place should also be recognised. Were it not for their foresight and appreciation of the importance of preserving our heritage for posterity, mixed with a good dose of the Australian penchant for collecting 'war trophies', this collection would not have come into being.

Finally, I thank my partner, Angela O'Neil, for her encouragement.

Using this book

Where possible, incidents involving the individual aircraft in question are recounted, followed by an 'in context' section containing a more general discussion about the type and its Australian connections. The latter has been kept minimal, as this information is in most cases readily available elsewhere. In the few cases in which little or nothing is known of the specific aircraft's war history, incidents and historical notes relating to the type more generally are expanded upon.

Where applicable, figures such as altitudes, bomb weights, armament calibres, fuel capacities and engine power are given in the contemporary (and, in some cases, continuing) aviation usage of imperial measurements. The conversions are as follows:

1 foot (ft) = 0.305 m
1 pound (lb) = 0.454 kg
1 horsepower (hp) = 0.746 kW
1 gallon (gal) = 4.55 l
1 mile per hour (mph) = 1.61 km/h

At the end of each chapter are three sections, as follows:

Timeline

This is a summary of the known chronology of the individual aircraft. Minor movements for repair or storage are not generally included.

Data

Where possible, data provided relates to the particular aircraft variant or sub-type in question. Production figures, for example, are for the variant rather than the general type unless otherwise stated. Data is taken from a variety of official sources as well as reputable publications, such as Jane's *All the world's aircraft* and relevant Putnam and *Aircraft in profile* aviation books. Owing to the variety of aircraft types covered, the data headings cannot be made entirely consistent throughout.

Notes on colour scheme

This section provides, in most cases, an overview of the paint scheme and markings currently applied (either original or replicated) to the individual aircraft. In cases in which the current scheme is inaccurate, this is stated and the correct wartime scheme given. Notes on markings are intended as a guide only and do not generally include exact locations and sizes, nor the more minor markings (such as handling stencils).

Introduction

The Australian War Memorial is custodian to one of the world's great collections of military aircraft. Because this institution is unique in the world, its aircraft collection is also unique in its purpose: to illustrate and enhance the story of Australians at war with examples of the air technology which our nation and its enemies used. For the most part they are not simply type examples, for the individual aircraft and their former crewmen have their own stories to tell. The aircraft are integrated into a much wider collection which not only tells their story, but also commemorates their sacrifice. In that sense, the collection is unlike that of any aviation or military air museum.

When the First World War ended in November 1918, the Australian War Records Section (from which the Memorial evolved) administered an exhibition at Australia House in London. Prominent among the displays were examples of some of the aircraft used in that conflict by both the Australian Flying Corps (AFC) and the German Air Service. Their inclusion not only graphically illustrated the technology that had brought war into the 'third dimension', but, equally importantly, allowed visitors to appreciate more fully the experience of Australians in the air war.

Three subsequent exhibitions brought these aircraft to an Australian audience before the Memorial itself was built. The first was at the Exhibition Building in Melbourne from 1920. Augmenting the aircraft previously displayed in London were a number of others still then in service with the renamed Australian Air Corps, which in 1921 became the Royal Australian Air Force. That same year, some of the aircraft went to Adelaide for exhibition by the Motor Traders' Association of South Australia. Then in 1925, after a fire destroyed some of the aircraft in Melbourne, many were transported to Sydney following the Memorial's relocation there. They remained there for a decade until the exhibition's closure for its ultimate display in the purpose-built Australian War Memorial in Canberra, which was delayed until 1941 by the Depression and the coming of the Second World War.

Incorporated into the design of the Memorial's new building was Aeroplane Hall (known for a time as Bradbury Aircraft Hall, then simply Aircraft Hall). Over some 70 years, this relatively small gallery space has played host to an impressive array of aircraft and artefacts illustrating Australia's part in air warfare. At first its focus was the First World War, but over the years, as the Second World War, Korea and Vietnam were added to the Memorial's collecting charter, these wars too have been represented.

When Aeroplane Hall first opened, the First World War machines exhibited were only about 25 years old, and the AFC veterans who knew them at first hand were in their forties. Those veterans are now gone, and the ranks of those from the following world war, represented in a major changeover of the displays in 1955, are also now rapidly thinning. The lasting legacies of all these airmen and women are the personal memorabilia and records they leave behind, nearly 10,000 of the 102,000 names on the Memorial's Roll of Honour, and the surviving aircraft they once flew in and serviced.

The size of Aircraft Hall allows only a small part of the Memorial's aircraft collection to be displayed at any one time. During the 1990s, an interim answer to this problem was to open to the public, for two days per week, the Memorial's Treloar Technology Centre storage facility in the Canberra industrial suburb of Mitchell. However, the long-term display capacity was enhanced by the development of a new purpose-built large technology display gallery at the rear of the Memorial's main building. Named ANZAC Hall, it was opened in 2001. In the Second World War and *Conflicts 1945 to today* galleries, particular aircraft are integral to the design layouts.

The aim of this book is to bring the Memorial's aircraft alive by relating some of the extraordinary events that surrounded them and those who served with them. Without such historical connections, the interest and relevance of these aircraft would be purely technological. Technology is, of course, a crucial element of warfare in its own right. In that respect, the collection can impart a great deal of understanding of how the aeronautical engineers of more than half a dozen nations, over nearly a century, have tackled a multitude of problems in the design and production of such machines. Some pertinent technological background is discussed, though not extensively. More thorough treatments are readily available elsewhere.

The most meaningful artefacts are often those associated with known personalities and events, as they can best provide an understanding of and an emotional involvement with the part played by Australians in aerial warfare. The following narratives record the tragedies of war as well as the adventures experienced by airmen. Most of the Memorial's aircraft are weapons of war, and should be viewed in that context. Many of the people whose lives crossed paths with them did not live to tell their stories, while others survived with memories they would rather forget. By learning of their experiences and hardships, we can gain a greater insight into the experience of war.

The Memorial's collection of aircraft is diverse, yet focused on examples with significant Australian wartime connections. In recent years, staff and the visiting public have seen exciting developments for the collection. Increased funding has allowed for better display facilities, including the complete refurbishment of Aircraft Hall during 1999–2000 and the subsequent opening of ANZAC Hall. Equally importantly, intensive conservation programs at the Memorial's Treloar Technology Centre and elsewhere are now allowing previously undisplayed aircraft finally to reach public view, many portrayed in evocative settings. With this increased exposure, it seems appropriate to tell their stories in one publication for the first time. By doing so, the Memorial's aircraft collection can be used together to provide a broad overview of the history of Australian wartime aviation up to the Vietnam War.

The conservation and restoration projects involved in preparing the aircraft for public display have, for the most part, not been covered in detail in this book. To do this work justice would require a book in itself. A great number of hours of planning and labour, both paid and unpaid, by Memorial staff and volunteers, engineering contractors, military personnel past and present, and enthusiasts has been spent in preserving each of them for future generations. In some cases, much of an aircraft's skin or fabric, and many of its components, have had to be remade. It is, however, the Memorial's policy to retain as much original material as possible. While many historic aircraft around the world tend to be restored to their appearance when first built (or better), one of the great strengths of the Memorial's collection is its originality. Indeed, it includes some of the world's most authentic examples of historic military aircraft.

You are invited to explore, in these pages and in the displayed aircraft if you are able to visit, some of the stories hidden beneath fabric and aluminium skins.

First World War
1914–1918

DEPERDUSSIN CFS.5

Point Cook, Victoria
9 MARCH 1914

Over the boggy coastal plain south-west of Melbourne, a frail but sleek-looking monoplane made its 50-m take-off run, then steadily gained height. It was a rare calm moment on the normally windswept landscape—a good time for a demonstration circuit of the aerodrome.

Perched on a light timber seat in the narrow fuselage, behind a small alloy fuel tank, sat a slightly built, 30-year-old Englishman and former solicitor. Lieutenant Henry Petre's hands clutched a wooden control wheel linked by wires to the elevators and to the rear undersides of the wings. By turning the wheel, the wires warped the linen-covered wings to change their angle of attack, banking the aircraft with frustrating slowness; at his feet was a pivoting bar linked by wire to the rudder. That was it, as far as control was concerned. As for instruments, they consisted of an oil 'pulsator' flow indicator, and the pilot's eyes and ears.

The 'dirty dustbin'.
Lieutenant Henry Petre, Instructor, Central Flying School

One of the two Central Flying School Deperdussins in the Point Cook assembly shop. AWM A03964

Petre had more flying experience than most (he had built his own aircraft and been a pilot at Brooklands for the company which built his present mount), but even he found the lack of response difficult to get used to. Although the Deperdussin had introduced some significant technological developments, the design was now four years old and there had been advances since it had been considered cutting-edge. The Wright-patented idea of wing-warp banking, for example, had by now generally been replaced by the more effective aileron technology (although the Germans were to employ wing-warp banking successfully well into the First World War with their Fokker monoplanes). Also, a 35-hp engine was no longer considered powerful enough, even in such a light airframe.

Australia's Minister for Defence, the Hon. Edward Millen, visiting Point Cook, looked on from the safety of the ground. The Anzani three-cylinder engine coughed and died, a not uncommon occurrence. The little monoplane immediately descended steeply, heading straight for some telephone lines. Petre turned sharply to avoid them before drag won over lift, and the Deperdussin side-slipped into the ground. He was not badly hurt, thankfully—probably just thrown into an embarrassing heap, as he had no seat belt—but his faith in the aircraft that was quickly earning the nickname 'dirty dustbin' was dashed, and he did not order its repair. Thus ended the week-long Australian army flying career of Deperdussin trainer CFS.4, leaving its sister machine CFS.5 at the Central Flying School as its (non-flying) monoplane trainer.

◄ ►

This ignominious end for the sole flying monoplane of the Australian Flying Corps (AFC) did nothing to allay the general belief among the higher echelons that military aviation was a useless and expensive fad. There were a few, however, who had the foresight both to see past such incidents and to appreciate the potential that aviation held. Fortunately they also had the influence to keep it alive during this crucial weaning period. From today's perspective, in comparison with the speed of development in later decades, it seems that aviation was slow to develop during the few years after the Wright Brothers' first powered flight in 1903. In fact, a great deal of experimentation was taking place and progress was being made, but these experiments often led to dead ends. By March 1914 there had been numerous advances in aerodynamics, airframe design and engine technology, but it would take a war to force more major breakthroughs. And that war was, in fact, just months away.

In August 1913 four army mechanics at Victoria Barracks in Melbourne had been given the task of uncrating and assembling what was at the time a very unusual consignment. Ordered a year earlier (three months, in fact, before the establishment of the AFC by Military Order No. 570 of 22 October 1912[1]), this shipment from Britain had arrived in Sydney at the end of May aboard the SS *Demosthenes*. It was Australia's first batch of military aircraft: two BE.2a biplanes, a Bristol Boxkite pusher-type biplane, and the two monoplanes from the British Deperdussin Company.

The Memorial's Deperdussin displayed in ANZAC Hall soon after its opening in 2001.
AWM RELAWM12614

When the crates were opened, it was found that the fragile aircraft had suffered in transit. The 'rolling-taxi' and 'flying-taxi' Deperdussins[2], which had cost the Australian government £450 and £480 respectively, had been packed in damp English conditions. In the heat of their voyage across the equator, the fabric had quickly rotted, and already needed replacing.[3] In December the aircraft were duly re-covered by the Commonwealth Clothing Factory.

In early 1913 Henry Petre and another eager flyer, 27-year-old Eric Harrison of Victoria, had begun the task of establishing Australia's first military flying school. Grazing land at Point Cook was procured for £6,000 and the Central Flying School was officially created on 7 March 1913. Harrison had learned to fly the Boxkite in Britain with just half an hour of tuition. It was another year before the Boxkite and the 'flying-taxi' (or 'school type') Deperdussin took to the air on Sunday, 1 March 1914, with Harrison and Petre at the controls, respectively. With these short flights, Australian military aviation effectively began.

The Deperdussin monoplane followed a basic layout similar to the 1909 Blériot XI, which was equally underpowered and sluggish. To be fair, most aircraft of the period had poor handling characteristics by later standards. In a slight gust of wind a wing could drop, requiring full opposite controls to recover. To avoid a wing stall the aircraft was turned mostly with rudder only in a flat skid; in any case, wing warping was much less effective than modern ailerons in banking an aircraft. Frank Tallman writes of flying the Blériot XI:

> There is still no experience in my years of flying to equal the sick feeling you have when a wing goes down in gusty air and you head for the ground, unable to pick up the wing in spite of full opposite control ... Beyond gentle turns, one is quite content to just fly along at about 40-odd mph [65 km/h] and enjoy the air-conditioned ride.[4]

Landing approach was made with a nearly 30-degree nose-down attitude, power off, directly into the wind if possible and while praying for no sudden crosswinds. Another limitation was the unreliability of the aero engines of the day, the air-cooled Anzani being no exception. Overheating during sustained flight was not uncommon. Louis Blériot was lucky that his Anzani continued to run for the whole 37 minutes of his historic 1909 crossing of the English Channel in his Blériot XI.

Harrison was present to oversee the completion of the Deperdussins in Britain and to receive them after testing at Farnborough by the certifier, Mr W.L. Brock, in February 1913. At Point Cook, CFS.5 was intended merely to familiarise students with taxiing and ground handling, its engine reportedly rigged for insufficient power to lift off. However, some students managed to break the rules (of both the army and physics) and hop it into the air. Spliced joins still evident on the four fuselage longerons are testimony to at least one incident of rough treatment. When not in use, the monoplanes were housed with the BE.2a biplanes in a tent hangar that was sheltered from wind by a small pine and gum tree plantation at the entrance to the property. The aerodrome had been a sheep pasture, now with long grass as the sheep had been moved away.

During the eight flying courses conducted at Point Cook during 1914–18, CFS.5 was derided by the less kind of its pupils. Nevertheless it gave them some of their first steps in aircraft handling in preparation for the rigours of combat flying in Mesopotamia and Egypt, and later on the Western Front. Each course lasted three months and consisted mainly of flying the Boxkite. Aircraft were then still a complete novelty; Richard Williams (later Air Marshal Sir Richard Williams KBE CB DSO) had seen his first aircraft only a few months before graduating from the first course with three other pilots in August 1914.

Henry Petre was soon promoted to captain. Just over a year after his first flight at Point Cook, he went off to command Australia's first air unit to see action, the Mesopotamian Half-Flight. He was later awarded the Distinguished Service Order and the Military Cross, before returning to law practice in London in 1919. Eric Harrison had led an even earlier but uneventful overseas expedition, to German New Guinea in September 1914, and later reached the rank of group captain in the air force. Along with Williams, both Petre and Harrison can legitimately be considered as the fathers of the RAAF.

The technological strides in aviation during the First World War made the surviving Deperdussin an obsolete curiosity well before the war ended. In 1920 it was transferred to the care of the Australian War Museum (as the Australian War Memorial then was) for display in the Exhibition Building, Sydney. Surviving a 1936 reduction of the Memorial's aircraft collection, its subsequent display in Canberra included a period during the 1980s suspended from the ceiling of the Memorial's Aeroplane Hall. It holds the distinction of being Australia's oldest surviving military aircraft.

The Deperdussin's open cockpit is the simplest of all the Memorial's aircraft. Forward of it is the fuel tank. AWM RELAWM12614

The Deperdussin in context

In 1910 entrepreneur Armand Deperdussin founded the Société des Aéroplanes Deperdussin near Reims, France, and employed engineer Louis Béchereau as his chief designer. Their early monoplane design (often cited, apparently unofficially, as Type A), of which CFS.4 and CFS.5 were examples, appeared the same year. Racing developments with up to 80-hp engines soon followed.

Numerous French aircraft companies also had British equivalents. In early 1912 the British Deperdussin Aeroplane Company was formed at Highgate in London by D.L. Santoni and Royal Navy Lieutenant J.C. Porte, both of whom later that year founded the British Anzani company, which built the Deperdussin's French-designed engines. It was from the British Deperdussin Aeroplane Company that Australia's two Deperdussins were ordered.

The Australian government's choice in July 1913 of a monoplane design for two of its military trainers was seen by some as a gamble. Deperdussin had made its name with record-breaking monoplane racers, the hot-rods of their day, which many considered to be structurally unsound because of their monoplane design. A fatal crash in Britain in September 1912 had, in fact, led to a five-month ban on flying monoplanes by the Royal Flying Corps (RFC).

In 1913, the year that the two Deperdussins were sent to Australia, the company's latest monoplane racers won two prestigious events: the first Schneider Trophy at Monaco, and the Gordon Bennett air race at Deperdussin's own aerodrome near Reims (by then a world aviation centre). In the latter event, the aircraft set a world absolute speed record of 204 km/h. By the time of the victory, Armand Deperdussin had been convicted of forgery and embezzlement. His fall from grace spelt the end of his involvement with the aircraft and eventually led him to take his own life. However, his company, which had grown to employ 180 workmen,[5] was saved in 1914 by a consortium led by none other than Louis Blériot. It became the Société Pour L'Aviation et ses Dérivés (SPAD), for which Béchereau was to design some of the most renowned scouts of the First World War.

TIMELINE—CFS.5

1912	(Jul) Ordered by Australian army
1913	(Feb) Tested at Farnborough, UK; (May) arrived Melbourne
1914	(Mar) First flown at Central Flying School, Point Cook, Vic.
1920	Transferred to Australian War Museum; displayed in Exhibition Building, Melbourne, and in Adelaide for the Motor Traders Association of SA; later to Exhibition Building, Sydney
1941–55	Displayed in AWM Aeroplane Hall, Canberra
1956	Loaned to RAAF Museum, Point Cook
1970	Returned for display in AWM Aeroplane Hall; suspended during 1980s
1990	Stored at AWM annexe, Mitchell
2001	Briefly displayed in AWM ANZAC Hall; returned to storage

DATA

Type	Rolling-taxi type monoplane
Designed by	M. Béchereau (Deperdussin, France)
Manufacturer	British Deperdussin Aeroplane Company, Highgate, UK
Role	Single-seat ground trainer
Used by	Australian Flying Corps
Type entered service	1910 (1913 in AFC)
Identification	CFS.5 (Australian Army Central Flying School No. 5)
Powerplant	British Anzani Company 3-cylinder 'Y' air-cooled engine of 35 hp driving a two-blade Rapid propeller
Wingspan	8.83 m
Length	7.62 m
Max. take-off weight	227 kg
Max. speed	80 km/h

NOTES ON COLOUR SCHEME

The fabric covering the wings, tailplane and tail, replaced in 1913, c. 1937 and again in the 1950s, is of linen finished in clear dope (originally Emallite) giving a bone colour. 'CFS 5' is believed to have been painted in black on the rudder. The dark varnished timber and wire fuselage structure is uncovered, although it may have been covered during its service, and metal fittings have been painted in black japan.

At least one photo believed to depict the flying trainer, CFS.4, in the air shows a covered fuselage. Interestingly, it has been said that an uncovered fuselage would enhance stability by virtue of the increased drag.

ALBATROS D.VA D.5390/17

Armentières–Deulement region of Flanders, northern France

1452 HOURS, 17 DECEMBER 1917

Six Albatros D.VA scouts of the Royal Prussian *Jagdstaffel (Jasta)* 29 were out in search of prey: perhaps a lone, lumbering British reconnaissance aircraft. Soon, as hoped for, one presented itself. It was an RE.8, a slower, heavier and less agile machine than the Albatros, and no match in combat for the sleek German scout.

The RE.8, sometimes called the 'Harry Tate' (after a contemporary Scottish music hall comedian) by its crews, had joined 69 (Australian) Squadron RFC,[6] six months earlier. In its reconnaissance role the plane served as an airborne observation platform to provide an elevated view of the battlefront. This was an absolute necessity for the hard-pressed artillery batteries, but it came at the price of extreme danger for its crew, as Lieutenant J. Lionel Sandy of Sydney and his observer Sergeant Henry Hughes of Melbourne, well knew.

> ## *The most gallant action he had seen.*
> *F.M. Cutlack, official Australian Flying Corps historian*

An early RE.8 of 3 Squadron AFC. This example flew more hours than any British aircraft on the Western Front, and was later taken into the Memorial's collection. It is thought to have been destroyed by fire in 1924. AWM P00355.045

Leutnant Clauss's Albatros after being brought to 3 Squadron's airfield at Bailleul. AWM E01684

The two men were flying an RE.8 numbered A.3816. Using a Sterling 'spark transmitter' radio, they sent coded instructions to a central wireless station for relaying to the howitzer battery stations. By observing the fall of the shells, and sending back corrections, the men in the air allowed the gunners to 'range' their shots on the target. Artillery cooperation was one of the primary roles the squadron had been performing over France for three months now. It was a particularly useful role in the winter months, which often brought poor ground visibility. The first snow had fallen a few days earlier, but this cold Monday afternoon was clear, and Sandy and Hughes were taking advantage of the good visibility to range 8-in artillery fire for the 151st Siege Battery, Royal Garrison Artillery.

Half an hour into their flight, the routine mood of the operation changed in seconds as the Albatros scouts came in for the kill. The RE.8 may have been slow and lumbering but it could turn well in skilful hands, and 'Old Sandy', a 32-year-old Gallipoli veteran, tried his best chance. At full throttle he banked into a tight circle to give Hughes a clear shot with his Lewis machine-gun. If he missed, Sandy himself might be able to manoeuvre into position for a chance with his forward-firing Vickers machine-gun. It was probably Hughes who managed to hit one of the German scouts, sending a bullet through its fuel tank and into the upper thigh of its pilot, 24-year-old *Leutnant* Rudolf Clauss.

With all but a few litres of fuel gone, and undoubtedly fearing a fire with fuel leaking into the fuselage, Clauss landed his Albatros intact between Armentières and Ploegsteert

Leutnant Clauss's overboots, souvenired by Major Reed. AWM RELAWM00668

The Memorial's Albatros in Aeroplane Hall in 1999 (with propeller spinner removed for conservation work), just prior to the hall's refurbishment. At right is the SE5a. AWM PAIU1999/157.01

Wood. The aircraft came to a halt just inside the lines of the 2nd Australian Division, near the dugouts of the 21st Battalion. Major Alf Reed, a company commander in the 21st, wrote:

> Before the pilot had time to destroy it we seized him and I placed a guard over the plane … The pilot, a young German officer wearing an Iron Cross,[7] was brought to my dug-out, and I advised Brigade headquarters of what had occurred. The prisoner had a flesh-wound in one leg caused by shrapnel from one of the 'archies' [anti-aircraft gunners]. We dressed the wound after we had searched him.[8]

Reed's souvenir of the occasion was the pair of fur-lined, thigh-length flying boots that Clauss had left behind, one sporting a blood-stained bullet hole. In 1920 he donated them to the Australian War Museum to join the Albatros.

While Clauss's fighting days were coming to an abrupt end, Sandy continued to throw his RE.8 around the sky in what was described by a watching artillery officer as

Lieutenant J. Lionel Sandy, pilot of the RE.8 which shot down the Albatros. AWM P03945.001

the most gallant action he had seen. A second RE.8 joined the duel, then a third. After 13 minutes, far longer than most dogfights in 1917, the remaining five Albatros scouts left the scene. Lieutenants Jones and Hodgson in the second RE.8 crew flew alongside A.3816, before returning to base at Bailleul for ammunition. Sandy and Hughes had seemed uninjured. Yet as evening approached, apprehension grew for the crew; they had not returned to base, and were not sending radio signals.

Meanwhile, 69 Squadron hatched an audacious plan to retrieve the Albatros. At 8.00 that night the squadron's equipment officer, Captain Roderick Ross, took a brave and determined team out from Bailleul to the front lines near Armentières. Ross found Clauss, still under guard by the 21st Battalion, in pain from his thigh wound but able to walk. Under heavy fire from howitzers, the team went out to retrieve the downed aircraft, which they decided not to attempt to fly out. The nearby allied artillery fire made the men understandably nervous, but the muzzle flashes also gave them some illumination as they took the Albatros apart. It was a particularly cold night, and Ross noticed the water from the radiator freezing as it dripped out. When the wings were off, they trucked both the aircraft and Clauss back to Bailleul. Next day on the base there was 'much interest all day in the racy-looking bus', wrote 3 Squadron's Sergeant Francis Latimer in his diary. Clauss was sent to Southampton[9] in Britain, and spent 1918 as a prisoner of war.

The following afternoon, nearly a full day after Sandy and Hughes had gone missing, a telegram arrived from a hospital near St Pol: an RE.8 had come down a few kilometres north-east of town, and two dead crewmen were with the aircraft. A single German bullet had passed through Hughes's left lung and into Sandy's head. Incredibly, their RE.8 had been carried some 80 km by a north-east wind, before running out of fuel and coming down more or less intact—a testament to the aircraft's stability in flight and robust construction. It had ground-looped before coming to a halt, its throttle still fully open.

According to Captain Ross, the frozen body of Hughes, the observer, was found lying on the lower wing. Although mortally wounded, he had apparently retained or regained consciousness, and fell out of his compartment as he collapsed. Sandy and Hughes were posthumously recommended, unsuccessfully, for immediate awards of the Military Cross and the Distinguished Conduct Medal respectively.

◄ ►

Both the British and Australians were more interested in the Albatros than in its pilot. To the British it was the first intact example of its type, and a potential test-bed for enemy technology and

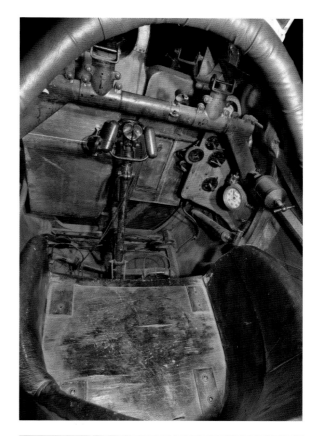

Cockpit of the Memorial's Albatros. AWM RELAWM04806.001

TIMELINE—D.5390/17

1917	(Aug) Built by Albatros Werke, served with *Jasta* 29; (Dec) force-landed in France
1918	Test flown in Britain; displayed in Australia House, London
1919	Shipped to Australia aboard the *Booral*
1920	Displayed at Melbourne Exhibition Buildings and in Adelaide for Motor Traders Association exhibition
1925–35	Displayed at AWM Sydney building
1927	AWM condition report lists many holes for repair, and a need for repainting
1941–66	Displayed in Aeroplane Hall
1966–68	Transported in RAAF Hercules from AWM store, Duntroon, to Sydney for restoration. Work begun by the Society of WW1 Aero Historians, and continued by Camden Museum of Aviation, including replacement of fabric and engine
1968–99	Displayed in Aeroplane Hall
1999–2007	Stored at AWM Treloar Technology Centre, ACT
2007–08	Restored and conserved at Treloar Technology Centre for *Over the front* exhibition, ANZAC Hall

DATA

Type	Albatros D.Va
Identity	D.5390/17 (German Air Service) G.101 (Royal Flying Corps)
Design firm	Albatros Werke GmbH, Johannisthal, Germany
Manufacturer	Albatros Werke
Role	Fighting scout
No. built	1,612 ordered by October 1917
Type entered service	1917 (October)
Powerplant	Daimler-built Mercedes D.III six-cylinder, water-cooled inline engine of 160 hp
Armament	Two Spandau-built 7.92-mm Maxim LMG08/15 machine-guns
Wingspan	9.05 m
Length	7.33 m
Max. speed	186 km/h
Endurance	2 hours
Max. take-off weight	937 kg

performance; to the Australians on the Western Front it was a war trophy, their first enemy aircraft captured intact.

The day after its capture the Albatros made a first stop in the convoluted route from Bailleul to Australia. By order of 2nd Brigade, RFC, it went to the headquarters supply depot at Saint-Omer. The Australians put in a claim for it to be allocated to the Australian War Museum, which was granted, but for the time being the British had more pressing need for it. After minor repairs and modifications, including a change of propeller, it was given the serial number G.101, painted with British national markings, and flown to Britain for test flying to ascertain its flight characteristics. After about 14 hours' flying by a number of RFC pilots, it was taken back by the AFC on 22 May and dismantled and packed, prematurely as it turned out, for shipping to Australia. It did not leave for over a year. After some time at D. Napier and Son Ltd, an aeroplane works at Acton, in London, it was again assembled for a display at Australia House in London after the Armistice in November.

Little is known of the operational history of D.5390/17 before it was forced down. It had been ordered in August 1917, and thus would have been a fairly new aircraft. As for *Leutnant* Clauss, this had not been his first brush with RE.8s. On 13 November, a month before his capture, he had shot one down west of Blankaart See[10]. As it was not uncommon for pilots to regularly be assigned the same aircraft, it is interesting to speculate on whether Clauss may have been flying this Albatros on that occasion, too.

The Memorial's example is today the more original of only two surviving Albatros D.Va's. The other is held by the US National Air and Space Museum and, interestingly, it also sports a bullet hole in its fuel tank.

Leutnant Clauss and *Jasta* 29

Clauss's unit, *Jasta* 29, had been formed through the training and replacement unit *Flieger Ersatz Abteilung* 5 at Hannover in December 1916. Clauss joined it the following June, although he was on transfer until November with the home defence fighter squadron *Kampf-Einsitzer Staffel* 1a, and also spent some time in hospital. In support of 6 Armee in northern France, the unit moved on 13 December 1917 from Emerchicourt to Bellincamps, from where Clauss presumably made his last flight. He was the unit's only member taken prisoner, although 13 men were killed in action and a further 12 wounded during the course of the war.

Jasta 29 later had more encounters with Australians. The month after D.5390/17 was captured, the Sopwith Camel pilots of 4 Squadron AFC had their first combat with *Jasta* 29, one Australian being shot down and taken prisoner. In May they met again, this time with two victories to the Australians for one Camel pilot lost. By war's end, *Jasta* 29 had claimed 79 aircraft shot down.

The Albatros in context

The Albatros company's sleek, streamlined scouts of 1916–17 were responses to the supremacy of French and British scouts, and in fact incorporated French Nieuport design features. The D.V was an improvement over the D.III and appeared in May 1917. However, despite its revolutionary appearance with its oval-section monocoque fuselage, the performance of the D.V and D.Va was unremarkable.

Worse still, the lower wings were prone to fail in the prolonged dives which were now an integral part of German dogfighting tactics. This unfortunate weakness, a carry-over from the earlier Albatros, restricted the aircraft's combat performance, as it limited how long and how fast the pilot could keep it in a dive. The problem was caused by vibrations induced by the position of the 'V' interplane strut attachment point aft of the wing spar. An attempt to solve the problem—a small strengthening brace where the wing struts joined the lower wing—distinguished the more numerous D.Va from the D.V. Other improvements were a strengthened lower main spar, and a reversion to the earlier aileron cable arrangement.

Despite the shortcomings of the D.V and the D.Va, Germany's air service needed an answer to the latest British and French designs, such as the SE5, the Sopwith Camel and the SPAD S.XIII, so the D.V was ordered into full-scale production. The service also needed to expand its air presence on the Western Front in preparation for an offensive in March 1918, and the D.V was adopted as the standard scout for the participating *Jastas*. As a result, it was widely encountered by Australians. Well over a thousand were in front-line service over the Western Front and Palestine by May 1918. In the latter theatre they were regularly encountered by Australians, particularly 1 Squadron AFC. Among the aces to fly the D.V on the Western Front was the legendary Red Baron, Manfred Freiherr von Richthofen, who disliked it and later exchanged it for his preferred Fokker Dr.I Triplane. The D.V/D.Va proved to be the last Albatros scout to see service before the superior Fokker D.VII appeared in mid-1918.

NOTES ON COLOUR SCHEME

While displayed at the Memorial prior to the 1960s restoration, the Albatros's complex paint scheme was recorded by aviation historian Bob Waugh. It is thought to have been largely as it was in 1917. A summary of his findings, augmented by those of Eric Watson during the restoration, is as follows (see also 1966 Waugh plans in Mikesh, *Albatros D.Va: German fighter of World War I*):

Wings: Upper surfaces of upper and lower wings were dark green and mauve disruptive camouflage (applied over the standard five-colour lozenge pattern); underside of upper wing was six-colour lozenge pattern (light blue, pink, light purple, red, green and sand) with mauve rib tapes; underside of lower wing was light blue; starboard aileron was lozenge pattern (presumably replaced in-service); interplane struts were grey (outer bay) and khaki (centre section). Iron cross national marking in black with white outline in four wing positions.

Fuselage: Propeller spinner, metal engine panels and metal access hatches were brown, and propeller blades varnished laminated wood. Upper and side fuselage surfaces rear of engine were dark green; lower fuselage surface, engine compartment sides and sub-plane were varnished straw-coloured wood; an iron cross national insignia had been overpainted on each fuselage side. Weight details were stencilled in black on port side of cockpit. Undercarriage struts were brown, and wheel covers grey.

Tail section: Fin was dark green with a varnished wood finish on its forward port section; rudder was dark green over lozenge pattern fabric; iron cross national insignia in black with white outline on fin and rudder sides; tailplanes had buff undersides and light blue upper surfaces (a unit marking) with dark green tips. Aircraft serial number in black over varnished wood on port side of fin only.

The national markings were overpainted in Britain after capture, firstly with RAF markings (roundels, red/white/blue rudder stripes and 'G.101' on the rear fuselage) for its flight trials, and then with iron crosses on the rear fuselage. In 1927 it was assessed that the aircraft was in need of an overall repaint, the report recommending that both the Albatros and Pfalz be repainted in one colour. Memorial staff replied that this would be a pity, as 'they are the only examples of practical camouflage of this nature which we possess'. Evidently this view held, as little if any repainting was done at that time. It was noted, however, that the wing and tailplane upper surfaces had earlier been repainted dark green.

In 1968 the original paint and fabric were removed and a spurious scheme applied, with replica fabric covering which approximated the original lozenge colours. Accurate replica lozenge-printed fabric, made in the original German factory, was purchased during the 1990s. During the 2008 conservation work the aircraft was repainted in a scheme as close as possible to the original.

12,000 ft over Marquion, Cambrai region, northern France
1705 HOURS, 15 SEPTEMBER 1918

After the big allied offensive began at Amiens, on what *General* Ludendorff later called *der schwarze Tag* (the black day), 8 August 1918, the death knell for Germany's war was beginning to sound. The latest generation of fighting scouts of the *Luftstreitkräfte* (Imperial German Army Air Service), though in many respects the equal of any allied aircraft, were outnumbered by at least three to one. The German aircraft industry could not produce the new types in the numbers that were needed, nor were there enough pilots available to fly them or fuel to fill their tanks. Nevertheless the best of the new breed, the Fokker D.VII, was feared enough to be labelled the next 'Fokker scourge'. Recently, it been joined in smaller numbers by the latest offering from Bavaria: the Pfalz D.XII.

Both types were now serving with the Royal Bavarian *Jagdstaffel (Jasta)* 23, commanded by *Leutnant* Heinrich Seywald. The new Pfalz had only just been delivered

> ### *A sluggish workhorse which fought the bridle.*
> *Leutnant Rudolf Stark (Jasta 35, German Air Service)*

Members of 4 Squadron AFC at Bickendorf aerodrome near Cologne, Germany, inspect a new Pfalz D.XII in December 1918. AWM P00355.017

to this *Jasta*, and on this day may have been on its first operation with the unit. It was instantly disliked, as it was difficult to fly and less manoeuvrable than the Fokker. It was therefore allotted to the more experienced pilots who might be able to handle it, despite not having been given an opportunity to get used to it. *Leutnant* Paul Vogel was in the 'experienced' category: he had served with the unit for several months, and thus qualified as a veteran. Perhaps his main claim to fame was that in July he had saved himself at least once, possibly twice, by parachuting out of a burning aircraft—a rare feat at the time. Whether he liked it or not, he had now been assigned a Pfalz.

Vogel was now out on a patrol with *Jasta* 23, which had encountered a flight of British Bristol F.2B Fighters and SE5a scouts. The Germans attacked first, but three SE5as and a Bristol turned and managed to get behind Vogel's Pfalz as it dived on the tail of an SE. Second Lieutenant D.E. Cameron of 1 Squadron RAF was one of the SE pilots who followed him down. Vogel tried to shake him off with half-rolls and turns, but his mount was not agile enough. Cameron closed in, firing bursts from his Vickers and Lewis machine-guns all the way down to a height of 100 ft near the small village of Recourt.

During the few minutes that the dogfight lasted, Vogel also had to contend with the Bristol on his tail. Belonging to 62 Squadron RAF, it was flown by a noted ace with 16 victories, Captain William 'Bull' Staton MC, with his observer, Second Lieutenant Leslie Mitchell. Bullets struck the Pfalz, and it made a rough crash landing and turned over on its back. It was claimed shot down by both Cameron and Staton. At the time, Cameron was unable to identify his prey; the Pfalz D.XII was not generally known to Allied pilots, having only appeared in quantity on the Western Front during the previous few weeks. Staton, however, landed nearby and apprehended *Leutnant* Vogel, who was badly injured. The aircraft, serial no. 2486/18, was salvaged for examination and allocated the British serial number G/HQ/6—the sixth enemy aircraft registered by General Headquarters. Shortly after being captured, Vogel died of his injuries.

No detailed account of an Australian encounter with a D.XII has been found. However, this British encounter illustrates two of the traits for which the design became known: its relative sluggishness in combat manoeuvres, and the difficulty of landing it, even in favourable conditions.

◄ ►

The serial number of Vogel's Pfalz is not very far from the example which was shortly to make its way into the Memorial's collection. The number of the latter, 2600/18, tells us that it is a late production D.XII, but its wartime history is unknown. We do know that when 4 Squadron AFC occupied Bickendorf aerodrome near Cologne a month after the armistice of 11 November 1918, among the 150 aircraft they found there were examples of the D.XII. Some of these aircraft were flown by the Australians, in between taking the squadron's Sopwith Snipes up for 'spins' which often turned into aerobatic demonstrations for the Germans.

John Kemister (Senior Conservator of Large Technology) applies dope to the aircraft's replica lozenge-pattern fabric wing covering in April 2008. The aircraft is being prepared for display in the *Over the front* exhibition in ANZAC Hall. AWM PAIU2008/047.02

Jamie Croker (Large Technology Conservator) scrapes back non-original paint on the Pfalz fuselage to reveal what lies beneath, April 2008. AWM PAIU2008/047.01

For some reason, 2600/18 was for many years confused in the records with a two-seat reconnaissance aircraft, an LVG C.VI, that was forced down on 9 October 1918 at Nieppe, France, by a pair of 4 Squadron Camels. Pfalz 2600/18 first appears reliably in allied records in June 1919, when it was among the many German aircraft gathered together at the RAF's No. 2 Aircraft Salvage Depot at Fienvillers, in the Somme region of northern France, for allocation to Australia under the terms of the armistice. It had been given the number EA15: the 15th enemy aircraft assigned to Australia.

Interest in late-war German aircraft technology was such that over 170 Pfalz D.XIIs were reportedly earmarked for handing over to the allies at war's end. In addition, all surviving Fokker D.VIIs were to be confiscated under the terms of the armistice. For Australia, the Administrative Headquarters of the Australian Imperial Force (AIF) made claims for seven of each enemy aircraft type captured—one for the Commonwealth and one for each state—as well as engines, bombs, flying gear … the list went on. The British Air Ministry allotted 70 aircraft, but the logistics of getting them to Australia were beyond what was considered reasonable even by the notoriously trophy-minded Australians. In the end the claim was reduced by half, and still less were actually shipped. Included in the original claims were seven 'old' Pfalz D.XIIs, meaning that they were used examples rather than newly delivered from aircraft parks. Only one D.XII, though, appears to have arrived in Australia, and there is no evidence that 2600/18 had seen action. It had at least fired its Maxim machine-guns, as spent ammunition cartridge cases were found in the airframe during restoration in the 1960s.[11]

From Fienvillers, Australia's war trophy aircraft were dispatched to RAF Ascot in August and September 1919 before sailing to Australia. At the original Australian War Museum buildings in Melbourne and later Sydney during the 1920s, the D.XII joined a Pfalz D.IIIa (German serial 8284/17, British serial G/5Br/13) and a Fokker D.VII (German serial 8371/18, British serial EA24) as well as examples of Halberstadt, Hannover, Rumpler, DFW, LVG and Albatros types. Of these, only the Albatros D.Va and Pfalz D.XII have survived to this day as examples of the penultimate and final stages, respectively, of First World War German aircraft technology. Only three other D.XIIs are known to exist.

The Pfalz D.XII in context

Pfalz *Flugzeug-Werke* (aircraft factory) was founded by the Eversbusch brothers at Speyer, Bavaria, in 1913. From the start it was financially assisted by the Bavarian government, which promoted its own aviation industry and air corps. The company's first design to enter service, the Pfalz E.II monoplane, flew in the Sinai campaign in 1916. The company's successful D.III saw widespread service from mid-1917 in Palestine and on the Western Front, where many Australians encountered it. The D.XII evolved from the D.IIIa, and was ordered into production by the *Idflieg (Inspektion der Fliegertruppen*, the aviation bureau of Germany's War Office) in March 1918. Its performance at a fighter competition in May 1918 was encouraging enough for

Factory-assembling an
early production Pfalz D.XII.
AWM P00355.006

operational trials to be carried out at Adlershof the following month. The Pfalz was chosen largely to augment Fokker D.VII production, which could not keep up with demand. Five D.XIIs were in service by the end of June, but problems with the radiator delayed quantity production while D.IIIa production was stepped up in the interim.[12]

It has been said that the Fokker company must have had better public relations people than Pfalz. When the Fokker D.VII had joined the front-line *Jastas* on the Western Front in May 1918 it was proclaimed a 'world beater', and all pilots wanted to fly it. By contrast, the operational debut of the Pfalz D.XII shortly afterwards was unheralded, despite the successes of the D.III; as a result, pilots generally had not heard of it and reacted much more sceptically. First-encounter reports by German pilots were almost invariably negative, focusing on its poor turning performance, slow climb rate and handling difficulties. 'No one wanted to fly the Pfalz except under compulsion,' wrote Rudolf Stark, commander of Bavarian *Jasta* 35 in September 1918.[13] The effect of the directive to fly what was considered an inferior aircraft was, naturally, demoralisation and anger.

Yet once they got used to it, many pilots got to like the Pfalz. *Oberleutnant* Ernst Udet (the most successful German air ace after Manfred von Richthofen) reportedly considered it a good performer, and his influence was a factor in its being pressed into production. The cockpit was well-enclosed, while still affording good visibility. In many respects, its performance matched that of the early Mercedes-engined version of the Fokker D.VII. Although not as manoeuvrable and having a slower rate of roll, the Pfalz was faster, particularly in a dive—an advantage utilised in combat with allied fighters. Pilots did not have to fear wing failure in a dive, a weakness that had plagued the Albatros D.V; the Pfalz had a stronger, double-spar, two-bay wing design based on the French SPAD (although the profusion of bracing wires substantially increased the ground rigger's workload). But those who grew to like the Pfalz's performance still conceded that it was not an easy aircraft to fly, and even worse to land. Its tendency to float in the 'ground effect' (see Glossary) before touchdown led to numerous landing accidents, some fatal. Once it did touch down, a gentle approach was advisable lest its weak undercarriage collapse.

However, perhaps the main reason for the aircraft's lack of success was that its performance fell well behind that of the later BMW-engined Fokker D.VII. The superior BMW was fitted experimentally to a Pfalz and boosted its performance considerably, but the decision was made that the engines would go into the Fokker instead. The Pfalz got the rough-running and noisy, though reliable, Mercedes D.IIIa engine. As there were not enough Pfalz D.XIIs to fully equip whole *Jastas*, the two aircraft generally served side by

Pfalz D.XII 2695/18, wearing a similar camouflage scheme to that of 2600/18, in British hands. AWM P00355.012

side. The pilots of the more maneouvrable Fokker flew higher as top cover, where they were in a better position to assist the Pfalz pilots in case of attack.

◄ ►

Like that of the D.III, the smooth, sleek appearance of the Pfalz D.XII's fuselage and its light yet strong structure depends upon a clever innovation: the 'semi-monocoque' form. In this design, structural strength lies mainly in the wooden shell itself, so that the internal framework of formers and longerons can be greatly reduced to save weight. Over sparsely spaced plywood formers and spruce longerons is a shell of two layers of three-ply, spirally wrapped in opposing directions, which had been formed in halves over a mould. The shell is covered in doped fabric. The design did, however, have disadvantages: its construction was labour intensive, and it was subject to warping if it got damp, which could lead to unwanted and even dangerous flight characteristics.

During the brief few months of its service before the war ended, at least 18 *Jagdstaffeln*, a number of them from Bavaria (whose government, evidently, was keen to push the local product), were equipped with the D.XII.[14] By October 1918, 180 were in service on the Western Front;[15] but there were four times as many Fokker D.VIIs, and as events transpired, the D.XII had little impact on the war. One Australian Bristol pilot with a British unit is recorded to have shot one down, but overall, few Australians are known to have encountered the type.

The Pfalz D.XII found wider fame years after the war on the silver screen than it ever had during the war. A few surviving D.XIIs that had been sent to America appeared in such Hollywood air epics as *Dawn Patrol* and Howard Hughes' *Hell's Angels*, released in 1930.

TIME LINE—2600/18

1919	(Jun) Recorded at 2 Aircraft Salvage Depot RAF at Fienvillers, France
1919	(Sep) Shipped from France to UK aboard the cross-Channel steamer ferry *Richbow*; to RAF Ascot for shipping to Australia
1920	Displayed at Exhibition Building, Melbourne, and Motor Traders' Association of South Australia
1924–35	Displayed at AWM, Sydney
1941–55	Displayed in Aeroplane Hall
1968–74	Restored by Australian Society for Aero-historical Preservation. All fabric replaced, and engine replaced with that of the AWM's Albatros. Damage to fuselage repaired.
1974–99	Displayed in Aircraft Hall
1999	Stored at AWM Treloar Technology Centre
2007–08	Extensively conserved for display in *Over the front* exhibition, ANZAC Hall

DATA

Type	Pfalz D.XII
Design firm	Pfalz Flugzeug-Werke, Speyer, Bavaria
Manufacturer	As above
Role	Single-seat scout
No. built	750–800
Type entered service	June 1918
Identity	2600/18
Powerplant	Mercedes D.IIIa six-cylinder, water-cooled inline engine of 180 hp (134 kW)
Armament	Two Spandau-built 7.92-mm Maxim LMG08/15 machine-guns
Wingspan	9 m
Length	6.35 m
Max. speed	190 km/h
Endurance	2 hours
Loaded weight	900 kg

NOTES ON COLOUR SCHEME

The 1970s restoration paint scheme was based on a British report of the crashed D.XII, serial no. 2486/18, which was only roughly similar to 2600/18's original appearance. Aviation historian Bob Waugh had, however, taken colour notes, scrapings and photographic slides during the 1950s and 1960s; he recorded the following scheme, including the banded fuselage camouflage which was unique to the Pfalz:

Fuselage camouflage, in sequence from nose to tail: chocolate brown lower nose with khaki engine covers; grey-green forward of cockpit; dark green around cockpit; apple green around fuselage crosses; dark green forward of tail; medium green below fin; and dark brown forward of rudder. Fabric covering wings, tailplane and fin was printed in the unique German 'lozenge pattern' (five-colour variety) overall. Tailplane dope had a brown tint (possibly through age). Straight late-war style crosses in four wing positions and on rudder and fuselage sides. Rudder white. Wings struts khaki or light chocolate. 'Pfalz DXII 2600/18' in small black lettering on rear fuselage sides.

During the 2008 conservation work the aircraft was repainted in as close a scheme as possible to the original, and the wings re-covered in accurate replica lozenge-printed fabric.

AVRO 504K A3-4

Central Flying School, Point Cook, Victoria
MARCH 1919

Nine months after it had been ordered, the largest aircraft consignment to date for the AFC was finally received from Britain. As the staff of the Aeroplane Repair Section uncrated 20 Avro 504K trainers and a dozen Sopwith Pup fighter trainers, a nasty surprise was awaiting them. The Avros' fabric surfaces were covered in mildew, their unpainted metal parts including bracing wires and control cables were rusted, and their wings showed handling damage. As the wings of aircraft H2174 were being attached the men decided to open them up for inspection, and found that moisture-weakened glue had resulted in some three-ply timber fittings delaminating.[16] Subsequent inspections showed five other examples to be similarly damaged. The aircraft intended to be the pride of the post-war AFC were not even airworthy.

The poor condition of the Avros was serious enough for a board of inquiry to be convened, and for the Chief of the General Staff, General J. Gordon Legge, personally to inspect them. Evidently, their period in storage in Britain and the subsequent sea

> *The Avro was a different proposition, it would stand almost anything.*
> Air Commodore A.H. Cobby CBE DSO DFC and 2 Bars GM

Another of the 55 Avro 504s sent from Britain during 1919–20, photographed at 1 Flying Training School, Point Cook, Vic., in 1926. AWM P00448.005

voyage had allowed long periods of dampness. In June the six worst affected aircraft were stripped of their wing fabric for repairs to be carried out, and rusted cables were replaced. By August several Avros had been repaired, and were in service with No. 1 Home Training Squadron at Point Cook. They were ready just in time to fly in the First Peace Loan tour of 1919.

Still bearing its Royal Air Force (RAF) serial number H2174, the aircraft destined for the Memorial's collection joined this barnstorming tour of Australia's eastern states to sell government bonds. The aircraft were flown by veteran wartime pilots, some of whom would reportedly have benefited from a refresher course. Marred by regular landing accidents in town showgrounds and even a home backyard, the tour was not a particularly glowing advertisement for aviation. Three Avros and a Pup, in fact, were written off. However, being the first occasion that most Australians had seen an aircraft up close, the tour generated a good deal of interest and funds. The Avros and Pups were the first military aircraft in Australia capable of aerobatics,[17] and crowds thrilled to the novel sight of aircraft looping, spinning and barrel-rolling across the sky.

H2174 is also believed to have taken part in the Second Peace Loan tour in August–September 1920. A major event of this tour was a long-distance race, which included four Avros. This time, the pilots had been given a refresher course at Point Cook. The early 1920s was a period of transition for Australian military aviation. The AFC briefly became the Australian Air Corps, then on 31 March 1921 the Australian Air Force, and later that year, the Royal Australian Air Force (RAAF). Attached to 1 Flying Training School at Point Cook and nearby Laverton, H2174 flew with the service under all these names. Sometime in 1922, following the formation of the RAAF, H2174 became A3-4: that is to say, the fourth example of the third type in the Australian aircraft series.

By 1929 the Avro was obsolete, replaced by the next generation of British biplane design: de Havilland's new Cirrus Moth. Together with the SE5a (see the separate chapter), A3-4 was selected for preservation at the Memorial.

The aircraft retained its original condition for another 35 years, and then from 1965 spent more than 20 years in a different guise. An agreement was made with Qantas to allow its conversion to the configuration of their first aircraft, registered G-AUBG, involving a repaint and the installation of a Sunbeam Dyak water-cooled engine. In this promotional role for television commercials and at airshows, the old Avro served as Qantas's most visible connection with its origins. It even went to the Oshkosh Airshow in the United States, flying ten times faster than it ever had for the RAAF—in the cargo hold of a Boeing 747.

Meanwhile, its original rotary engine (which, interestingly, had earlier powered a number of Sopwith Camel scouts) was refurbished at RAAF Fairbairn, ACT, in 1983. Five years later, Qantas restored the aircraft to its original configuration in time for its display at the Bicentennial Airshow at RAAF Richmond, NSW.

Following its refurbishment, the Memorial's Avro was displayed at the Bicentennial Airshow at RAAF Base Richmond in 1988 (AWM PAIU1988/175.06)

Today, the Memorial's Avro is the sole original example of its type in Australia, and the oldest surviving aircraft known to have flown with the RAAF. Retaining almost all of its original structure and some 70 per cent of the original fabric, it is one of the most authentic of about ten surviving examples of the 504K world-wide. It is also the Memorial's only aircraft fitted with a rotary, an engine with radially arranged cylinders which rotates with the propeller. Although an unusual design from today's perspective, it was a common powerplant during the First World War.

The Avro in context

The slender Avro 504 design of 1913 epitomises the simplicity of the early years of Australian military aviation, in terms of both construction and handling. Nevertheless, it was the first trainer to be fully aerobatic, allowing complex maneouvres to be incorporated into the training curriculum for the first time. In fact, it was customary for pilots to loop the Avro during their first solo flight,[18] a practice which would be almost unheard of today.

With the 504K model of 1918, a universal engine mounting system allowed a variety of engines to be fitted. These included the rotary powerplants of fighter aircraft onto which trainee pilots would soon convert. The Avro was also robust, a necessary attribute in training schools. It was an ideal choice of trainer for men destined for service in fighters, leading to its mass production on a scale unrivalled in Britain during the First World War, with 504K production reaching 80 machines per week before war's end.

As the standard training aircraft for the RFC[19] and the Royal Naval Air Service (RNAS), the Avro paved the way in the development of a proper syllabus for flying training. In particular, the wartime School for Special Flying at Gosport in Britain, established by Major Robert Smith-Barry, used Avros to develop the RFC's first systematic flying instruction—the Gosport System (which also gave its name to the Gosport speaking tubes through which instructor and student communicated). The Avro had the right flying qualities for a trainer, being easy to fly and forgiving of the trainee pilot's elementary flying skills. It was sensitive on the rudder, although it had a sluggish roll rate. The instructor and his student were each faced with just half a dozen basic instruments. Throughout a typical flight, the trainee pilot had more to worry about with engine management than with handling. The throttle was a simple 'blip'

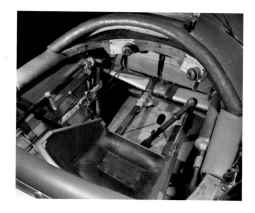

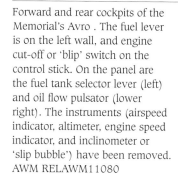

Forward and rear cockpits of the Memorial's Avro . The fuel lever is on the left wall, and engine cut-off or 'blip' switch on the control stick. On the panel are the fuel tank selector lever (left) and oil flow pulsator (lower right). The instruments (airspeed indicator, altimeter, engine speed indicator, and inclinometer or 'slip bubble') have been removed. AWM RELAWM11080

An AFC officer with an Avro 504K at Point Cook, Vic., c. 1919–20. AWM DAAV00150

TIMELINE—H2174/A3-4

1918	Built by A.V. Roe & Co, UK
1919	Shipped to Australia aboard SS *Berrima* and damaged in transit; reconditioned on arrival. Served with 1 Home Training Squadron of the Central Flying School, AFC, at Point Cook, Vic.
1919–20	Participated in First and Second Peace Loan tours
1921	Joined the newly formed RAAF with 1 Flying Training School, Point Cook, Vic.
1925	Loaned to 1 Squadron RAAF
1929	Donated to AWM ex-Laverton, Vic., by the Air Board, together with the AWM's SE5a, and displayed at Exhibition Buildings, Melbourne; reconditioned at 1 Aircraft Depot, Laverton, Vic.
1936	(Jun) Trucked to Canberra
1941–55	Displayed in AWM Aeroplane Hall, Canberra
1955–65	Held in AWM store, Duntroon, ACT
1965	Loaned to Qantas, flown by DC3 to Sydney and converted to represent the airline's first aircraft
1987–88	Restored to original appearance by Qantas technical staff, and displayed at Bicentennial Airshow, Richmond, NSW
1989–2008	Stored at AWM Trelor Technology Centre, ACT, apart from brief displays
2008	Displayed in *Over the front* exhibition, ANZAC Hall

DATA

Type	Avro 504K
Design firm	A.V. Roe & Co, UK
Manufacturer	A.V. Roe & Co, Park Works, Manchester, UK
Role	Two-seat trainer
Type entered service	1914 (Avro 504); 1918 (Avro 504K)
Number in RAAF service	61 (55 UK-built plus 6 locally built)
No. built	6,350 (total Avro 504 production: 8,340)
Identity	A2-4 (RAAF); H2174 (RAF/AFC)
Crew	2 (instructor and trainee)
Powerplant	Le Rhone 9C 9-cylinder rotary engine of 80 hp
Wingspan	10.97 m
Length	8.96 m
Max. speed	145 km/h
Range	400 km
Loaded weight	830 kg

switch on the control column which cut out the magneto ignition, and it could be very temperamental. Engine failure gave little time to turn into the wind, which was crucial for such a light but relatively large aircraft, and select a flat piece of ground for a 'controlled crash' landing.

The Avro 504 was the first aircraft encountered by many Australian trainee pilots. During the final year of the war the four AFC training squadrons of 1 Training Wing at Minchinhampton and Leighterton, in Britain, were equipped with more than 120 Avro 504Js and Ks. In a show of national identity, many were distinctively painted with such Australiana as kangaroos, emus and boomerangs. Initial training on the Avro was generally followed by intermediate instruction on the likes of the Sopwith Pup, and finally advanced training on high-performance types such as the Camel and Snipe.

Following the delivery of the first 20 Avro 504Ks to Point Cook in 1919, a further 35 were received in mid-1920. These formed part of the 128 aircraft of Britain's Imperial Gift sent to help get the RAAF off the ground; they served in 1 Flying Training School (formerly Central Flying School) at Point Cook throughout the 1920s. The Avro also holds the distinction of being the first military aircraft to be factory-built in Australia. As an initiative to encourage local aircraft manufacture, six were ordered for the RAAF from the Australian Aircraft and Engineering Co. Ltd. at Mascot, Sydney, in 1921.

Although its primary use was as a trainer, the 504 has some early claims to fame in combat during the First World War. One example flying in France recorded the RFC's first air-to-air victory with a machine-gun. Three others of the RNAS carried out one of history's first successful bombing operations, attacking the German Zeppelin airship shed at Friedrichshafen in November 1914. Later, in the home defence role, it hunted Zeppelins in the skies over Britain.

NOTES ON COLOUR SCHEME

H2174 was delivered in British PC.10 khaki green nitro-varnish finish. In about 1927 it was overpainted in 'V.84' silver finish, which was more conducive to Australian conditions as it reflected heat. This finish, which is currently replicated on the aircraft, was as follows: Silver Glaucous or aluminium nitrate dope over Clarke's Britannia dope, finished in clear varnish. Standard RAF-style blue/white/red roundels in six positions (fuselage roundels white-outlined), and blue/white/red vertically striped rudder. Semigloss black undercarriage, tubular steel wing struts (which replaced wooden struts in Australia) and details. Skids are varnished wood finish. Fabric covering on outer section of propeller blades is medium grey. Serial number 'A3-4' is in 20-cm black figures on rear fuselage sides.

14,000 ft over the Bray–Villers-Bretonneux region, France

0805 HOURS, 2 JUNE 1918

Four kilometres above the countryside of northern France, the pilots of nine SE5a scouts of 2 Squadron AFC were out on patrol to hunt down German aircraft. Though breathing the thin air was laborious, it was safer here at a height where the aircraft performed as well as the best of Germany's scouts. Their hopes for combat were met when six Pfalz D.III scouts presented themselves. Captain Roby Manuel attacked and sent two down in succession, one flipping onto its back and losing a wing. As a Pfalz lined up on Manuel's aircraft, flight commander Captain Henry Forrest in aircraft C9539 dived down and fired at it. It fell in a series of stalls and sideslips before it was lost. The remaining German scouts fled after the brief encounter; but there was more to come.

Over Albert an hour later, the Australians came upon another eight D.IIIs. One German fired at Lieutenant Copp, but Forrest surprised him by firing from out of the sun, sending the Pfalz down out of control. It was Forrest's 11th aerial victory in just over two months; it was also his last, as he was about to be posted to the Home Establishment. During the mêlée Manuel and Lieutenant Adams sent another two down, but Lieutenant Rackett was

> ### *Beautiful to fly.*
> Sir Raymond Garrett, 1 Squadron RAAF

Another Imperial Gift SE5a at Point Cook during the 1920s. AWM P02413.013

hit and descended to make a forced landing, and was captured. The fight soon drifted over the British lines, and the remaining Germans departed.

◄   ►

The Memorial's SE5a, serial no. C1916 (later re-serialled A2-4), was not involved in that action, although it was built in the same batch as some of 2 Squadron's aircraft. However, in 1970, in time for a visit to the Memorial by the Queen, it was repainted as the mount in which Captain Forrest claimed all his aerial victories.[20] Most noteworthy of those markings was the white boomerang on its fuselage, a reminder that Australia was the only British dominion to establish its own flying corps during the First World War, albeit under the control of British wings.

C Flight of 2 Squadron AFC at Savy aerodrome, France, in 1918. At centre, Captain Henry Forrest DFC and Bar is standing by the wheel of his SE5a, C9539, the aircraft which later lent its paint scheme and markings to A2-4. AWM E01881

After the war the Australian Air Corps (as the flying corps was renamed) remained dependent on Britain. In 1920, Britain supplied Australia with the bulk of its aircraft and equipment: the 'Imperial Gift' which enabled Australia to form an air force. In all, 128 gift aircraft bolstered the existing holdings of 20 Avro 504Ks, 12 Sopwith Pups and six Fairey IIID seaplanes. There were DH.9s and DH.9as, additional Avro 504Ks, and 35 SE5as, of which A2-4 was one. Although there were now more than enough aircraft to form Australia's air force, there was far from enough manpower: just 21 officers and 130 men were enlisted to fly, service and administer the aircraft. Apart from the lack of personnel, finance was inadequate to operate the whole fleet. Fourteen of the SE5as were not even unpacked. Nevertheless, in 1920 sufficient aircraft to equip the newly formed 1 Flying Training School at Point Cook near Melbourne were erected and test flown in a series of loops, rolls and spins. Trainee pilots looked forward to the thrill of converting from the docile Avro 504K onto the powerful SE5a during the latter part of their courses.

The SE5a displayed in ANZAC Hall in 2001. AWM RELAWM11091

In March 1921, Australia became the first dominion to form an air force independent from the army and navy, and the SE5as formed the bulk of its fighter strength. The new Australian Air Force replaced what had been the army's Australian Air Corps, and six months later, in August 1921, the prefix Royal was added to form the RAAF as we still know it today.

One of the first public appearances of the SE5a in Australia was at the 1922 Aerial Pageant in Sydney, where a display by a detachment from RAAF Point Cook awed the crowd with mock combat and aerobatics. Three years later, the RAAF began forming its first squadrons—1 Squadron at Point Cook, and 3 Squadron at Richmond near Sydney. For the opening of Parliament House in 1927, SE5as were flown from Point Cook and Richmond to Canberra, landing on a new strip south-east of town which would later become RAAF Base Canberra. The trip was marred by a number of accidents, including a fatal crash during one of the ceremonial flyovers. The pilot involved, Flying Officer Francis Ewen, was buried in the historic cemetery at St. John's Church of England in Canberra.

In 1929 the remaining five SE5as at Point Cook were clearly obsolete, and were phased out of RAAF service, to be replaced by Bristol Bulldogs. A2-4 had been stored at Point Cook until 1926, and so had only been flying with the training school for three years. It was approved for destruction by burning, which became the fate of the other four, but at the Memorial's instigation the Air Board approved its preservation together with the Avro 504K. During their RAAF service, the SE5as had been substantially rebuilt. Their original bungee-cord undercarriage suspension was considered inadequate for the stresses of hard landings by trainee pilots, and was retrofitted with pneumatic oleo legs; the original style would be refitted to A2-4 on display 40 years later. The aircraft came without machine-guns, but in 1939 a Lewis gun and a Vickers gun, no longer required by the RAAF, were made available for its display in Canberra.

The SE5a in context

The wing-tips of the [main] planes, ten feet away, suddenly caught my eye, and for a second the amazing adventure of flight overwhelmed me. Nothing between me and oblivion but a pair of light linen-covered wings and the roar of a 200-hp engine! There was the fabric, bellying slightly in the suction above the plane, the streamlined wires, taut and quivering, holding the wing structure together, the three-ply body, the array of instruments, and the slight tremor of the whole aeroplane. It was a triumph of human intelligence and skill—almost a miracle.[21]

Cockpit of the Memorial's SE5a.
AWM RELAWM11091

Thus RFC pilot and author Cecil Lewis described taking his first SE5a flight at 22,000 ft over the English countryside in 1917. It was a real 'pilot's aeroplane', and had few vices. Its rate of climb was a respectable 300 metres per minute. Its positive rudder response was a distinct asset. Considerable engine torque made snap-rolls to the right quick and easy, although pilots had to remember that attempting this to the left could end in a stall. Taxiing on rough ground took some care, as it was nose heavy and prone to tip over, but paradoxically it flew slightly tail-heavy. For cooling the powerful V8 engine, a flat radiator with shutters looking like venetian blinds was positioned up front, giving the aircraft a distinctive flat-nosed appearance.

The SE5a is often acclaimed as the best British fighting scout of the First World War, an accolade to which many of the war's greatest fighter pilots would attest (see table). British air ace Major James McCudden called it 'a most efficient flying machine … far and away superior to the enemy machines of that period'. Ironically, its original production version, the SE5 (meaning the Royal Aircraft Factory's Scout Experimental design No. 5), was disliked by many when it first appeared over the Western Front in small numbers during 'Bloody April' 1917, a particularly bad month of losses for the RFC. Captain Albert Ball VC DSO and 2 Bars MC, who died while flying an SE5 the following month, had initially called it 'a dud … a rotten machine' in comparison with his Nieuport 17. Evidently he got used to the SE5, as he shot down 11 enemy aircraft while flying it. What Ball did not live to see was that by June, after it had equipped only one squadron, its problematic 150-hp Hispano-Suiza V8 engine would be replaced in production by a more reliable, 200-hp version. The better-engined SE5a then joined the French SPAD S.XIII and Sopwith Camel in taking back the advantage in the air for the allies. Further improvement came with the Wolseley Viper engine, a British license-built high-compression version of the Hispano-Suiza. Many pilots preferred the SE5a to the famed Camel, as it was easier to fly, faster, more stable, and sturdier, if not quite as manoeuvrable. Perhaps most telling is the longevity of its service during a period when other new designs were quickly outdated. Many pilots were still having success with it after Germany introduced the feared Fokker D.VII, a year after the SE5a had entered service. In all, it equipped 23 squadrons, including two American and one Australian.

As a scouting unit, the primary aim of 2 Squadron AFC was the destruction of enemy aircraft. Under the command of Major Allan Murray Jones MC, the unit converted from the rotary-engined Airco DH.5 scout to the SE5a in December 1917, when enough engines had become available to increase deliveries of the aircraft. The pilots explored its strengths, and developed tactics to exploit them. It excelled in dives and zooming climbs, and performed especially well at high altitude. Its armament of one Vickers and one Lewis machine-gun was adequate; the Lewis, mounted on a curved rail on the upper wing, could be aimed upwards, although it was normally pointed ahead owing to the difficulty the pilot had re-aiming it while trying to keep control of the aircraft.

The Australian pilots soon became highly adept at flying the SE5a in combat, although they never encountered quite so many enemy aircraft as did 4 Squadron, which was actively competing with it for numbers of enemy aircraft shot down. In all, 2 Squadron produced 16 air aces (listed below) and an additional 24 pilots who recorded victories. Together they claimed nearly 160 enemy aircraft destroyed or sent down out of control. In addition to those of 2 Squadron, other Australians flew the type with British squadrons. Most legendary of these was the colourful Queensland-born Major

The SE5a's Lewis gun could be pulled back on its Foster mount for upward firing. AWM H11941

Stan Dallas, commanding officer of 40 Squadron RAF. On 1 June 1918, Dallas was promoted and taken off flying duties, but the news had not reached him when he took off that morning in an SE5a to patrol the front line. South-east of Lens he encountered three Fokker Dr.I triplanes of *Jasta* 14, and was shot down and killed by their commander, *Leutnant* Hans Werner. He was buried where he crashed near Lieven.[22]

Most successful SE5a air aces, 1917–18

(In alphabetical order; the number of aerial victories while flying the SE5/SE5a is shown in parentheses.[23] † Denotes died in service)

2 Squadron AFC

  Lt Frank Alberry DCM[24] (7)
  Capt Gregory Blaxland (9)
  Capt Alexander Clark (5)
  Capt Adrian Cole DFC MC (10)
  Lt George Cox (5)
  Capt Eric Cummings DFC (9)
  Lt Ernest Davies DFC (7)
  Capt Henry Forrest DFC MID (11)
† Lt Richard Howard MC (7)
  Capt Roby Manuel DFC and Bar (12)
  Capt Robert McKenzie MC (5)

† Maj Roy Phillipps DFC MC and Bar (14)
Capt Eric Simonson (5)
Capt Francis Smith DFC MC (16)
Lt Charles Stone (7)
Lt James Wellwood DFC (7)

Australians serving with British units

Capt Andrew Cowper MC and 2 Bars, of 24 Squadron (17)
† Maj Roderic (Stan) Dallas DSO DSC and Bar *Croix de Guerre,* of 40 Squadron (9)
Capt Harold Hamersley MC, of 60 Squadron (13)
Capt Harry Rigby MC, of 1 Squadron (6)
Capt Eric Stephens DFC, of 41 Squadron (13)
† Lt John Turnbull, of 41 and 56 Squadrons (5)

Other Empire nations

Capt Andrew Beauchamp-Proctor VC DSO DFC MC and Bar, of South Africa (54)
Maj Billy Bishop VC DSO and Bar DFC MC, of Canada (36)
Capt Geoffrey Bowman DSO MC and Bar, of Britain (30)
Capt William Claxton DSO DFC and Bar, of Canada (37)
Capt Percy Clayson DFC MC, of Britain (29)
Capt James Jones DSO DFC and Bar MC, of Wales (37)[25]
† Maj Edward Mannock VC DSO and 2 Bars MC and bar, of Britain (46)
Capt Frederick McCall DSO DFC MC and Bar, of Canada (32)
† Maj James McCudden VC DSO and Bar MC and Bar MM, of Britain (51)
† Capt George McElroy DFC and Bar MC and 2 Bars, of Ireland (47)

TIMELINE—A2-4	
1917	(Aug) Construction contract for 200 SE5as (C1751–C1950) signed; built at Addlestone, Surrey, UK
1920	Sent to Australia with Imperial Gift aircraft, and stored
1926–29	Attached to 1 Flying Training School, Point Cook, Vic.
1928	Forced landed twice, at Laverton and near Werribee, Vic.
1929	Forced-landed at Point Cook. Approved for destruction when retired from service, but issued to AWM in July and displayed at Exhibition Buildings, Melbourne
1941–99	Displayed in Aeroplane Hall
1970	Repainted as 2 Squadron AFC aircraft C9539; RAAF pneumatic undercarriage replaced with 1918-period style
2001–08	Displayed in ANZAC Hall
2008	Re-displayed in ANZAC Hall in *Over the front* exhibition

DATA

Type	Scout Experimental SE5a
Design firm	Royal Aircraft Factory, UK
Manufacturer	Air Navigation Co Ltd, Addlestone, Surrey, UK
Role	Single-seat fighting scout
Type entered service	June 1917
No. built	5,205 (total SE5/SE5a British production)
Identity	A2-4 (RAAF); C1916 (RAF)
Powerplant	Wolseley Viper V8 water-cooled engine of 210 hp (157 kW)
Armament	One fuselage-mounted Vickers Mk I* .303-in machine-gun, and one wing-mounted Lewis Mk II .303-in machine-gun on a Foster rail; 45-kg bomb load
Wingspan	8.11 m
Length	6.38 m
Max. speed	222 km/h
Range	547 km
Max. take-off weight	900 kg

NOTES ON COLOUR SCHEME

Delivered to Australia in PC.10 khaki green scheme with varnished, unpainted wing undersides; standard six British roundels; red/white/blue rudder stripes. Serial no. C1916 in light grey on rear fuselage sides, later replaced with A2-4. Repainted in RAAF 'V84' silver dope scheme in the late 1920s. Propeller grey.

In 1970 A2-4 was repainted in khaki green overall, with markings representing SE5a serial no. C9539 of 2 Squadron AFC, flown by Captain H.G. Forrest DFC, as follows: national markings as above, white 'V' and horizontal boomerang (2 Squadron's insignia from December 1917 to March 1918) aft of the fuselage roundels, 'V' repeated on upper wing, and the serial number (outline only) in white on both sides of fin.

In 2008, for the *Over the front* exhibition, the aircraft's markings were repainted to represent another 2 Squadron aircraft (with white serial no. D6950 on sides of fin), the fuselage boomerangs were deleted, and a vertical white bar was added forward of each fuselage roundel.

DH.9 F1278 ('PD')

Moulmein racecourse, Burma
APRIL 1920

Although we were travelling at 75 miles an hour, the natives were too quick for us. They rushed from all directions and swarmed on to the course … the engine suddenly gave out completely, and we had to descend. They had only left a small circular space for us to land in, and seemed to imagine the plane would drop down like a bird on the ground.

I had to decide between two alternatives on the instant, either to land and plough a way through the people, killing many of them, and even then, perhaps crash also, or to stall down in the small circular piece left and crash. I chose the latter, and the result was fortunate. We merely wiped off the undercarriage, broke the propeller, crumpled up the radiator, and crushed the petrol and oil tanks… [but] we really thought at that moment that our flight was finished.[26]

> ## Not in my lifetime has there been so careless an adventure.
> *W.E. Davidson, Governor of New South Wales*

'PD' with smashed undercarriage after its hard landing at Moulmein, Burma, in April 1920. AWM P00281.012

Lieutenants Parer and McIntosh with 'PD' just before leaving Hounslow, London, in January 1920.
AWM P06429.001

Thus Lieutenant Ray Parer of Melbourne described in 1921 one of the many harrowing moments which had almost become the norm during this epic flight from England to Australia. The DH.9's Puma engine, which had run uncharacteristically well thus far, had caught fire while off the coast of Burma, and Parer was forced to bring the biplane in to Moulmein racecourse. The crowd of locals burst into cheers and applause, perhaps assuming this to be the usual way of settling a flying machine onto the ground. Following the crash, the radiator had to be replaced with two smaller units from cars. Over a six-week period Parer and his Scottish-born mechanic and relief pilot, Lieutenant John McIntosh, their anger and frustration having subsided, toiled in the tropical heat to make the remaining repairs.

◄ ►

As an incentive to the development of air travel between Australia and the mother country, in March 1919 Prime Minister Billy Hughes had offered the almost unheard of sum of £10,000 to the first Australian airman to fly from England to Australia. The aircraft had to be of British Empire origin, and the journey was to be completed in 30 days any time before 1 January 1921. AFC officers Parer and McIntosh, the latter an AIF veteran of Gallipoli who had dreamed of such a flight, found a sponsor after much searching: Glasgow whisky distiller and millionaire, Peter Dawson. Next they needed an aircraft. One soon materialised, courtesy of the Aircraft Disposals Board's depot at Croydon Park in London and Dawson's £900 cheque, in the form of a war surplus DH.9 bomber. The Australian military authorities in London forbade the proposed flight, which was seen as foolhardy in a single-engined aircraft. That directive was disregarded.

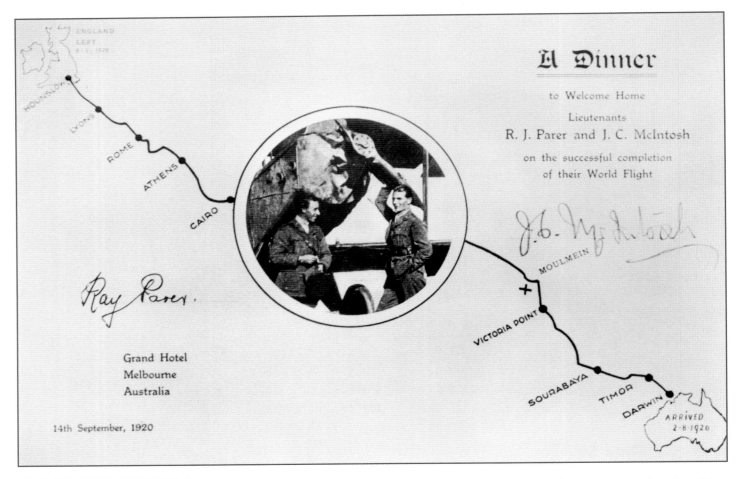

El Dinner

to Welcome Home

Lieutenants

R. J. Parer and J. C. McIntosh

on the successful completion
of their World Flight

Grand Hotel
Melbourne
Australia

14th September, 1920

Signed by Parer and McIntosh, this September 1920 'welcome home' dinner menu cover shows the DH.9's route. AWM P06429.002

Parer had Dawson's initials 'P.D.' emblazoned in large white letters on the aircraft's fuselage for the flight. Having stripped 'PD' of armament and fitted it with an extra fuel tank, the two airmen left on their epic journey from Hounslow, London, on 8 January 1920. By then, the Smith brothers in their twin-engined Vickers Vimy bomber registered 'G-EAOU' (which they interpreted as 'God 'elp all of us') had already won the race. Parer and McIntosh went ahead with the venture anyway, despite having no prospect of collecting the prize money. Five other aircraft made the attempt, all unsuccessfully; en route two planes crashed, killing both two-man crews: Douglas and Ross just six minutes into their flight, Howell and Fraser off Corfu. Parer and McIntosh survived trials and adventures that could fill a book; in fact, they filled two, *The record flight from London to Calcutta*, which they compiled in 1920, and *Flight and adventures of Parer and McIntosh*, which Parer wrote the following year.

Their first setback was bad weather in France, which delayed them by three weeks. Then over Mt Vesuvius, the aircraft was nearly lost when it went out of control in the hot, turbulent air rising from the volcano. Near Taranto, their maps blew away in a gale. They made two forced landings in the Iraqi desert, where they were nearly killed by armed Arabs. Following the crash in Burma, engine problems caused two more weeks'

64

delay in Malaya. Singapore saw the fourth propeller change, Grisee in Java a fifth, and one wing was nearly wrecked in a thunderstorm.

With the constant engine noise, communication in the air between the two crewmen was limited to hand signals and written notes handed forwards and backwards in the slipstream. McIntosh in the rear cockpit had a removable joystick, with which he could control the aircraft if Parer needed a rest.

After their longest over-water leg, from Timor, 'PD' arrived in Darwin with dry fuel tanks on 2 August 1920. It had taken 206 days to make the first single-engined flight from England to Australia. Importantly for Peter Dawson, despite all the crew's trials and tribulations, his promotional bottle of scotch remained intact. Prime Minister Billy Hughes presented the two crewmen with a cheque for £1,000, slightly more than the aircraft had cost Dawson.

With a crash landing at Culcairn, New South Wales, en route to Melbourne, Parer's 'dear old bus' ended its flying career on its back. Not long afterwards, McIntosh died in an air crash in Western Australia. As for 'PD', Parer followed Dawson's advice to 'sell the machine or museum it'. In 1921 it was bought by Norman Brearley, founder of Western Australian Airways, which flew Australia's first scheduled air service (from Geraldton in December that year). It was not long in Brearley's hands, as the Memorial bought it the following year for £250. The Smith brothers' Vimy also joined the collection, and was displayed with 'PD' until 1955, when it was replaced by the Lancaster. It is now displayed at Adelaide airport.

◄ ►

Grounding the DH.9 after its last crash didn't keep it out of harm's way indefinitely. Sixty-six years later, in 1986, near the end of a decade-long restoration project by a Canberra group of enthusiasts called the Australian Society for Aero-historical Preservation (ASAP), a wayward car skidded off the road at Duntroon, ACT, and crashed through the side of the Memorial's fibro storage shed. Much of PD's rear fuselage and tail section was reduced to splinters, setting the project back by two years.

The ASAP effort, both before and after the accident, was one of the most ambitious restorations undertaken on a Memorial aircraft at the time. It was completed on a shoestring budget and with minimal specialist equipment. Replica fuselage longerons were made from the smashed remains, and bent with the help of steam from a kettle while held to shape on a workbench, before being spliced to the aircraft. Replacements for the cockpit instruments, long since souvenired, were searched out far and wide. Tyres came courtesy of Dunlop, who found some tractor tyres of the right size and ground off their tread to match the smooth originals. The pilot's seat had to be rebuilt. The paint colours, duplicating its appearance on leaving

Forward cockpit of the Memorial's DH.9. AWM RELAWM07919.001

The Memorial's DH.9 stored at the Treloar Technology Centre in 2000. AWM PAIU2000/182.16

London, were matched to fabric fragments found inside the aircraft. One timber panel was left unpainted where the original RAF serial number, F1278, could still be read.

'PD' was ready in time for display at the 1988 Bicentennial Airshow at RAAF Richmond, New South Wales, and officially unveiled two years later on the seventieth anniversary of the flight. It is now one of just a handful of surviving DH.9s worldwide, and Australia's sole example. It is a fitting tribute to the daring and ingenuity of two young adventurers who took on the challenge of a remarkable journey against all odds of completing it.

The DH.9 in context

The DH.9 bomber evolved from the DH.4 which had entered service in March 1917, and was intended to fly faster and further while carrying a greater bomb load. In fact, it proved in many ways inferior, owing to its problematic engine, the Siddeley Puma, which lacked power and leaked oil. Nevertheless, the DH.9 was pressed into mass production by no less than 14 British manufacturers by war's end. First flying in July 1917 and reaching squadron service in November, its slowness and a high rate of engine failures led to some severe loss rates (80 per cent on one raid into Germany on 31 July 1918). Although it served with some 35 operational RAF squadrons, from the Western Front to Palestine and Russia, production still exceeded requirements. 'PD' was one of the many surplus DH.9s available for cheap purchase after the war.

As a type example, it represents an operational wartime bomber flown by, and in company with, Australians in the RAF. Although none of the wartime AFC squadrons flew the DH.9, at least one RAF squadron came under the command of an Australian. From June 1918 Lieutenant Colonel 'Dicky' Williams (later Air Marshal Sir Richard Williams KBE CB DSO) led 40 (Army) Wing of the Palestine Brigade, RAF. As well as his own 1 Squadron AFC, the wing comprised three RAF units, including 144 Squadron flying DH.9s, supported by Australian Bristol Fighters. Here, in the desert war against the Turks, the DH.9 proved more successful than on the Western Front. Bombing raids against rail centres and enemy headquarters greatly assisted the forces of General Sir Edmund Allenby and Colonel T.E. Lawrence, more famously known as Lawrence of Arabia.

After the war, the more powerful and successful DH.9a served through the 1920s as one of the RAF's main workhorses, protecting British colonial interests far and wide. In Australia, 28 DH.9s (bonus aircraft sent as compensation for aircraft donated by the nation for RAF service during the war) and 30 DH.9as arrived for the air corps in 1920. Together they made up nearly half of the Imperial Gift which made possible the formation of the RAAF the following year. The DH.9's primary role in the new air force was initially as an advanced trainer with 1 Flying Training School, Point Cook, Victoria, but later as an army cooperation aircraft with 1 and 3 Squadrons, with tasks such as artillery spotting and message retrieval. Long-range survey and mapping flights, as well as some night flying, were also performed. By 1929 the aging DH.9s and DH.9as were considered obsolete, and replaced by Westland Wapitis.

'PD' is something of a special case in the Memorial's collection, as it was preserved in light of a peacetime feat. However, the England-to-Australia air race had strong links to the First World War. The participating airmen were AIF personnel who had not yet returned home after the war's end in November 1918. Those who did not survive the flight are commemorated in the Australian War Memorial's Roll of Honour, as they died before the disbandment of the AIF which occurred on 31 March 1921. Two who were barred from the race, Charles Kingsford Smith and Bert Hinkler, were soon to become arguably Australia's most famous airmen.

Importantly, the race was also part of the wider Australian advancement of peacetime pursuits. The development of global air travel, with the specific aim of linking Britain with Australia, was seen as one of the primary means towards national prosperity in the wake of the devastation and horror of the First World War. Thus, the DH.9 fits well within the Memorial's charter, including its secondary mission to record the enduring impact of war on Australian society. The flight's 70th anniversary in 1990, for example, saw a commemorative world vintage air rally from England to Australia for pre-1950 aircraft. Locally, commemorative activities such as the unveiling of a memorial to Ray Parer at Bathurst Airport in February 2003, help to hold the achievement in the public memory. In a global sense, of course, the airliners which repeat the journey daily are its most obvious legacy. There have been few events as pivotal as the 'great air race' in the development of world air travel with its far-reaching consequences.

TIMELINE—'PD'	
1918	Built by Waring & Gillow furniture company, Hammersmith, London
1920	(Jan–Aug) England–Australia flight
1922	(Dec) Purchased 'in a very dilapidated condition' by the AWM for £250, and displayed at AWM Exhibition Buildings, Melbourne
1925–35	Displayed in AWM Sydney exhibition; by 1926 it was reportedly 'reduced to a shabby skeleton'
1927	Some refurbishment work done
1941–55	Displayed in Aircraft Hall, AWM, Canberra
1955–65	Stored at AWM store, Duntroon, ACT
1965–70	Moved to Bathurst, NSW, and stored at Parer's school, St. Stanislaus' College, where its condition further deteriorated
1970	Returned to Duntroon store. Australian Society for Aero-historical Preservation proposal to restore aircraft
1975	Restoration begun at Duntroon store
1986	Badly damaged by a car crash during restoration
1988	Restoration largely completed; displayed at Bicentennial Airshow, RAAF Richmond, NSW
1990	Official unveiling following restoration. Stored at AWM annexe, Mitchell, ACT
2008	Displayed in *Over the front* exhibition, ANZAC Hall

DATA

Type	DH.9
Design firm	G. de Havilland for Aircraft Manufacturing Co (Airco) of Hendon, London
Manufacturer	Waring & Gillow at Hammersmith, London
Role	Two-seat bomber
No. built	UK production: DH.9: more than 3,232 (500 by Waring & Gillow) DH.9a: more than 2,300
Type entered service	1917
Identity	F1278 (RAF)
	G-EAQM (UK civil)
Crew	2 (pilot, observer)
Powerplant	Siddeley-Deasey Puma 6-cylinder water-cooled engine of 230 hp (171 kW)
Armament	(operational bomber): 200-kg bomb load (two 230-lb bombs) One fixed .303-in Vickers and one Scarff-ring mounted .303-in Lewis machine-guns
Wingspan	14.3 m
Length	9.4 m
Max. speed	176 km/h
Endurance	4.5 hours
Max. take-off weight	1,510 kg

NOTES ON COLOUR SCHEME

The paint scheme applied during restoration was largely based on photographs, as much of the original fabric and the rear fuselage plywood had been replaced during the 1920s. The scheme chosen was the standard RFC scheme for DH.9s of pigmented cellulose PC.10 khaki green, with blue-grey on plywood section of fuselage, and aluminium nose and engine cowls. Additional markings include sponsor's initials 'P.D.' in large white letters, black-shadowed, on fuselage sides; civil registration 'G-EAQM' in black against white rectangle on rear fuselage sides and upper wings; and black letter 'G' in a white square on rudder sides. Photographs taken at Moulmein, Burma, in 1920 show sponsors' names, 'Shell' and 'Firestone', painted on the undersides of upper and lower wings, respectively.

War in Europe
1939–1945

SPITFIRE MK II P7973

12,000 ft over Mardyck–Bethune region, northern France
1130 HOURS, 9 AUGUST 1941

In wild and sudden elation, Blue kicked his controls and gave him the lot, burnt through his gun-patches for the first time and fired continuously for five seconds, point-blank. The enemy tail-fin disintegrated before his eyes, the elevator peeled off like paper and the [Messerschmitt Bf] 109 tripped in its stride and fell. Blue went after it, fiercely, down and down, until it passed vertically into cloud like a meteor a thousand feet above the earth.[1]

Pilot Officer Keith 'Bluey' Truscott, flying as Green One with 452 Squadron RAAF, had just shot down his first confirmed German aircraft. His mount was a Supermarine Spitfire Mk IIa, serial no. P7973, which had been delivered to the RAF eight months earlier. In this fast-advancing technological war, eight months was a long time, and the Mk IIa had already been made obsolescent by the more powerful Mk V now coming into service with the squadron. It was still, nevertheless, a formidable opponent in the right hands. After his victory Truscott dived down to strafe the harbour at Boulogne,

The supreme fighter aircraft.
Ivan Southall, Bluey Truscott

Spitfire P7973 served with RAF Central Gunnery School at Catfoss, Yorkshire, during 1944. It still wears this paint scheme today. AWM 148873

A flight of 452 Squadron Spitfires sets out from Kirton-in-Lindsey, Lincolnshire, mid-1941. AWM SUK15120

anti-aircraft fire following him out to sea as he headed home. The powerfully-built, red-haired Melburnian was still better known to the Australian public as an Australian Rules footballer, but that was set to change over the next few months as he became the best known pilot in the RAAF. Years later, the aircraft he flew that day would become known to visitors at the Australian War Memorial as Truscott's Spitfire.

The operation this day was a 'circus' escort. Several squadrons of fighters, hoping to lure the *Luftwaffe* up for a fight, greatly outnumbered the five bombers they were escorting. It paid off: just before arriving over the target, Gosnay in Pas-de-Calais, the escort wing ran into a hundred Messerschmitt Bf 109s. Within seconds it was a free-for-all. Truscott's friend and mentor, 20-year-old Irishman Flight Lieutenant 'Paddy' Finucane DFC[2] (Red One), shared in the destruction of one enemy aircraft with Pilot Officer Donald Lewis (White Two), another with Pilot Officer Ray Thorold-Smith (Yellow One), and shot down a third himself. When the flight returned to base at Kenley in south London, the commanding officer, Squadron Leader Bob Bungey (Blue One), found cannon holes in his Spitfire. Meanwhile Sergeant Richard Gazzard (White One) brought his crippled Spitfire, its propeller damaged, in to Lympne just across the coast of Kent.

Senator Justin O'Byrne visits his old
Spitfire at the Memorial in 1976.
AWM 043790

Senator Justin O'Byrne visits his old
Spitfire at the Memorial in 1976.
AWM 043790

Within two years, all these young pilots would be dead. Two others, Sergeants
Christopher Chapman and Gerald Haydon (Green Two, Truscott's No. 2 man), were shot
down and killed that very day. A third man missing from this operation, Pilot Officer
Justin O'Byrne (Blue Two, Bungey's No. 2 man) of Tasmania, who had flown P7973
previously, as had Bungey, was later found to have been captured and hospitalised at
Saint Omer, France. He was soon a prisoner in *Stalag Luft III* at Sagan, Germany (now
Poland). He was still there in March 1944, waiting in an underground tunnel during the
Great Escape when the German guards discovered the attempt. Fifty officers, Australians
among them, were killed for their audacious efforts. O'Byrne, who later became a
Tasmanian senator, helped to erect a memorial to them outside the barbed wire.

◄   ►

Truscott was a foundation member of 452 Squadron. Its pilots formed a close-knit and
dedicated band, and several would later become household names. His flight on 9
August came just a month after 'first blood' for this, the first Australian fighter squadron
in Britain. It was also Truscott's last operation in P7973 before the squadron converted
fully to the Spitfire Mk V. A number of other pilots, some destined for fame had also
flown P7973. Thorold-Smith had flown its first operation with the squadron, and would
later shoot down six enemy aircraft in other Spitfires, before being killed in action
against the Japanese in March 1943. Flying Officer Andrew Humphrey (later Chief of
the British Defence Staff, Sir Andrew Humphrey GCB OBE DFC AFC and 2 Bars) had
destroyed a Bf 109E while flying P7973 near Cherbourg on 24 July. The day before,
Truscott had been piloting it when he sent a Bf 109 into a dive, although he was not

able to confirm that it crashed. On 7 November Truscott himself was shot down in another Spitfire, but baled out and soon rejoined the squadron.

Keith 'Bluey' Truscott

After captaining his school football and cricket teams and attending the youth organisation Lord Somers' Camp and Power House, Truscott played for the Melbourne Football Club and worked as a clerk. Joining the RAAF in July 1940, he began learning to fly at the Elementary Flying Training School at Essendon in Melbourne. While his flying abilities were assessed as below average to average, he was 'outstanding in all essential qualities as an officer' and 'would have plenty of fight'. In action, his sheer tenacity and good marksmanship made up for unexceptional flying ability.

In January 1942, after seven months with 452 Squadron, Flying Officer Truscott was promoted to acting squadron leader to take command of the unit. Awarded a Distinguished Flying Cross and Bar, in March he was posted back to Australia with the squadron. While on leave, for old times' sake he played a game with the Melbourne Football Club in May, declaring at the end of it, 'Not for me. Too dangerous.'[3] His next posting was to 76 Squadron RAAF in Queensland, which was re-forming with Kittyhawk fighters.

As a supernumerary acting squadron leader, Truscott was in an invidious position in the unit.[4] Unfairly, a pilot's experience in Europe held no weight among squadron personnel in the Pacific war, and it was expected that he would revert to his substantive rank. In Truscott's case, public opinion ensured that he remained a squadron leader. He took part in the fighting at Milne Bay, Papua (see Kittyhawk chapter); when the squadron's commanding officer, Peter Turnbull, was killed in August 1942, Truscott took over command and showed outstanding leadership during the attempted Japanese invasion. He was Mentioned in Despatches, and the squadron received a unit commendation from US Major General George Kenney, commander of the Allied Air Forces in the Pacific. Truscott's destruction of 16 German and Japanese aircraft (unofficially 20.5) made him the RAAF's equal-third most successful fighter pilot of the war.

In a twist of fate, in March 1943 Truscott was flying a Kittyhawk in a practice attack on a US Catalina flying boat in Exmouth Gulf, Western Australia, when he misjudged his height over the glass-calm water and flew into the sea. Pilot Officer Loudon in a second Kittyhawk saw the aircraft lose its propeller and rebound 60 m into the air, before rolling over and diving vertically into the water on fire. The remains of the fighter were found and raised from 10 m of water the following day, Truscott's body still strapped in.[5] An airfield in northern Western Australia was named after him, as was a street in Canberra near the Australian War Memorial.

'Bluey' Truscott in October 1942. He was killed six months later. AWM 013061

The watch Truscott was wearing when he was shot down in a Spitfire on 7 November 1941 is held by the Memorial. AWM RELAWM32038

Its two months in action with 452 Squadron was not the end of P7973's career. Shortly after Truscott's victory it went to 313 (Czech) Squadron RAF, flying from Portreath in Cornwall. The Czech pilots had escaped from their homeland after the Nazi invasion and, tenacious in fighting spirit, went to England to join the RAF; 313 was the third Czech squadron in the RAF.

On 28 September 1941 the squadron flew an escort mission to France for four Whirlwind fighters, on a low-level attack against Morlaix aerodrome. On the return trip, Sergeant Arnost Mrtvy in P7973 was busy avoiding anti-aircraft fire when he was dazzled by tracer and explosions, and flew the Spitfire into a telegraph pole. The other pilots heard his urgent call of distress, in Czech, in their headsets: 'Spearhead blue four. I've bought it! The whole aircraft is shaking. I don't think I will make it, chaps. Give my love to my wife.'[6] Two pilots were sent back to find Mrtvy and escort him home. By now his engine was overheating and losing power, and Mrtvy was in shock and not feeling well. His voice on the radio was unsteady. When his fellow pilots found his aircraft over the Channel, they could see half a metre of telegraph pole protruding from the port wing, and engine oil covering the underside. Remarkably, he managed to bring the crippled Spitfire in to Predannack airfield in Cornwall, and was given two days' leave to visit his wife. Spitfire P7973 saw no more action against the enemy, but two and a half years later Mrtvy (whose name means 'dead' in Czech) was shot down and killed in Belgium.

By 1942 the Mk II variant of the Spitfire was obsolescent, and although P7973 had a partial upgrade to Mk V standard (its propeller spinner, canopy and ailerons, for example, being changed), it was relegated to the pilot instruction role. Training new pilots could also be hazardous, and at least four crash landings are recorded. On 19 July while with 57 Operational Training Unit (OTU) at Hawarden, North Wales, the unit which had supplied most of 452 Squadron's initial pilots, Sergeant Booth was taking off in P7973 when a tyre burst. He got the aircraft airborne and came back around for a landing, but on touchdown could not hold the Spitfire on its good tyre. The aircraft ground looped and nosed over, and although damaged it was soon repaired.

Another flying accident, with 61 OTU at Rednal, Shropshire, in December, was potentially more serious. Belgian Pilot Officer Duchateau was following the twists and turns of the River Dee during a low flying exercise, when he made such a violent turn that he blacked out. The subsequent inquiry relates that 'the pilot's lack of English precludes an accurate description of the accident, but he presumably hit some object yet to be identified'. A damaged propeller necessitated a forced landing, and again P7973 was repaired.

By May 1944, the now aging Spitfire was serving with the RAF Central Gunnery School at Catfoss, Yorkshire. Its 452 Squadron service was still on record, and when the RAAF requested a Spitfire that month for eventual preservation by the Australian War Memorial, a natural choice was one flown by Truscott. Although it had finished its fighting early in the war, it would commemorate not only the Australian Spitfire pilots who fought the *Luftwaffe*, but now also those fighting the Japanese on the other side of the world. (See 'The Spitfire in context' below.)

In surviving the war, P7973 was more fortunate than several of the men who flew it. Twenty-four-year-old Pilot Officer Bill Willis of Melbourne was killed in action near Rouen, France the month after flying it. Truscott, as described here, died accidentally in March 1943. Perhaps the saddest story is that of his fellow 452 Squadron commander and a Battle of Britain veteran, Wing Commander Bob Bungey DFC, 'the man who made the Australian Spitfire squadron', in Truscott's words. Three months after Truscott's death, Bungey was found dead on Brighton beach in Adelaide, a .38 revolver near his body.[7] After losing so many of his squadron friends, he had lost his English wife to illness a fortnight before. Their baby son was taken into care by his parents.

452 Squadron RAAF

This was the first of the Australian squadrons to form in Britain during the Second World War, in compliance with Article XV of the Empire Air Training Scheme. Starting out at Kirton-in-Lindsey, Lincolnshire, in April 1941 it began operations with the Spitfire Mk IIa[8] in south-east England with 11 Group, RAF Fighter Command, the next month.

The squadron's operations included defensive patrols over England and the Channel as far as occupied France and Belgium, escorting bombing raids, and flying fighter sweeps in search of enemy aircraft. During its year fighting the *Luftwaffe*, it established itself as one of the most successful squadrons in Fighter Command, destroying 62 enemy aircraft and damaging another 17. Shipping was also a target: on 11 February 1942 the squadron strafed and severely damaged a German destroyer during the dash through the English Channel made by the German battlecruisers *Scharnhorst*, *Gneisenau* and *Prince Eugen*. For his part in this operation, Truscott earned a Bar to his DFC.

Squadron Leader Bob Bungey DFC in mid-1941. AWM SUK15123

The squadron finished operations in Britain in March 1942. It sailed for Australia as one of the three Spitfire squadrons requested by Prime Minister Curtin for the country's defence. The squadron re-assembled at RAAF Richmond near Sydney in September, and after re-equipping with new Spitfires it returned to front-line service the following January. It was based at Batchelor, south of Darwin, then at the nearby Strauss and Sattler airstrips. Meanwhile, 457 Squadron was stationed at Livingstone, and 54 Squadron RAF at Darwin. Apart from a brief period in March 1943, when it was deployed to reinforce the air defences of Perth, 452 remained in the Darwin area until December 1944. During the latter half of the year, a new RAF squadron defended Darwin, relieving 452 to range out to the Netherlands East Indies on ground attack sorties.

The squadron next joined the 1st Tactical Air Force and relocated to Morotai to support Australian operations in Borneo, and to the island of Tarakan in May and June 1945. Following the Australian landing at Balikpapan on 1 July, a detachment moved there to support the land campaign. The squadron's last sorties of the war were flown on 10 August 1945, and it was disbanded two months later.

OPERATIONS FLOWN BY SPITFIRE P7973 WITH 452 SQUADRON RAAF, 1941		
Date	**Pilot**	**Comments**
19 June	PO Thorold-Smith	Dusk patrol. No incident
26 June	Sqn Ldr Bungey	Dusk patrol. No incident
27 June	Sqn Ldr Bungey	Dusk patrol. No incident
28 June	PO Willis	2 x convoy patrol. No incident
30 June	PO Willis	2 x convoy patrol. No incident
2 July	Sqn Ldr Bungey	Dusk patrol. No incident
3 July	Sqn Ldr Bungey	Dusk patrol. No incident
14 July	PO Truscott	Scramble—Kirton-in-Lindsey to North Coates and return. No incident
22 July	FO Humphrey	Cover over Channel for returning bombers. No incident
22 July	FO Humphrey	Wing sweep at 10,000 ft. St Valory to Le Croty. No incident Squadron moved to Kenley
23 July	PO Truscott	Channel sweep to Saint Omer. Bf 109 shot at with a quick burst; it dived almost vertically, result unknown
23 July	PO Truscott	Sweep
24 July	FO Humphrey	Sweep Kenley to Merston
24 July	FO Humphrey	Operation Sunrise 2 to Cherbourg. Destroyed Bf 109E during return
26 July	FO Humphrey	Convoy escort
31 July	FO Humphrey	Bomber escort. No incident
3 August	FO Humphrey	Sweep to Saint Omer. Bf 109s attacked
6 August	PO O'Byrne	Sweep[9]
7 August	PO O'Byrne	Close escort for Blenheims. Heavy flak
7 August	PO Truscott	High cover for Blenheims
9 August	PO Truscott	Destroyed Bf 109 between Mardyck and Bethune. (Squadron claims five Bf 109s; three Spitfires missing)
12 August	Sgt Tainton	Patrol to Saint Omer. Moderate flak. Enemy aircraft attacked

The Spitfire in the Second World War gallery in 2001. Like the Memorial's Bf 109, its paintwork is original.
AWM PAIU2001/270.17

The Spitfire in context

Britain's most famous aircraft, the Spitfire was the brainchild of Supermarine's chief designer, R.J. Mitchell. Mitchell had already made his name designing entrants in the Schneider Trophy seaplane race, culminating in the Supermarine S.6B which in 1931 set a world air speed record of 655 km/h. The experience gained from these projects was mated with the new Rolls-Royce Merlin engine to produce the Spitfire prototype, designated F.37/34. Its first flights, in March 1936, proved it to be the world's fastest military aircraft. The RAF could see that this was going to be a world beater, and it was ordered into mass production.

During the Battle of Britain in the summer of 1940, the Spitfire flew beside the Hurricane against the *Luftwaffe* onslaught to turn the tide of the war. While fitted with the same engine and armament as the Hurricane, its lightweight, stressed-skin design and thin, low-drag elliptical wings gave it the edge in speed and high-altitude performance. It went on to see service around the world, in all Allied air forces, including those of the United States and the USSR, throughout the war. Australians flew Spitfires in the Battle of Britain, Europe (including support of the D-Day landings), the Middle East, Burma, the defence of the Northern Territory, the Netherlands East Indies and finally in the Borneo campaigns. Although most famous in its air superiority/interceptor role, the Spitfire's tasks also included ground attack and photo-reconnaissance.

RAAF SPITFIRE SQUADRONS		
Squadron	First operational with Spitfires	Operational base areas
452	May 1941	England, Darwin, Morotai, Tarakan
457	June 1941	England, Darwin, Morotai
453	June 1942	England, France
79	June 1943	Goodenough Island, Morotai, Darwin
85	October 1944	Perth
451	February 1944	Corsica, France, Italy, England
ROYAL AIR FORCE SPITFIRE SQUADRONS IN AUSTRALIA		
54	October 1942	Darwin
548	July 1944	Darwin
549	July 1944	Darwin

In May 1942, British Prime Minister Winston Churchill agreed to the release of three UK-based Spitfire squadrons for the defence of Australia. The cannon-armed Spitfire Mk Vc aircraft ordered for them were assigned a codename (Capstan, a brand of cigarette) so that the Japanese would not be alerted to their arrival. After the first examples arrived in secrecy in October, they began joining the formerly UK-based 452 and 457 Squadrons RAAF and 54 Squadron RAF. Together forming 1 Wing RAAF under Group Captain Clive Caldwell, they finally became operational at Darwin and its satellite fighter strips in January 1943. This was nearly a year after the first Japanese raids on Darwin, during which time American and Australian Kittyhawks had been defending the town and nearby airfields. Nevertheless, the Spitfires saw eight months of intense action against Japanese bombers, fighters and reconnaissance aircraft before Japan's final raid on the Northern Territory in November 1943.

Although it saw much success in the war against Japan, the Spitfire had limitations in this war theatre which had not been so apparent in Britain and Europe. Its limited fuel capacity greatly restricted its radius of operations. Also, despite having a tropical filter fitted to its air intake, the Mk Vc was not well suited to the northern Australian conditions of heat, dust and humidity, and engine overheating was common. The narrow-track undercarriage made the aircraft unstable on rough airstrips. In September 1943 the latest Spitfire model, the Mk VIII, arrived with its high-altitude two-stage supercharged engine, four-blade propeller and redesigned tail. It made up the majority of the 656 Spitfires delivered to the RAAF.

By war's end, more Spitfires had been built than any other aircraft among the western Allied nations. After the war, the type stayed on in RAF service until 1952. The number of its variants ran to 24, in addition to numerous versions of the navalised Seafire. The final variant, the Griffon-engined Seafire FR.47, bore little resemblance to the original Mk I, neither in appearance nor in capabilities: although 25 per cent heavier, the FR.47 had twice the rate of climb of the Mk I, 140 per cent more power, and cannon armament producing three times its weight of fire.

TIMELINE—P7973

1940	Built at Castle Bromwich Aircraft Factory, Birmingham, UK
1941	(Jan) Test flown and delivered to RAF
1941	(Apr–May) Served with 222 (Natal) Squadron RAF, Coltishall, Norfolk; flew 10 operations, mostly 'kipper' patrols
1941	(Jun–Aug) Served with 452 Squadron RAAF, Kirton-in-Lindsey, Lincolnshire (12 Group RAF) and Kenley, Surrey (11 Group RAF); flew 24 operations
1941	(Aug–Sept) Served with 313 (Czech) Squadron RAF, Cornwall; flew 18 operations
1942–44	Served with 57, 61 and 42 Operational Training Units RAF. Damaged several times. Repaired at Hamble, Feb 1942
1944	(May) Served with RAF Central Gunnery School; selected for Australian War Memorial
1945	(Mar) Despatched from Liverpool on SS *Port Adelaide* to Melbourne. Stored at Werribee, Vic., then RAAF Canberra, and issued to AWM in 1950
1955–99	Displayed in Aircraft Hall
2000–	Displayed in Second World War gallery

DATA

Type	Spitfire Mk IIa
Design firm	Supermarine (subsidiary of Vickers-Armstrongs) UK
Manufacturer	Vickers-Armstrongs at Castle Bromwich Aircraft Factory, Birmingham, UK
Role	Single-seat fighter
Used by	RAAF and RAF
No. built	921 (Mk II); 20,334 (Spitfire total)
Subtype entered service	Sep 1940
Identity	P7973 (RAF)
	Constructor's number CBAF 492
Powerplant	Rolls-Royce Merlin XII V-12 liquid-cooled engine of 1,175 hp (876 kW)
Armament	Eight .303-in Browning machine-guns
Wingspan	11.23 m
Length	9.12 m
Max. speed	570 km/h
Range	800 km
Loaded weight	2,870 kg

NOTES ON COLOUR SCHEME

During its service with 452 Squadron RAAF in mid-1941, P7973 wore the temperate land scheme: dark earth and dark green upper surface camouflage, and sky (light grey) undersides and spinner. Fuselage code letters 'UD-N' in medium sea grey. RAF roundels type A (underwing), type B (wing upper surfaces) and Type A1 (fuselage). On rear fuselage: duck-egg green band and black serial number. Fin flash in red/white/blue.

Prior to this, the aircraft may have displayed the 222 Squadron code letters 'ZD', and afterwards the 313 Squadron code letters 'PY', in place of 'UD'.

In August 1941, at the time P7973 left 452 Squadron, a new day fighter camouflage scheme intended to make the aircraft less visible at high altitude came into effect: ocean grey and dark green upper surface camouflage, and medium sea grey undersides. In 1944 the fuselage code letters 'R-H' of the RAF Central Gunnery School were painted in medium sea grey. These camouflage and markings, together with the roundels, fin flash, fuselage band and serial number described above, are the scheme it still bears.

As with the Memorial's Messerschmitt Bf 109, part of the significance of P7973 is that it retains its Second World War–period paint. In this respect, it is almost unique among the 100 or more remaining Spitfires.

LANCASTER W4783 'G FOR GEORGE'

9,000 ft over Peenemünde rocket research facility, off the Baltic coast of Germany

0145 HOURS, 18 AUGUST 1943

The bomber crews had never seen anything like this. On most nights the danger was hidden in darkness, but tonight, under a full moon, they could clearly see German fighters everywhere. Newspapers later described it as 'the greatest night air battle the war has seen' with 'fighters hopping in and out of the stream of bombers like they were crossing the road'.[10]

The final wave of 560 British Lancasters, Halifaxes and Stirlings had just released their bombs and turned for home when they were caught by the German *Nachtjagdgeschwader* (NJG) night fighter wings. Some 200 twin- and single-engined fighters were in the air that night: Messerschmitt Bf 110G-4s, Junkers Ju 88s, Dornier Do 217s, Messerschmitt Bf 109G-6s, Focke-Wulf Fw 190s. Many were operating as free-ranging interceptors, the so-called *Wilde Sau* (wild boar), which searched out the bombers visually without the use of radar.

Two Bf 110s, piloted by *Leutnant* Peter Erhardt and *Unteroffizier* Walter Hölker of 5/NJG5, were trialling the new radar-assisted *Schräge Musik* cannon installation. They followed the bomber stream west on its homeward leg and, moving into position in the

> *An indispensable contribution to victory.*
>
> Noble Frankland, Bomber offensive: the devastation of Europe

'G for George' at RAAF Laverton, 14 November 1944, after arriving from Britain. AWM VIC1753

blind spot beneath each targeted aircraft, remained undetected. With their two upward-firing cannon they shot down six, including an Australian Lancaster,[11] the crewmen never knowing what hit them. Nearby, using conventional forward-firing armament, *Leutnant* Dieter Musset of II/NJG1 shot down another five bombers in less than 15 minutes[12] before being shot down himself. Earlier, five other Bf 110s of NJG1, flown by experienced night fighter aces, had headed out over the North Sea and engaged five Beaufighters on an intruder mission to German airfields. Leading the Beaufighters was RAF ace Wing Commander Bob Braham, who shot down two of the enemy; leading the Messerschmitts was *Leutnant* Heinz-Wolfgang Schnaufer, who before war's end would destroy 121 aircraft to become Germany's most notorious night fighter ace.

Despite its successes against the bombers, the *Luftwaffe* had arrived too late to protect Peenemünde—a disgrace which soon led its chief of staff, *Generaloberst* Hans Jeschonnek, to commit suicide. The fighter attack came just after 5 and 6 Groups RAF in the third and final wave had completed their bombing of the experimental works. The German air response had been delayed by a decoy raid on Berlin by Mosquitos, and it was there that most of the fighters had first gone. Had they not been thus deceived, the raid could well have failed and Bomber Command would probably have suffered its worst loss of the war.

By the time the fighters did arrive, 18 Lancasters of 460 Squadron RAAF in the second wave of the attack were on their way home. Although their crews reported nine aerial combats and two night fighters probably destroyed, only one of the squadron's aircraft was hit: the Lancaster flown by Flight Sergeant Danny Rees, badly shot up by both flak and a Ju 88 fighter. After losing 2,500 l of fuel from bullet holes in the main fuel tanks, Rees managed to get the bomber back to Britain.

Flight Sergeant Don Moodie's crew, an experienced team comprising mostly Australians, was among those lucky to miss the fighters. It was their first time in Lancaster W4783, callsign 'G for George'. The bomber had almost been written off in a ground explosion six weeks earlier, but its senior fitter, Flight Sergeant Harry Tickle, was not to be beaten and 'George' was repaired in time for this maximum effort.

At 12.35 am, an hour before the main fighter force arrived, Moodie's bomb aimer, Flight Sergeant Stanley Bethel, had checked the switches on his bomb selection panel, and knelt in concentration in the bomber's nose. He peered through the Mk XIV bombsight, release button in hand. Light cloud drifted past in patches, and a smoke cloud, the Germans' attempt to screen the complex, was blowing east of the target. It was a long, agonising run low over the anti-aircraft defences towards the target as Bethel checked and re-checked the patterns of buildings here and there in the wooded landscape below. Moodie relayed over the intercom the bomber's course and altitude, as Bethel fed the numbers into the computer at his side. 'Left... right... steady...' he instructed the pilot. 'Bomb doors open.' In the moonlight he had a clear view of the factory workshops through the bombsight glass.

A tail fin from Major Heinz-Wolfgang Schnaufer's Messerschmitt Bf 110G-4 records the 121 British bombers he destroyed at night, including RAAF Lancasters and Halifaxes. AWM RELAWM35144

The Pathfinders and their 'master bomber',[13] which circled the target directing the attack, had accomplished their task. In the bombsight, green target indicators seemed to be concentrated right on target, and Bethel was satisfied. He pressed the bomb release button, and nine 1,000-lb bombs fell to explode among the markers. The F-24 camera exposed a picture, and Moodie banked the bomber to turn for home.

Each of the three waves of bombers attacked a different part of the Peenemünde complex: the living quarters for the scientists and workers, the experimental station, and the rocket factory workshops. Tragically, 7 km away, the camp for the slave labourers was mistakenly bombed, and over 500 were killed in addition to the 180 Germans who died in the residential area.

◄　►

The choice of a moonlit night removed the bombers' best defence against night fighters, and the low altitude ordered (less than half that of most operations) exposed the bombers to increased accuracy from enemy anti-aircraft fire. These two calculated risks taken by the raid's planners highlighted the importance of accurate bombing, and made it clear to the crews that Peenemünde was no ordinary target. They had also been told that if they did not severely damage the target they would be back the next night—a frightening prospect after the defences had been alerted. Nevertheless, they had no idea of the target's true nature. The story fed to them had been that it was a research station developing new radar defence countermeasures for use against them. The rocket development work was not divulged, as it was vital that British intelligence about the complex and its work be kept secret.

That intelligence had brought to light some alarming developments. Fragments of information, beginning with the 'Oslo Report' of November 1939, spoke of the development of self-guided, long-range rocket bombs. However, it was not until March 1943 that the British had made any follow-up investigations. Aerial photographs taken by reconnaissance Mosquitos not only confirmed that the rockets existed, but showed that they could almost be ready for operational use.

In fact, the first successful experimental launch of an A-4 (soon to be known as the V-2[14]) self-guided rocket at Peenemünde had been made six months earlier, on 3 October 1942. Wernher von Braun's design[15] was proven. Hitler was soon convinced of its merits, and authorised the allocation of vast resources to it. The British photographs and other evidence also pointed to flying bombs and rocket-powered fighter aircraft (see the Me 163 chapter) at the *Luftwaffe* airfield on the other side of the peninsula. If the German scientists were left to perfect these new technologies for large-scale production, it could seriously hamper the Allied war effort. Despite the view of some (including the top scientific adviser to the Prime Minister and the War Cabinet) that it was all an elaborate hoax, and that the Germans were not capable of developing an operational rocket, the evidence was considered reliable enough to launch an all-out attack.

A Lancaster silhouetted over the burning city of Hamburg, Germany, during a night bombing raid.
AWM 044855

The cost to RAF Bomber Command on the night of 17–18 August 1943 was 40 bombers and over 200 men killed, with a further 35 aircraft badly damaged. The Command's chief, Sir Arthur 'Bomber' Harris, considered the loss of 7 per cent of the force acceptable in light of the target damage assessment, and hailed the Peenemünde raid as a fine demonstration of the ability of bombers to search out and destroy key targets in the face of strong enemy defences. It was the only successful precision attack by a large force that RAF Bomber Command made. Thereafter, Harris's force continued in its attempt to destroy Germany's great cities and their war industries by 'area bombing'.

The Americans, continuing what they regarded as precision daylight attacks on German industry, were suffering even worse loss rates. On the same day as the Peenemünde raid they launched a two-pronged attack on the ball-bearing plant at Schweinfurt and the Messerschmitt aircraft factory at Regensburg. Despite achieving heavy damage to the factories, the loss of a disastrous 16 per cent of the force (60 out of 376 B-17 Flying Fortresses), with hundreds of crewmen killed, provoked a strategic rethink of unescorted missions over Germany.

The RAF crews had done their job: the damage to the Peenemünde complex was assessed as sufficiently serious that the force would not be obliged to return. Numerous medals were awarded to crewmen after the raid, including a Conspicuous Gallantry

At Binbrook in the early hours of 26 June 1943, Flying Officer Bob Henderson's crew leaves 'G for George' after a bombing raid on Gelsenkirchen, Germany. A few days later the aircraft was badly damaged by an explosion on the tarmac. AWM P03173.004

Medal to Flight Sergeant Rees and a Distinguished Flying Medal to Flight Sergeant Moodie.

The damage assessment may have been premature; although Peenemünde's housing estate was heavily damaged, the experimental and production works had suffered only moderate damage. An important post-war US report went so far as to conclude that the raid was ineffective. That view, however, must be considered overly pessimistic, as the Germans themselves estimated that the V-2 experimental program had been set back for two months or more. The raid also killed the V-2's chief propulsion scientist, Dr Walter Thiel, and precipitated the relocation of V-2 production to the *Mittelwerk* underground facility near Nordhausen,[16] with all the disruption that this entailed. All this considered, the raid may have saved London and Antwerp, in particular, from 700 or more potential V-2 rocket attacks which could have been launched in the year before the rocket's actual operational deployment in September 1944. It also reduced the scale of the eventual assault, although by how much is a matter of conjecture.

The campaign against Germany's V-weapons continued for the rest of the war. The following year the complex was attacked again, this time by a thousand American B-17s in three consecutive raids. The attacks on Peenemünde, and other factors including fuel shortages, so hampered the production and deployment of the V-2 that by war's end, the combined destructive power of all the V-2s launched did not exceed that of just one large Bomber Command raid. Nevertheless, they did have a disproportionately disruptive effect on daily life in the targeted cities, London and

Antwerp in particular. The V-2s could not be predicted or be seen approaching, nor could they be readily attacked in the air.

The D-Day invasion in June 1944 started the Allies' inexorable push east which, together with Russia's push west to Berlin, ended with Germany's defeat. Throughout that push, Operation Crossbow conducted a campaign both of attacking German rocket production and of defence against the V-1 flying bomb. Peenemünde itself links Lancaster 'G for George' with the two V-weapons in the Memorial's collection; the V-2 was developed there and the V-1 was test-flown there. 'George' is also linked with Schnaufer's Messerschmitt tail fin, and with the Messerschmitt Bf 109G-6. All serve in different ways as reminders of Hitler's vengeance weapons: the forces deployed to defend them, the thousands of people they killed, and their frightening potential, had their development and production continued unhindered.

◄ ►

The effectiveness of Bomber Command's campaign throughout the course of the war is more difficult to quantify than the results of one raid. For a start, it must be considered in light of the deaths of 55,000 British and Commonwealth crewmen, including some 3,500 Australians, as well as more than a quarter of a million civilians in Germany and occupied countries. Undoubtedly Bomber Command played a crucial part in Germany's defeat, but it did not win the war on its own, as 'Bomber' Harris had hoped.

'G for George' over the main street of Murray Bridge, near Adelaide, during the Third Victory Loan fundraising tour in March 1945. Some 2,000 passengers were taken aloft during the tour. AWM P03710.001

'G for George' was half way through its operational career at the time of the Peenemünde raid. In April 1944, after a year and a half of active service, it flew the last of its 89 operations. By then its operations had shifted to pre-invasion attacks on Nazi transportation systems in France. Through the dedication and skill of its maintenance and flight crews and a good deal of luck, 'George' had made it through Bomber Command's most dangerous period, surviving the battle of the Ruhr Valley (Germany's industrial hub) before Peenemünde, the battle of Berlin immediately after it, and in 1944 two disastrous raids on Leipzig and Nuremberg, which between them cost nearly 180 bombers and their crews. The flight of 'George' to Australia, and the hundreds of passenger flights it made in 1945 to sell war bonds, must have seemed like milk runs in comparison.

'G for George' and 460 Squadron RAAF: 'Strike and Return'

460 Squadron was formed at Molesworth, Cambridgeshire, in November 1941 in accordance with Article XV of the Empire Air Training Scheme agreement. With a mix of Australian, British and other Commonwealth personnel, the squadron joined RAF Bomber Command in the strategic bombing campaign against the industry, infrastructure and cities of Germany, Italy and the occupied countries. Initially flying Vickers Wellington bombers, it mounted its first raids in March 1942, operating under 1 Group of Bomber Command from RAF Breighton and, later, RAF Binbrook.

Over the next three years the squadron was in constant action, sometimes committing its full complement of 24 to 28 bombers on 'maximum effort' operations. Although it had originally been planned to re-equip it with Handley Page Halifaxes in September 1942, the squadron only used the Halifax for training and converted to Lancasters the following month.

'G for George' was among the first Lancasters to join the squadron. The bulk of its operations formed part of the strategic bombing offensive against Germany, although in the months before the D-Day landings in June 1944 it supported the preparatory operations for the Allied invasion. The diary of its senior ground fitter, Flight Sergeant Harry Tickle, records some of 'G for George's' close calls, including damage from flak and fighters on 20 occasions. The entries from 1943 include 'Nearly wrecked aircraft' (27 March), '17 flak holes' (16 June), 'Incendiary bomb went through tailplane' (31 August), 'Fighter came close, read the letter 'G' and left smartly' (16 December). As the squadron's oldest surviving aircraft, 'George' was retired from service in April 1944 to fly to Australia for a publicity tour and, thereafter, to join the Memorial's collection.

'460' was acclaimed as the most efficient of the Australian bomber squadrons, maintaining consistently high serviceability rates among its aircraft. As one of the larger and longest-serving RAAF bomber squadrons, it flew the most raids and dropped the greatest tonnage of bombs (some 25,000 t). In so doing, the squadron suffered heavily, losing 1,018 men killed or missing, including 589 Australians, and 181 aircraft on operations.

OPERATIONS FLOWN BY LANCASTER W4783 'G FOR GEORGE'

Year	Operation number	Date	Target	Captain	Bombers despatched	Bombers lost
1942	1	6 Dec	Mannheim	Flt Sgt J.A. Saint-Smith	272	14
	2	8 Dec	Sea mining off Denmark	Flt Sgt A. McKinnon	80	5
	3	9 Dec	Turin	Flt Sgt A. McKinnon	272	3
	4	17 Dec	Sea mining off Denmark	Flt Sgt J.A. Saint-Smith	50	–
1943	5	16 Jan	Berlin	Flt Sgt J.A. Saint-Smith	201	1
	6	3 Feb	Hamburg	Flt Sgt J.A. Saint-Smith	263	16
	7	7 Feb	Lorient	Flt Sgt J.A. Saint-Smith	323	7
	8	11 Feb	Wilhelmshaven	Flt Sgt J.A. Saint-Smith	177	3
	9	13 Feb	Lorient	Flt Sgt J.A. Saint-Smith	466	7
	10	14 Feb	Milan	Flt Sgt J.A. Saint-Smith	142	2
	11	16 Feb	Lorient	Flt Sgt J.A. Saint-Smith	377	1
	12	21 Feb	Bremen	Flt Sgt J.A. Saint-Smith	143	–
	13	26 Feb	Cologne	Flt Sgt J.A. Saint-Smith	427	10
	14	28 Feb	St Nazaire	Flt Sgt J.A. Saint-Smith	437	5
	15	1 Mar	Berlin	Flt Sgt J.A. Saint-Smith	302	17
The battle of the Ruhr						
	16	5 Mar	Essen	Flt Sgt J. Murray	442	14
	17	8 Mar	Nuremberg	Flt Sgt J. Murray	335	8
	18	9 Mar	Munich	Flt Sgt J. Murray	264	8
	19	11 Mar	Stuttgart	W Cdr C. Martin	314	11
	20	12 Mar	Essen	Flt Sgt J. Murray	457	23
	21	22 Mar	St Nazaire	Flt Sgt J. Murray	357	1
	22	26 Mar	Duisburg	Flt Sgt J. Murray	455	6
	23	27 Mar	Berlin	Flt Sgt J. Murray	396	9
	24	29 Mar	Berlin	Flt Sgt J. Murray	329	21
	25	3 Apr	Essen	Sgt P. Coldham	348	21
	26	4 Apr	Kiel	Sgt P. Coldham	577	12
	27	9 Apr	Duisburg	Flt Sgt J. Murray	104	8
	28	10 Apr	Frankfurt	Sgt J. Williams	502	21
	29	13 Apr	Spezia	Flt Sgt J. Murray	208	4
	30	16 Apr	Koblenz*	Flt Sgt J. Murray	327	36
	31	18 Apr	Spezia	Flt Sgt J. Murray	186	1

			OPERATIONS FLOWN BY LANCASTER W4783 'G FOR GEORGE'			
Year	Operation number	Date	Target	Captain	Bombers despatched	Bombers lost
	32	20 Apr	Stettin	Flt Sgt J. Murray	339	21
	33	27 Apr	Duisburg	Flt Sgt W. Rose	561	17
	34	4 May	Dortmund	FO J. Henderson	596	31
	35	27 May	Essen	Sgt D.J. Strath	518	23
	36	29 May	Wuppertal	Sgt D.J. Strath	719	33
	37	11 Jun	Dusseldorf	FO J. Henderson	783	38
	38	12 Jun	Bochum	FO J. Henderson	503	24
	39	14 Jun	Oberhausen	FO J. Henderson	203	17
	40	16 Jun	Cologne	FO J. Henderson	212	14
	41	21 Jun	Krefeld	FO J. Henderson	705	44
	42	22 Jun	Mulheim	FO J. Henderson	557	35
	43	24 Jun	Wuppertal	FO J. Henderson	630	34
	44	25 Jun	Gelsenkirchen	FO J. Henderson	473	30
	45	28 Jun	Cologne	FO J. Henderson	608	25
		3 July	Aircraft badly damaged in ground explosion at Binbrook			
	46	17 Aug	Peenemünde	PO D. Moodie	596	40
	47	22 Aug	Leverkusen	Flt Sgt H. Carter	462	5
	48	27 Aug	Nuremberg	Flt Sgt H. Carter	674	33
	49	30 Aug	Mönchengladbach	Flt Sgt H. Carter	660	25
	50	31 Aug	Berlin	Flt Sgt H. Carter	622	47
	51	3 Sep	Berlin	Flt Sgt H. Carter	320	22
	52	5 Sep	Mannheim	Flt Sgt H. Carter	605	34
	53	6 Sep	Munich	Flt Sgt J. Goulevitch	404	16
	54	22 Sep	Hanover	Flt Sgt H. Carter	711	26
	55	23 Sep	Mannheim	Flt Sgt H. Carter	628	32
	56	27 Sep	Hanover	Sqn Ldr A. Nichols	678	39
	57	29 Sep	Bochum	Flt Sgt H. Carter	352	9
	58	2 Oct	Munich	Flt Sgt H. Carter	296	8
	59	3 Oct	Kassel	Flt Sgt R Power	547	24
	60	4 Oct	Ludwigshaven	Flt Sgt H. Carter	66	–
	61	7 Oct	Stuttgart	Flt Sgt H. Carter	343	4
	62	8 Oct	Hanover	Flt Sgt H. Carter	504	27

OPERATIONS FLOWN BY LANCASTER W4783 'G FOR GEORGE'

Year	Operation number	Date	Target	Captain	Bombers despatched	Bombers lost
	63	18 Oct	Hanover	Flt Sgt H. Carter	360	18
	64	20 Oct	Leipzig	PO N. Peters	358	16
	65	22 Oct	Kassel	Flt Sgt W. Watson	569	43
	66	3 Nov	Dusseldorf	WO H. Carter	589	18
The battle of Berlin						
	67	18 Nov	Berlin	WO H. Carter	444	9
	68	22 Nov	Berlin	Flt Sgt R. Douglas	764	26
	69	23 Nov	Berlin	Flt Sgt R. Douglas	383	20
	70	26 Nov	Berlin	WO H. Carter	450	42
	71	2 Dec	Berlin	Flt Sgt K. Goodwin	458	40
	72	3 Dec	Leipzig	Flt Sgt R. Douglas	527	24
	73	16 Dec	Berlin	PO H. Carter	493	54
	74	20 Dec	Frankfurt	PO H. Carter	650	41
	75	23 Dec	Berlin	PO H. Carter	379	16
	76	29 Dec	Berlin	Flt Lt A. Wales	712	20
1944	77	1 Jan	Berlin	PO J. Howell	421	28
	78	5 Jan	Stettin	PO J. Hills	358	16
	79	19 Feb	Leipzig	Flt Sgt J. McCleery	823	78
	80	20 Feb	Stuttgart	FO T. Leggett	598	14
	81	24 Feb	Schweinfurt	FO T. Leggett	734	33
	82	25 Feb	Augsburg	FO T. Leggett	594	21
	83	18 Mar	Frankfurt	PO K. Morgan	846	22
	84	22 Mar	Frankfurt	PO K. Morgan	816	33
	85	26 Mar	Essen	Flt Sgt R. Allen	705	9
	86	30 Mar	Nuremberg	Flt Sgt V. Neal	795	95
Lead-up to invasion						
	87	9 Apr	Villeneuve St. George	FO J. Critchley	225	–
	88	10 Apr	Aulnoye	FO J. Critchley	132	7
	89	20 Apr	Cologne	FO J. Critchley	379	4

*Target was Pilsen; 'G for George' could not locate flares, and bombed Koblenz.
Note: 90 operation symbols are painted on the aircraft. Squadron and log book records indicate one less, although records are occasionally contradictory.
Sources: 460 Squadron Operations Record Book, and Middlebrook and Everitt, *The Bomber Command war diaries*

'G for George' in ANZAC Hall, 2004. AWM PAIU2004/111.01

The Lancaster in context

By the mid-1930s, the RAF could see the need for a heavy bomber capable of carrying a large load of bombs well into Germany. Three of Britain's main aircraft manufacturers, Short Brothers, Handley Page and A.V. Roe (Avro), put forward designs which eventually went into production. These heavy bombers—the Stirling, Halifax and Manchester respectively—all flew over Germany, Italy and occupied Europe during the war.

The twin-engined Manchester came from the drawing board of Avro's chief designer, Roy Chadwick, and flew its first operations in February 1941. By then it was already clear, however, that its two Rolls-Royce Vulture engines were unsatisfactory and the aircraft was underpowered, so the design had been re-examined. The modified aircraft which emerged was basically a Manchester fitted with four Rolls-Royce Merlin engines. It was called the Lancaster.

Wartime pressures made for a speedy development program; the Lancaster was flying operationally just over a year after the prototype's first flight in January 1941. The 'Lanc' soon had a reputation as one of the outstanding aircraft of the war. It could be adapted to carry a wide range of loads, including passengers and cargo—but more importantly, a variety of bomb loads.

The Lancaster was designed with economy and speed of production in mind. Sub-assemblies were built and fitted out as self-contained units for ease of assembly and transport. There were several other factors in the Lancaster's effectiveness as a warplane. Its Merlin engines were highly reliable, and provided sufficient power for the extreme loads often carried. The bomb bay could accommodate 15,000 lb (6,800 kg) of bombs without modification, considerably more than that of its American contemporary, the B-17. Bomb loads were generally a mix of incendiaries (for starting fires) and a 4,000-lb Cookie blast bomb; for attacks on factories or fortifications, 500- or 1,000-lb general purpose bombs were used. For special operations the load could consist of a single massive bomb: Barnes Wallis's bouncing bomb (of Dambusters fame), the 'Tallboy', and the 10-t 'Grandslam', although 'G for George' was not modified to carry these.

RAF Bomber Command's 'area bombing' attacks on cities were intended to weaken the will and ability of the German populace and industry to wage war. Painted on the nose of an ex-RAAF Lancaster preserved at the Royal Air Force Museum in London is a quote by *Luftwaffe* leader and Hitler's second in

A wartime photo of the pilot's instrument panel in 'G for George'. At left is the control column and trimming wheel, and left of centre the throttle quadrant and propeller speed control levers for the four Merlin engines. AWM 044733

Flying Officer Clive Tindale DFM (left) tunes in the T1154/R1155 radio set while Flying Officer Wilf Gordon DFC studies his navigational charts in 'G for George', October 1944. The aircraft is about to leave Scotland for Australia. AWM UK2052

command, Reichsmarschall Hermann Göring. Reading 'No enemy plane will fly over the Reich territory', it is made poignant by being accompanied by the aircraft's tally of 137 operations symbols in the form of bombs. Göring stated that if he was proved wrong, 'you may call me Meyer' (a Jewish name). The German people remembered this during 1942–43 and, at the sound of air raid sirens, a catch-cry was often heard: 'Can you hear Meyer's hunting horn?', a reference to Göring's preference for stag hunting rather than ensuring that Germany's cities were defended.

Three England-based RAAF squadrons of Bomber Command, numbered 460, 463 and 467, flew the Lancaster. In four years of operations, including 5,700 sorties in Lancasters from late 1942 to May 1945, 460 Squadron alone lost over a thousand men, many of them Australian.

A container of incendiary bombs is winched into the bomb bay of 'G for George' at Binbrook, Lincolnshire, in June 1943. AWM P03173.001

NOTES ON COLOUR SCHEME

Dark green and dark earth on upper surfaces in a disruptive pattern; special night black on lower and side surfaces. Yellow/blue/white/red roundels on fuselage sides; red and blue roundels on upper wing surfaces. Red/white/blue flashes on outside of fins. 460 Squadron identification 'AR-G' ('UV-G' prior to mid-1943) in large red letters either side of roundel, both sides. Small 'G' in red, outlined white, on each side of nose just aft of blister. Red handling stripe on lower nose. Serial number stencilled in red on rear fuselage sides. Operations tally on port side of nose, consisting of 90 yellow bomb symbols with various crew insignia ('Saint' stick-figures, cherries, red stripes and blue 'V's) and decorations denoting the DFM, CGM and DSO.

The aircraft received a partial repaint before leaving the UK in 1944, and was repainted in an approximation of the original scheme in 1977. It was repainted accurately in 2002.

TIMELINE—W4783

1942	(Oct) Joined 460 Squadron RAAF of 1 Group RAF at Breighton, UK
	(Dec) Began bombing operations
1943	(May) Moved with squadron to Binbrook, Lincolnshire, UK
	(Jul) Badly damaged in ground explosion at Binbrook
1944	(Apr) Completed operations
	(Oct–Nov) Flew from Scotland to Australia
1945	(Mar–Apr) Flew as flagship of Third Victory Loan tour, then stored at RAAF Canberra, both hangared and outside
1955	(Jun) Installed in AWM Aeroplane Hall
1999	(Mar) Relocated to AWM Treloar Technology Centre, ACT, for conservation and repainting
2003	(Dec) Displayed as centrepiece of *Striking by night* exhibition in ANZAC Hall

DATA

Type	Avro 683 Lancaster Mk I
Design firm	A.V. Roe & Co, UK
Manufacturer	Metropolitan-Vickers, Manchester
Role	Heavy bomber
No. built	3,399 (Mk I)
	7,366 (Lancaster total)
Type entered service	1942
Identity	W4783 (RAF) A66-2 (RAAF)
Crew	7 (pilot, navigator, bomb aimer, flight engineer, wireless operator, mid-upper gunner, rear gunner)
Powerplant	Four Rolls-Royce Merlin 24 V-12 engines, each of 1,280 hp (955 kW)
Armament	6,350 kg of bombs Eight .303-in machine-guns in three turrets
Wingspan	31.09 m
Length	21.13 m
Max. speed	443 km/h
Combat range	2,670 km
Max. take-off weight	30,844 kg

MESSERSCHMITT BF 109G

163824

En route to Russelheim, Germany
0205 HOURS, 26 AUGUST 1944

Of the seven crewmen in Lancaster ND864 'X for X-ray' of 460 Squadron RAAF, two were especially watchful. Sergeants H.W. Marchant in the rear turret and V.C. Perris in the mid-upper were the eyes of the crew, scanning the night for enemy fighters. In the moonless sky at 12,000 ft, it was hard enough to make out nearby Lancasters; enemy fighters would appear as just a small fleeting silhouette against a sky that was almost as dark. On nights like this, the bomber's Fishcake radar warning device came into its own.

Suddenly there was a blip: fighter at 600 m, port quarter below. Before anyone had time to get a visual on the enemy, the pilot threw the Lancaster into a violent corkscrew dive to port. Sergeant Marchant picked up the fighter on his Village Inn tail-warning radar when it had closed to 400 m. As he lined up his gyroscopic sight with the radar blip and began firing his machine-guns, the enemy's cannon and machine-guns opened up and raked the bomber.

Two of the Lancaster's fuel tanks and lines were hit. The number four engine spluttered as its throttle control was severed. Sergeant Perris cursed as the hydraulic line

> ## Once I had climbed into its claustrophobic cockpit it felt lethal!
> Captain Eric Brown, Royal Navy test pilot

Werknummer 163824 at Bankstown airport c. 1964, when it was in the Sid Marshall collection.
AWM P05491.001

was cut, disabling his turret, but fortunately no one was injured. In seconds, the fighter had closed to 200 m. As it broke away to starboard from its attack run, the Australian pilot caught a brief glimpse of the dark shape of a Messerschmitt Bf 109. With leaking fuel tanks the Lancaster only made it as far as the Normandy beach-head, where its pilot, Flying Office Neville Twyford, made a forced landing.

Although it was a day fighter, from July 1943 the Bf 109G saw night use on many occasions such as this. The devastation of Hamburg by RAF and RAAF night bombers that month caused fear in the German high command that a prolonged series of such raids could mean defeat. Along with the heavy raids came a new British innovation: Window, radar-jamming foil strips dropped from the aircraft, which proved disastrous for the radar-controlled German 'box system' of air defence. Until a countermeasure could be developed, the Germans tried a recently developed tactic: free-ranging single-seat fighters, which now augmented the twin-engined radar-equipped night fighters. The pilots of the single-seaters had to rely on visual identification, making use of the light from the fires below, ground searchlights and air-dropped flares to spot and home in on individual bombers. It was a somewhat desperate measure, as it meant using day fighters at night, resulting in a high rate of accidents on take-off and landing.

These fighters were nicknamed *Wilde Sau* (wild boar) and included Bf 109G-6 day fighters. As shown in the Memorial's *Striking by night* display, they frequently attacked night bombers crewed by Australians, such as the Memorial's Lancaster, and accounted for hundreds shot down. In the intensive first few weeks of Bomber Command's battle for Berlin at the end of 1943, for example, the night fighter units defending Berlin, largely with G-6s, made claims of 123 British bombers brought down. It was supposed to be a short term tactic, and its success declined in 1944. Nevertheless, *Wilde Sau* augmented the *Zahme Sau* (tame boar) night fighters for the remainder of the night bombing campaign. The continuation of this tactic for longer than planned is indicative of the state of the *Luftwaffe* in 1944–45.

◄   ►

Twice Australia nearly lost its only example of this, the most important German aircraft of the Second World War. The first time was the result of official indifference and a lack of somewhere to put the aircraft; the second was an attempted export that was foiled in the nick of time.

In 1946 crates labelled 'RAF Display Unit' arrived in Melbourne, apparently originating from the RAF maintenance unit at Brize Norton, Oxfordshire, UK. They contained, upon inspection, two Messerschmitts: a Bf 109 and an Me 163, both complete and in original paint work, thanks to a directive that they were to remain in original condition for display use. Painted on the port side of the tail of each was its identifying *Werknummer* (its *Luftwaffe* serial number)—163824 in the case of the Bf 109. Its subtype was conveniently identified on the small identification plate on its fuselage as Bf 109G-6. Distinguished by its later-style *Erla Haube* clear-vision canopy, it however lacked such refinements as the taller tail and cockpit pressurisation which appeared on a number of G-6s.

The Messerschmitts were transferred to nearby RAAF Laverton, and for at least the next eight years there is no record that they were uncrated. By 1954, hangar space at Laverton was at a premium, and the crates were transferred to RAAF Tocumwal, New South Wales, the following year. One report indicates that they were re-assembled at Laverton before leaving, but were soon re-crated for transport.

No information accompanied either aircraft. Even how they came to be allocated to the Memorial is unknown. An RAAF collection team was active in the UK at the end of the war, and it is possible that they organised the aircrafts' allocation to Australia. Perhaps they were gifts from Britain in recognition of Australia's contribution to the air war in Europe. The Memorial's original catalogue entry for the Bf 109—'the Spitfire of the German Airforce'—was of little help.

Both the Me163 and the Bf 109G were unique in Australia. An earlier Bf 109, the E series 'Yellow 7' of the fighter unit III/JG3 and a casualty of the Battle of Britain, had been scrapped. Sent to Australia in 1941 it had toured eastern Australia as a fundraising and recruitment exhibit. More than a quarter of a million people turned out to see it. With Australia's entry into the Pacific war, however, interest in it waned and it ended its days at Werribee, Victoria. Interestingly, on the same day that 'Yellow 7' had been shot down over Kent, 5 September 1940, *Luftwaffe* ace *Leutnant* Franz von Werra suffered the same fate, also in Kent. (Von Werra's intriguing story of escape was later told in the 1956 book, *The one that got away*, and the film of the same name.)

The Memorial's Bf 109 nearly got away too: first from the collection and then, years later, from the country. In 1963 a senior instructor with Illawarra Flying School at Bankstown in Sydney wrote to the Memorial to ask if he could buy the Bf 109 for display. Interest in historic military aircraft in Australia was at this time quite limited, and the Memorial's Board of Trustees, conscious of a lack of storage space and seeing little prospect of displaying the aircraft, sold it to him for £100, less than its scrap metal value.[17] It was not long before it changed hands again, this time to Sid Marshall, also of Bankstown, to add to his collection which included a Japanese Oscar (also a former Memorial machine), a Spitfire, and Douglas DC-2 transports. For much of its time with the Marshall collection, the aircraft was displayed suspended in his hangar.

After his death, the sale of Marshall's collection began in 1975. The Bf 109 was sold in 1979 to a British aircraft collector, reportedly for $100,000, many times its sale value just 15 years earlier. The new owner even arranged for it to be allocated the British civil registration G-SMIT. Fortunately for the Australian public, restrictions governing the export of historic aircraft had been introduced not long before, and the Bf 109—the sole example in Australia—was seized by Australian Customs. Pending a court decision on its future, Customs impounded the aircraft and stored it at No. 2 Stores Depot, RAAF Regents Park in Sydney.

During its impoundment, the Memorial made representations for the aircraft on the basis of its historical importance and rarity. In 1987, the aircraft's circuitous path was completed when it was awarded to the Memorial.

It was then that investigations into the history of *Werknummer* 163824 began. Correspondence from Germany during the early 1990s shed some light on its probable early movements. The story illustrates how Messerschmitt's production facilities were dispersed owing to constant Allied aerial bombardment of the major centres, and how recycled components were used in production. Dispersal, however, did not mean reduced production, and over 14,000 Bf 109Gs were built in 1944 alone. As the war progressed and fuel became scarce when the Allied bombing focused on the Nazi oil industry, many of these aircraft sat at their airfields, hardly used.

Airframes completed at the main Messerschmitt factory at Regensburg went by road, in pieces, to Waldwerk Hagelstadt—a concealed final assembly plant in the forest—or to Regensburg-Obertraubling. Under cover of darkness, the disassembled aircraft were then trucked to nearby Puchhof airfield to the south-east. There, test pilots would take the brand new Bf 109s into the air to put them through their paces. Two such pilots, *Feldwebeln* Lohmann and Ertl, flew aircraft with serial numbers very close to

Allied gun cine-camera image of a Bf 109G being shot down. AWM SUK15206

Werknummer 163824 in May 1944, so it is reasonable to speculate that one of them may have taken it on its first flight. As Bf 109G-6 production had given way to the G-10 the previous month, 163824, constructed in April, would have been among the last G-6s made.

Of its subsequent wartime history, little is conclusively known. One report[18] states that on 12 August while attached to the headquarters ferry flight unit *Flzg.ÜberführG*.1, and presumably before delivery to an operational unit, it was heavily damaged at Rheine airfield in a taxiing collision with another G-6. A small painted inscription below the canopy indicates that it was refurbished in December, reportedly by Ludwig Hansen & Co at Münster, not far from Rheine. It appears to have been an extensive refit, as the starboard wing and fuselage sternframe were replaced. It is believed to have been fitted with the high-altitude DB 605AS engine until this refit. The canopy, probably a replacement, is from a dive-bombing variant—indicated by angled red lines which were visual horizon markers for the pilot. Intriguingly, a curse written in Cyrillic script has been found inside the fuselage, indicating that Russian prisoners of war were used as labour in the refurbishment.

It came to light in 2003[19] that the two aircraft with serial numbers either side of 163824 saw operational service. *Werknummern* 163823 and 163825 flew with the

fighter unit I/JG5 and were both lost in action on 27 May 1944, probably within a month of delivery. Perhaps 163824 also flew with this unit.

In May 1945, at the end of the European war, advancing British troops moved into the *Luftwaffe* airfield at Eggebek in Schleswig-Holstein, northern Germany. From British records, the known history of *Werknummer* 163824 begins the following September, when it departed Eggebek for the UK with three other aircraft. What it had been doing there, and whether it had been assigned to a unit, remains unknown.

Despite its hazy origins, 163824 is believed to be the most complete and original Bf 109 of the dozen or so in existence. It is also probably unique in retaining its wartime *Luftwaffe* paint scheme intact [20] (see Colour Notes), which tells of a complex history of refurbishment and repair and strongly suggests that it saw service despite the lack of unit or tactical markings.

As with the Me 262, there is more direct evidence that this aircraft had seen combat action: what appear to be battle damage repairs on the fuselage. The most telling are two small patches to its metal skin, one in the cockpit's rear bulkhead and the other in the upper fuselage just below the loop aerial. They are strongly suggestive of a bullet having passed through, narrowly missing the pilot's head, and shrapnel damage to the pilot's armoured seat is also evident. A section of rear fuselage skin has been replaced, and various replacement components show battle damage. Until the relevant *Luftwaffe* records come to light, if they ever do, we can only speculate about the origin of these repairs.

The Comptroller-General of Australian Customs awarded the aircraft to the Memorial on condition that it 'ensure the restoration and preservation of the aircraft ... and that the aircraft will be maintained on display for the general public'. The opportunity to comply came with the construction of ANZAC Hall, and in 2003 the Messerschmitt was finally on display, elevated in a dramatic flying attitude as though attacking Lancaster 'G for George'. There it forms an integral part of a major 'object theatre' presentation on the air war in Europe.

The Bf 109G in context

The Bf 109 first flew in 1935 and entered service two years later. A modified example attained a landplane speed record of 610 km/h, also in 1937. Throughout its development, progressive modifications greatly increased its engine horsepower and armament.

The Bf 109G 'Gustav' series introduced in 1942 was the most numerous, with the G-6 of 1943 being the most-produced sub-variant and reportedly accounting for the most Allied aircraft losses. The *Luftwaffe*'s fighter leader, *General* Adolf Galland, urged all-out fighter production to combat the Allied bombers which were destroying Germany by day and night. A response to these demands, the G-6 introduced more power, speed and armament, with a resulting higher wing loading (leading to somewhat more sluggish control) than the earlier Bf 109 models. However, it climbed well and at over 25,000 ft was a nimble and pleasant aircraft to fly. The Allies' answer was to bomb the Messerschmitt factories. In August 1943 a US daylight raid included the Regensburg factory where the G-6 was now in large-scale production. The cost to the Allies was one of the worst US losses of the war: 60 bombers, mainly downed by G-6s, some of which were fitted with 21-cm mortars, and by Focke-Wulf Fw 190As after the bombers' escort fighters had reached their fuel range and turned back.

A Bf 109G-6 was landed in error at Manston, Kent, in July 1944, its pilot unaware that he was on the wrong side of the English Channel. The British were thus handed the opportunity to evaluate it against the latest Spitfire and Mustang, as they had done with earlier 109s. Despite a number of faults—poor roll rate at high speed, the cramped cockpit, and poor visibility for the pilot (the clear Galland canopy of the Memorial's example addressed the latter problem)—it was found to be the equal of the Allied aircraft in some respects, such as climb rate. In general agility, it was marginally inferior.

More generally, the Bf 109 as a type was probably the most important Luftwaffe aircraft type Australians fought, beginning with the crucial Battle of Britain and continuing on all fronts for the next four and a half years. The Memorial's Spitfire, for example, shot down three Bf 109s. In the Mediterranean and North Africa, numerous RAAF squadrons, as well as AIF troops, regularly encountered them. More Bf 109s were built than any other military aircraft in history bar one, the Russian Il-2. Only one other Bf 109, also a G-6, is held in Australia: a restoration project recovered from a Russian lake in 1990 and owned privately in Melbourne.

Oberleutnant Erbo von Kageneck, recipient of the Knight's Cross of the Iron Cross with Oak Leaves, with his Bf 109E and ground crew of III/JG27 in Sicily, 1941. Von Kageneck claimed 69 Allied aircraft destroyed, but was wounded in action in North Africa in December, probably by RAAF ace Flying Officer (later Group Captain) Clive Caldwell of 250 Squadron RAF. He died of his wounds a few weeks later. AWM P00323.001

TIME LINE—WNR 163824

1944	(Apr–May) Built as a Bf 109G-6AS at Regensburg; probably trucked to Puchhof airfield for test flying
	(Aug) Ground accident while attached to delivery unit
	Possibly flew with JG5
	(Dec) Underwent a major refurbishment, including return to G-6 standard
1945	(Sep) transported from Eggebek, Germany, to RAF Sealand, UK
1946	To RAF Brize Norton and later RAF South Cerney or Little Rissington, UK (details for Air Ministry AM229); shipped to Australia and stored at RAAF Laverton, Vic.
1955	Moved (crated) to RAAF Tocumwal with Me 163, then to AWM store, Duntroon, ACT
1963	Sold to a member of Illawarra Flying Club, Bankstown, NSW
1963	Sold to Sid Marshall collection, Bankstown, NSW, and displayed
1975	Changed hands following Sid Marshall's death
1979	Sold to UK aircraft collector; confiscated by Australian Customs following export attempt. Stored at RAAF Regents Park, Sydney.
1987	Awarded by court to AWM and transported to AWM store, Mitchell, ACT
2002–03	Conservation carried out for display in *Striking by night* exhibition in ANZAC Hall

DATA

Type	Bf 109G-6
Design firm	Messerschmitt GmBH, Germany
Manufacturer	Messerschmitt GmBH at Regensburg
Role	Single-seat fighter
No. built	Approx. 23,000 (Bf 109G)
	32,461 (total Bf 109[21])
Type entered service	Mid-1943 (G-6)
Identity	*Werknummer* 163824
Powerplant	Daimler-Benz DB 605A inverted V-12 engine of 1,475 hp
Armament	One 20-mm MG 151 cannon
	Two 13-mm MG 131 machine-guns
	Up to 300-kg bomb load when configured
Wingspan	9.92 m
Length	8.84 m
Max. speed	620 km/h
Range	563 km on internal fuel; 1,000 km with drop tank
Max. take-off weight	3,678 kg

NOTES ON COLOUR SCHEME

The aircraft's factory paint scheme was somewhat altered during its service with the replacement of major components (including one wing), presumably during its refurbishment in December 1944. It probably entered service in the following scheme: RLM75 *Grauviolett* (grey-violet) and RLM83 *Dunkelgrün* (dark green) upper surface camouflage in a roughly-sprayed, irregular splinter pattern (still to be seen on the port wing), with RLM81 *Braunviolett* (brown-violet) replacing the RLM75 on the upper fuselage. RLM76 *Lichtblau* (light blue) on sides and undersides. Fuselage sides and rudder have mottling of RLM81 and RLM83 or similar.

Subsequent variations are numerous. Sides and undersides of fuselage, tailplane and port wing are now a greenish grey, while the starboard wing underside, elevator undersides, lower cowls and rudder remain RLM76 *Lichtblau*. The starboard wing has light grey in place of RLM75, and the wing tip has underlying yellow, possibly an Eastern Front marking. Landing flaps are grey.

Upper wing *Balkenkreuze* crosses are thin white outlines only. Underside crosses are black filled; fuselage crosses are filled in RLM83. Black *Hakenkreutz* (swastika) with white outline on each side of fin, and *Werknummer* in black on port side of fin only. No unit markings are carried. Spinner is longitudinally divided into 2/3 black-green and 1/3 white, with a rough spiral in white.

Prior to its export attempt the aircraft was coated in a plastic protective film which was painted silver, apparently to pass it off as a Mustang. Most of this was removed by the time it came to the Memorial.

(With reference to notes by Brett Green)

MESSERSCHMITT ME 262

Over north-west Czechoslovakia
1400 HOURS, 8 MAY 1945

Oberleutnant Hans Fröhlich had at his disposal the world's most advanced aircraft. By pushing its two throttles to their limit he could reach 800 km/h at low altitude, then pull back on the stick to enter a zooming climb at more than one vertical kilometre per minute. Flattening out in the thinner air at 20,000 ft, he could get an extra 70 km/h out of the jet engines. In comparison with conventional piston-engined aircraft there was little noise or vibration: 'like being pushed by an angel' is how former *Luftwaffe* fighter leader *General* Adolf Galland described the sensation of flying the Messerschmitt Me 262.

Had he met an Allied aircraft on that last day of the war, Fröhlich might have had little trouble disposing of it with the four 30-mm cannon mounted in his aircraft's nose. If he so chose, he could instead have outrun it with a 120 km/h speed advantage over the fastest piston-engined fighter he might have encountered.[22] He was more likely to have had the opportunity to fire his cannon in a strafing attack on columns of advancing Russian troops. However, the goal occupying his mind now was to make it to northern Germany, where he intended to surrender himself and his aircraft to the western Allies. The irony in handing over such a prize to the enemy was presumably not lost on him, but Germany had lost the war—of that there was now no doubt.

Two weeks earlier most of Fröhlich's unit, II *Gruppe* of *Kampfgeschwader* (*Jabo*) 51 (II/KG (J) 51), had been overrun at Straßkirchen airfield by General Patton's 7th Army.

> ## *Its beautiful yet sinister lines reminded me vividly of those of a shark.*
> *Captain Eric Brown CBE DSC AFC, Royal Navy test pilot*

Me 262 'Black X' (at left) under armed guard at Fassberg airfield, Germany, after the May 1945 surrender. The middle aircraft is *Werknummer* 111690 'White 5' of *Jagdgeschwader* 7. AWM P01605.009

While the remaining Germans set fire to any unairworthy Me 262s, *Oberleutnant* Wolfgang Bätz and six other pilots took off for Landau, not far south. They joined up with I/KG(J)51 before moving on to Austria and finally to Zatec in Czechoslovakia. Among them was Fröhlich.

At the Ruzyne airfield complex at nearby Prague, the remnants of several Me 262 units had formed into an improvised combat group, *Gefechtsverband Hogeback* under *Oberstleutnant* Hermann Hogeback, which continued to fly close-support sorties in the face of the Russian onslaught. Possibly Fröhlich and the other Me 262 pilots at Zatec lent a hand. On 2 May, capitulation was imminent. As related by aviation historians John Foreman and Sid Harvey, the surrender conditions were not to their liking and, unwilling to become guests of the Soviet Union, *Leutnant* Batel, Häffner and Fröhlich, under *Hauptmann* Abrahamczik, made a run for Germany while they still had the means.[23]

It was an action soon justified, as those of Fröhlich's friends who remained at Zatec were captured by the Russians and never heard of again. Leaving in the early afternoon of 8 May, the four pilots split up. Abrahamczik and Häffner landed at Munich-Riem and surrendered to the Americans. Batel flew 500 km and belly-landed his jet at his hometown near Hanover. Fröhlich headed for Fassberg, south of Hamburg, which was now in British and Canadian hands. In all likelihood he signified his surrender in the recognised way, lowering his undercarriage and flaps early, before touching down on the airfield at 2.50 pm. He taxied to a halt, switched off his engines, and surrendered.

Fröhlich's sleek mount joined a number of other intact examples of this, the revolutionary jet that had come as such a shock to Allied aircrews nine months earlier. Distinguishable by a black X painted on its fuselage, it had two bomb pylons under its nose; KG(J)51 was a fighter-bomber unit. The British at Fassberg by now had several Me 262 variants to examine: a few *Jabo* or *Sturmvogel* (stormy petrel) fighter bombers like this, numerous *Schwalbe* (swallow) fighters, and two-seat *Nachtjäger* night fighters.

The story of Fröhlich's reception, or lack of it, says much about the mood of the time. In high spirits following the announcement of the armistice, the Allied troops were too busy drinking and singing to take much notice of him. Author Wolfgang Dierich relates in his history of KG51 that 'it was two days before their heads cleared sufficiently for someone to suggest that this 'enemy airman' ought to have his pistol taken away and handed over to the Army'.[24]

The British arranged to send nine of their Me 262 war prizes (three each of the fighter, fighter bomber and night fighter variants) over the Channel to the Royal Aircraft Establishment (RAE) at Farnborough for evaluation. Three weeks after its capture, with its *Luftwaffe* crosses now overpainted with British roundels, 'Black X' was flown out of Fassberg in company with two other jets. In the cockpit was the head of the RAE Aerodynamics Section, Squadron Leader Tony Martindale. First stop was the RAE collection point at Schleswig airfield. Continuing into Holland, Gilze-Rijen was the

The Memorial's Me 262 and Me 163 together at RAAF Point Cook in 1973. Courtesy of John Hopton

next stop, followed by Melsbroek, where brake and other problems held the aircraft up for three months. The next available pilot was Captain Eric 'Winkel' Brown, veteran test pilot with the Fleet Air Arm and RAE. Brown had first taken an Me 262 aloft at Schleswig at the end of May, after taking the precaution of interrogating Messerschmitt's chief Me 262 test pilot about its idiosyncracies. On 28 August he took 'Black X' over the sea to England, landing at Manston for an unscheduled stopover due to hydraulic problems. He continued to Farnborough the following week. Brown later described the Me 262 as one of the most exciting aircraft he had flown.

After replacement of its radios and other equipment with British equivalents, in October and November 1945 'Black X' made 11 flights at Farnborough. A few of these were demonstration flights to show the British public what their RAF airmen had been up against, but the majority were evaluation flights. The RAE pilots were keen to see if the Me 262's performance lived up to the claims of its German pilots. They were intrigued to learn, for example, the flight characteristics of an aircraft with swept-back wings—an innovation not yet used on Allied production aircraft—particularly at speeds approaching that of sound. The pilot was again Martindale, with Brown taking his place for one flight.[25]

As with many of the early jets, the Me 262 suffered from unreliable engines. The British had been told by *Luftwaffe* pilots that the maximum flying life of a Jumo jet engine was 25 hours, with an overhaul required after just ten. Not wishing to push its luck, the RAE soon curtailed its Me 262 flight program. As it was unknown how long the engines in 'Black X' had been run, after five and a half hours in the air at Farnborough its flying days were over. In 1946, it was selected as a gift from Britain to Australia for the nation's part in winning the European war. It arrived by ship at Melbourne on 22 December, and still crated, was trucked to nearby RAAF Base Laverton.

◄   ►

Thirty-five years elapsed before a detailed analysis of the Memorial's Me 262 was made. In 1981 *Luftwaffe* expert Ken Merrick led a project to examine the aircraft, and it proved to be a veritable time capsule of German production techniques during the last desperate months of the war. Every expedient had been employed to push aircraft through production lines and out of the factories and assembly plants, which were largely staffed by unskilled and slave labour. Leftover metal scraps still lay in the fuselage. Aluminium skin panels had been hastily riveted, and the rear fuselage join was misaligned. Timber was used for hatches, undercarriage doors and cockpit consoles in preference to scarce aluminium. The undersides were largely left unpainted, apart from steel or timber components, to save precious production time. Filler was roughly applied over screw holes and steel screw heads primed, but there was no overall undercoat. The camouflage paint was thinly and roughly applied.

The Me 262's markings revealed by rubbing back overlying paint, from left to right: original German cross insignia, British roundel, replica cross, 'P' prototype symbol, British Air Ministry number 81, and (faintly visible on the tail) the serial number '500200'. AWM PAIU1992/210.02

Of particular interest were the aircraft's painted markings, as they should reveal its identity. This had been hidden since the RAAF had repainted it prior to its public display at the Memorial in 1955, and had not been recorded. The time consuming job of sanding back the overlying paint revealed a number of things. Not least of these was the aircraft's serial number; previously thought to be either 500210 or 112372[26], it was revealed as 500200. It has now come to light that Me 262s with serial numbers close to this were assembled at Waldwerk Stauffen near Fliegerhorst Obertraubling, an assembly plant administered from Regensburg, and that in January and February 1945, *Feldwebel* Heinz Lohmann test-flew numerous examples in the 500200 serial range at Obertraubling and ferried them to units.[27] Interestingly, Lohmann may also have flown the Memorial's Bf 109 in May 1944 after its assembly at Obertraubling, making for a possible early connection between these two Messerschmitts.

As the overlying paint was rubbed back, the black 'X' and *Luftwaffe* crosses were also revealed; but over these had been painted British markings. There were RAF roundels, prototype symbols (applied to aircraft with unfamiliar flight characteristics), and the aircraft's number 81, assigned by the Air Ministry. It was only after this work that Memorial staff and aviation historians were able to piece together the story of 'Black X', by then one of just ten surviving examples of the world's first operational jet aircraft.

Another find was a half-inch bullet hole in the wing: 'Black X' had seen combat, which is not surprising considering that KG(J)51 lost more than 170 men during its jet period. The extent of this action during the aircraft's brief operational life may never be known. Attempts to correspond with Fröhlich during the early 1980s brought no reply, and his unit's operations records, which were probably destroyed at war's end, have not come to light.

What of the Me 262's relevance to Australia? Numerous Australian bomber crews and fighter pilots encountered them in the air during the last few months of the war. A Lancaster rear gunner with 463 Squadron RAAF, Flight Sergeant Peter Dale, recorded one encounter during a daylight bombing raid on Hamburg on the afternoon of 9 April 1945. While 617 (Dambuster) Squadron dropped 'Grandslam' and 'Tallboy' bombs on U-boat pens, Wing Commander Keith Kemp DFC led a force of 40 Lancasters at 18,000 ft. The force, made up of 463 and 467 Squadrons RAAF and 9 and 61 Squadrons RAF, flew in 617's slipstream, headed for German oil storage tanks. Several aircraft were hit by radar-aimed anti-aircraft fire, but the flak ceased just after bombing. The crews soon discovered why, and tightened up their formation:

> We were attacked by a group of 30 Me 262 jet fighters from behind. They mainly attacked Lancasters on the edge of the gaggle, though many flew right up the centre of our formation and attacked at random. One, armed with 12 spin-controlled 50-mm rockets slung under the wings, was lining up on us from the rear, well back and slightly out to starboard. It was closing in at a great speed, in excess of 800 km/h, when fortunately for us it veered slightly to starboard and lined up on a Lancaster of 61 Squadron which was dropping back from our formation and losing speed, no doubt as a result of previous damage received. The jet hit the Lanc with either cannon or rockets, and instantly its starboard outer engine exploded in a ball of flame. It and the outer section of the wing broke off, sending the crew to their deaths in a tight, spiralling spin ... not one parachute was seen opening out.
>
> Our Spitfire and Mustang escort fighters above made many attempts to intercept them with vertical dives, but had no chance at all of engaging them. In desperation, some Mustangs dropped their disposable petrol tanks from high above us, luckily falling just in front of us. The Mustangs then came hurtling down with added speed, but all to no avail. They were no match for the Me 262s. The Mustangs got their revenge, however, as the jets began running out of fuel.

Clearly below I saw several jets being shot up and exploding as they attempted to land on a runway. There were many more explosions along the runway and airfield buildings.

The gunners felt demoralised by the firepower and speed of these jets. Our miserable .303-in Brownings were no match at all, except in cases of close-in attacks. The rotation of our turrets was also too slow. The pilots of the jets were protected by 4-in thick armoured glass windscreens, and our bullets would just ricochet off them. Seven Lancasters of 463 and 467 Squadrons reported attacks.[28]

In addition to the Lancaster from 61 Squadron RAF, the Me 262s of JG7 shot down another from 50 Squadron RAF that day.

The month before, two 460 Squadron air gunners, Flight Sergeant Harold Joyce and Flying Officer Leslie Lewarne, had been credited with probably destroying one of the jets. In the early hours of 19 March, during a night raid on Hanau from 11,500 ft, Joyce in the rear turret of Lancaster RF196 'E for Easy' spotted the engine glows of a twin jet about 1,500 m behind. From its silhouette as it flitted through a searchlight beam, he identified it as an Me 262. Over the crew intercom, he called for his pilot to 'corkscrew' the bomber in a spiralling dive to starboard, and tracking the engine glows with his gyroscopic gunsight, fired 600 rounds from his machine-guns as the jet closed to a kilometre. Lewarne in the mid-upper turret fired 80 rounds. The next thing they saw was a 'trail of sparks', ending as a ball of fire on the ground. If the gunners did in fact hit this aircraft, it was through extraordinarily skilful or lucky long-range shooting.

An Australian fighter pilot had a confirmed victory over an Me 262, coincidentally a fighter-bomber of KG(J)51. On the afternoon of 14 February 1945, Flight Lieutenant F.A.O. (Tony) Gaze DFC and Bar,[29] flying with 610 Squadron RAF, was leading an attack on Arado Ar 234 jet bombers near Nijmegen in Holland. His mount was a Spitfire Mk XIV, its maximum speed of over 720 km/h making it one of the few Allied aircraft which had a chance of catching an Me 262. After firing at the Arados without result, Gaze climbed through cloud and emerged to find three Me 262s carrying bombs. Pushing his throttle to its limit, he

followed them flat out … with just about only the canopy sticking through the clouds and finally got close enough to shoot at the starboard one of the three. Pieces flew off the starboard engine which caught fire. The aircraft dived into cloud and my No. 2 called to say it had gone straight in near Emmerick.[30]

The German pilot, *Feldwebel* Rudolf Hoffmann, was killed. Just before war's end, Tony Gaze had an even closer encounter with Me 262s. After landing his Meteor jet on the autobahn at Schleswig, he audaciously ordered the Germans to prepare a 262 for him to fly. He sat in its cockpit, a *Luftwaffe* unit commander quite pleasantly instructing him on its finer points, but in the end he did not fly it. Later at Fassberg, he got as far as taxiing

The Me 262 in ANZAC Hall in 2007. The number '200' is just visible below the nose cannon ports. AWM PAIU2007/021.06

one out to the runway, but was ordered not to take off, as another Me 262 had just suffered a nosewheel collapse on landing and caught fire. Gaze did not record the serial number of the Me 262 he came so close to flying, but 500200 was at Fassberg for three weeks after the war.

The Me 262 in context

Before looking briefly at the broader Me 262 story, a few of the early milestones of jet aviation development will help to place it in context. Germany had taken the lead, its Heinkel He 178 making the world's first turbojet-powered flight just before the outbreak of war. Italy followed in 1940 with its unsuccessful Caproni N.1. Britain's Gloster E 28/39 flew in May 1941. Then, following the two-year development of the Junkers Jumo engine, the Me 262 (originally designed as the P.1065 in mid-1939) made its first fully turbojet-powered flight in July 1942. America's unspectacular XP-59A Airacomet followed in early October.

It is the Me 262, however, which holds the distinction of being the world's first turbojet-powered aircraft in service. Its debut in July 1944 was met with alarm among Allied airmen. Although Britain's own jet, the Meteor, was ready for use against V-1 flying bombs later that month, the Me 262 was evidently superior to it. In August KG51 proved the effectiveness of the fighter-bomber variant after converting from piston-engined bombers. In air combat, the Me 262's record was mixed. Although the jet pilots claimed some 350 Allied aircraft destroyed during its nine months of service,[31] their main opponent, the US Eighth Air Force, records only 62 aircraft lost to jets.[32] By contrast it is believed that perhaps 200 Me 262s were lost and 150 pilots killed,[33] owing to a number of factors including its vulnerability during take-off and landing, engine failures, and a lack of adequate training for its pilots.

This remarkable aircraft is a reminder of Germany's potentially war-winning designs which never got the chance to fully prove themselves or to have a major impact on the war. To begin with, the Junkers Jumo jet engine's development was protracted, and problems with its reliability and short flying life were never ironed out. The aircraft itself faced competing production and development priorities, set by Germany's conservative air ministry. For example, the concentration of Messerschmitt's resources into producing and improving the conventional Bf 109 meant that by the time Minister for Armament Albert Speer gave the Me 262 program top production priority, in December 1943, it was too late. The final obstacle was the Allied bombardment of Messerschmitt's factories, which necessitated the decentralisation of production and all the logistical headaches which this entailed.

Adolf Galland, himself an Me 262 pilot and a fighter ace with 104 victories, estimated that had the Me 262 and its engines been ready for deployment in early 1943, before the Allies gained control of the air, it could have tipped the balance in Germany's favour. The Allies' hard-won control of the air would have been difficult to maintain. With Allied bombers facing large numbers of jet fighters, the bombing campaign against Germany could well have been drastically reduced in scale by unsustainable losses.

All this is, however, academic speculation. The 'foremost warplane of its day', as Eric Brown called it,[34] was held back by all the difficulties described, and ultimately by a lack of fuel and pilots to fly it. The vast majority of those produced either did not reach operational units, or sat idly at their airfields. As it was, the greatest legacy of the Me 262 was the influence it had on jet research and high-speed aircraft design among the Allied nations. In particular the swept-back wing and moveable tailplane were soon found on many high-speed aircraft of the immediate post-war period.

As a fighter-bomber variant, the Memorial's *Werknummer* 500200 has another level of significance. An oft-cited hindrance to Me 262 deployment was Hitler's view that the aircraft should, at least initially, be a bomber rather than a fighter, which is what its design dictated. Knowing that an Allied invasion of France was approaching, he considered that bombing would be the most valuable role to counter it. In December 1943 he called for the Me 262 to be produced as a high-speed *Blitzbomber*, and the following June ordered that production of the fighter version be suspended. In August, however, he authorised every twentieth Me 262 to be produced as a fighter, and the following month allowed for the bulk of production as fighters. In November 1944 the bomber directive was rescinded, although the fighters were still to be capable of carrying bombs.[35]

What effect did these decrees have on Me 262 fighter deployment? Probably not a decisive one, as they were not strictly adhered to. While it was certainly delayed to some extent by the development and modifications necessary to turn the aircraft into a bomber, three-quarters of Me 262s produced were fighters even while the order was in effect. Writes Manfred Boehme, 'Everyone kept quiet about the fact that production planning was still focused on the pure fighter version.'[36] Only about 60 bomber variants were delivered to the bomber wing, KG(J)51, prior to Hitler's November order. In light of this, it cannot be said that bomber production decisively reduced fighter production. The earlier delays were undoubtedly more significant.

TIMELINE—WNR 500200

1945	(Feb?) Test flown after assembly at Regensburg-Obertraubling. Flown by 4 *Staffel* of II/KG(J)51. Possibly flew missions in the Speyer and Kaiserslautern areas under *Major* Grundmann before moving south to Furth in early March, then to Straßkirchen and to Zatec, Czechoslovakia, in April.
1945	(May) Attached to *Gefechtsverband* (battle unit) *Hogeback* at war's end
1945	(May) Captured at Fassberg and flown to RAF Farnborough, UK, for evaluation flights
1946	Shipped from Liverpool to Australia aboard *SS Waipawa* and stored at RAAF Laverton, Vic.
1948	Stored/displayed at RAAF Base Canberra
1955–70	Repainted by the RAAF; displayed in Aeroplane Hall
1970–1981	Loaned to RAAF Museum, Point Cook, Vic.
1981–82	Aircraft examined, areas of paint sanded back, and identity established
1982	Some restoration work carried out by Government Aircraft Factory, Melbourne
1988	Returned to AWM annexe, Mitchell, ACT
1990s	Fuselage briefly displayed in Aircraft Hall
2003	(Dec) Displayed in ANZAC Hall

DATA

Type	Me 262A-1a *Jabo*
Design firm	Messerschmitt GmBH, Germany
Manufacturer	Messerschmitt
Role	Fighter-bomber
Used by	Germany (*Luftwaffe*)
Type entered service	1944 (Jul)
No. built	Approx. 1,430 (Me 262 total excluding Czech production)
Identity	*Werknummer* 500200, coded 9K+XK (*Luftwaffe*)
	Air Ministry 81 (UK)
	RAF serial no. VP554
Powerplant	Two Junkers Jumo 109-004B axial-flow turbojets, each of 1,980 lb (860 kg) static thrust
Armament	One 500-kg or two 250-kg bombs
	Four MK 108 30-mm belt-fed cannon
Wingspan	12.5 m
Length	10.6 m
Max speed	868 km/h
Range	1,050 km
Max take-off weight	7,045 kg

NOTES ON COLOUR SCHEME

As noted above, portions of the RAAF paint applied prior to the aircraft's display in 1955 were sanded back in 1981–82, revealing much of the original camouflage and markings. However, as the original paint was sprayed only thinly, the colours cannot be conclusively identified. The following is believed to be the most likely scheme. For further details see Green and Evans, *Stormbird colours: construction, camouflage and markings of the Me 262* (EagleFiles No. 5).

Post-February 1945 Me 262 scheme of RLM81 *Braunviolett* (brown-violet) and RLM 80 medium green or 82 *Hellgrün* (light green) in splinter pattern; underside aluminium areas unpainted, with RLM76 light blue, a very light bluish grey, or similar applied to steel (e.g. the nose and engine nacelles) and timber components. Dark grey filler and primer over panel joins show through the thin paint application. Some mottling of RLM76 and RLM81 on tail surface. *Balkenkreuze* crosses are white outline on fuselage and wing upper surfaces, and black outline on wing undersides. Black *Hakenkreutz* (swastika) each side of fin. Unit markings: black X outlined in white on fuselage sides forward of crosses, and repeated twice on nosewheel door; red tips to nose and tail to indicate 4 *Staffel*. *Werknummer* on port side of fin above tailplane. '200' in black on each side of nose.

Over this scheme, after capture, were painted the following RAF markings: RAF roundels in yellow/blue/white/red on wings and over the fuselage crosses, and aft of these a P in circle (prototype insignia) in yellow. After arrival in UK, this was overpainted with the UK Air Ministry marking 'AIR MIN 81' in white.

MESSERSCHMITT
ME 163B *KOMET* 191907

27,000 ft over Leipzig, Germany
1800 HOURS, 10 APRIL 1945

Like sparrows darting among vultures, several nimble rocket-powered interceptors had penetrated a daylight bomber formation with such speed that no air gunner could effectively track them. Two hundred and thirty Lancasters, Halifaxes and Mosquitos of RAF Bomber Command were attacking the Leipzig railway yards, and the pilots of I *Gruppe* of Germany's only *Komet* wing, *Jagdgeschwader* 400 (I/JG400), were doing their best to stop them. As the bomber crewman concentrated on their tasks, they put their trust in their Mustang top fighter cover. They could do little else.

Leutnant Fritz Kelb's *Komet* shot up the rear turret and tail of a Royal Canadian Air Force (RCAF) Halifax. Its pilot managed to bring the crippled bomber back to Britain, earning a Distinguished Service Order in the process. Kelb then headed for the lead Halifax, NA185 of 415 Squadron RCAF, Flying Officer Evans' crew oblivious to the danger rocketing past, a hundred metres beneath them. The *Komet* was fitted with an experimental weapon system: the SG 500 *Jägerfaust*, a battery of four upward-firing 50-mm cannon in each wing that was activated by a photoelectric cell as it flew into the bomber's shadow. Eight shells shot up into the bomber's belly, blowing it apart. Flaming wreckage and seven crewmen plummeted to earth.

> ## I realised we were looking at the future.
> *Flying Officer W. Ralph Clark DFC, RAAF*

Werknummer 191907 while on loan to the RAAF Museum at Point Cook during the 1970s when it still wore its original wartime paint. AWM 136092

Despite the intense cold of altitude, Kelb climbed and came upon a group of Mustangs coming down to attack him. His main concern was fuel; he had taken off with just eight minutes' worth, and had precious little left for a dogfight. In any case, his mission was to down bombers, not fighters. He used his remaining fuel to continue the climb through them, then turned and dived vertically past a Mustang towards Leipzig's Brandis airfield. Dumping what little fuel that might have remained in his tanks, he extended his landing skid and brought the rocket fighter down onto the grass field. He climbed out of the cramped cockpit and examined his aircraft: shrapnel holes from the exploding bomber had peppered its fabric-covered plywood wings and aluminium fuselage.

'Green 1', Flying Officer John Haslope of Melbourne, was piloting one of the Mustang escort fighters of 165 Squadron RAF. Up ahead, as a *Komet* attacked a bomber and climbed vertically, he jettisoned his underwing fuel tanks and pushed the throttle to its limit to give chase. As the German turned towards him, he too turned and fired his six wing-mounted 0.5-in machine-guns at a range of a kilometre. He followed the *Komet* into a vertical dive and caught up with it, fired again, and saw pieces of the aircraft break away as bullets struck its wingroots. The Mustang pulled up sharply to avoid colliding with the *Komet* before overshooting it. Witnessed by Polish Mustang pilots in the vicinity, the rocket fighter dived out of control into the ground and exploded.[37]

Haslope, however, did not witness its end. He had momentarily blacked out in his high-G pull-up; when he regained consciousness, his aircraft was down to 8,000 ft, its wings bent and wrinkled from the tremendous forces his Mustang had endured. As flak from Brandis aerodrome burst around him, he climbed back to rejoin his unit.

◄ ►

Haslope's victory was the last of seven Me 163B *Komets* brought down by Mustangs during the final year of the war, and the only one by a Commonwealth pilot. Few Australians had even seen one. Likewise, Kelb's victory was probably the last for a *Komet*.

At this time, the *Luftwaffe* units to the east were retreating from the advancing Russians. The previous month the *Staffeln* of I/JG400's sister *Gruppe*, II/JG400 under *Hauptmann* Rudolf Opitz, had moved from Stargard near Stettin in Germany's north-east to airfields in its west. At Salzwedel farmers helped to hide the *Komets* in barns around the countryside, and to save tractor fuel, the aircraft were towed to their take-off positions by ox. The next move was to Nordholz, where preparations for combat operations were constantly interrupted by Allied fighters. On 10 April, the day of Haslope's victory at Leipzig, came the final move to Husum airfield in Schleswig-Holstein. This was the most northerly of some 21 airfields[38] used by the Me 163. The move was accomplished by trucks to the port at Cuxhaven, then by ship to Husum. The few aircraft ready for flight were aerotowed by Messerschmitt Bf 110s, one of which was shot down by a Spitfire.

Meanwhile, I/JG400 had stayed at Brandis in defence of the oil refineries in the Leipzig area. In mid-April US troops captured the airfield and discovered 33 wrecked *Komets* there, destroyed by the Germans as they left. At Husum, the aircraft of II/JG400 were largely grounded through lack of fuel, and the unit officially disbanded on 20 April. On 8 May, when British forces over-ran the airfield, they discovered numerous examples of the little interceptors—but unlike those at Brandis, some 30 had remained intact by order of the German high command. Half were disassembled but the rest were combat ready, giving the British troops a close-up look at the world's fastest aircraft. The personnel of *7 Staffel* (7/JG400) were instructed by the British to pack them and their spare parts into containers. There was no animosity; the war was over, and the German airmen accepted their task. They were even issued with passes and allowed to inspect the British Spitfire Mk 21 and Tempest fighters which soon arrived.[39]

The *Komet* displayed in ANZAC Hall. The dolly wheels were jettisoned after takeoff. AWM REL/08386

Werknummer 191907 and 22 other Me 163Bs were transported from Husum to the Royal Aircraft Establishment at Farnborough for ground evaluation. One later went to Wisley and Wittering for gliding tests. Meanwhile, American forces had captured a few others and sent them Stateside, one of which was towed aloft behind a B-29 bomber for gliding trials. The US also imported Alexander Lippisch himself. Neither the British nor the Americans ended up flying the *Komet* under power. They did, however, study it in detail. Both nations had more than a passing interest in this, the pinnacle of German high-speed aviation technology, while investigating the possibility of transonic flight.

After examination of their airframes and engines at Farnborough, the *Komets* were sent to Brize Norton west of London (now the RAF's largest air base) to await distribution. Forwarded to the RAF maintenance unit at Wroughton in England's south, 191907 was crated for shipping to Australia in 1946. Together with the Memorial's Bf 109G, the aircraft became a gift to the nation for Australia's role in the defeat of Germany. Lacking somewhere to be displayed it remained crated at the Memorial's store until 1970, when it was loaned to the RAAF Museum at Point Cook, Victoria, and put on public view for the first time.

The Me 163 in context

'It may sound strange, perhaps, but in our own way we loved the *Komet*,' reminisced Me 163 unit commander *Leutnant* Mano Ziegler.[40] Strange, yes, because the unassuming little aircraft may have been responsible for the deaths of more of his friends and colleagues than of the enemy. In ten months of limited operations they shot down perhaps nine Allied bombers, but lost 14 of their own number in combat. However, combat losses were not the main concern.

Of the *Komet's* many liabilities, the main one was that posed by its two exotic fuels: hydrogen peroxide and hydrazine hydrate in methanol, chemicals which sound dangerous enough but were positively lethal if combined accidentally or spilt onto the pilot. As a protective measure, special asbestos-mipolamfibre flight suits were worn. Explosions were a constant threat, the fuel in tanks inside and behind the cockpit being prone to detonating if subjected to a hard landing. The other fuel limitation was the voracious rate at which it was consumed. Just eight minutes of engine power limited the aircraft's role to that of 'point defence', allowing it only to attack bombers within a few minutes' flying time from base. (After the war, this role would be filled by the surface-to-air missile.)

Another limitation was the *Komet's* armament. A high-speed interceptor ideally needed weapons that were reliable and had reasonably high muzzle velocity and rate of fire. The MK 108 *Maschinenkanonen* (automatic cannons), one mounted in each wingroot, although of heavy 30-mm calibre, had neither of the other attributes.

 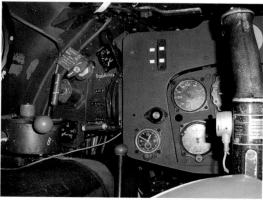

Left: Instrument panel and control column of the Memorial's *Komet*. Courtesy of Alan Scheckenbach

Far left: The *Komet* cockpit's right side wall, including a fuel tank (below) and oxygen regulator. Courtesy of Alan Scheckenbach

The Memorial's *Komet* stored at the Treloar Technology Centre in 1997, showing its advanced swept wing design. Thrust came from the rocket motor in the tail; the nose 'propeller' is in fact an impellor simply for turning the generator to provide electrical power for radio, instruments, etc. AWM PAIU1997/217.05

However, this and the aircraft's other problems may well have been ironed out had the resources been available for a dedicated refinement program, or instead for development of its intended replacement, the Junkers Ju 248. Following Allied air raids, the dispersal of Me 163 production facilities into the Black Forest hindered production; but perhaps the real downfall of the Me 163 lay in its unorthodoxy. In common with most of the jet projects begun by Germany's aircraft designers, resources for its full development were scarce. Instead, production of the conventional Bf 109 and Fw 190 took priority. Messerschmitt itself was not dedicated to the aircraft, and delayed production to the point where it was transferred to Klemm in October 1943 and to Junkers the following September.

The *Komet* had been the brainchild of Professor Alexander Lippisch, an aerodynamicist working for Messerschmitt at Augsburg, in January 1939. Lippisch had been experimenting with 'tailless' (lacking a horizontal stabliser) or 'flying wing' type gliders since 1921. Evolving from his DFS 194 design which made its first powered flights in June 1940, the basic concept was for an interceptor so fast that it could not be shot down, and to this end the Walter company developed its rocket motor. The German-pioneered swept-wing concept was also integral to the high-speed design, and elevons controlled both roll and pitch in lieu of a tailplane. The fuselage was made of light alloy, and the Walter rocket motor concealed within its rear.

Following gliding tests, in August 1941 two Me 163A prototypes began powered flight trials at Peenemünde-West. A world speed record of 1,004 km/h was soon set.

The day after the massive RAF bombing raid on the facility on 17 August 1943 (see the Avro Lancaster chapter), the Me 163 test unit moved south.

It was March 1944 before the specially formed JG400 began receiving examples of operational Me 163Bs. In May, *Komets* saw some limited operations against US Eighth Air Force B-17 Flying Fortresses. In I/JG400's combat debut on 28 July, five aircraft made ineffective attacks on a B-17 formation. On 24 August, however, eight *Komets* shot down four B-17s, and bolstered by this success, JG400 was expanded. By year's end it had over a hundred Me 163Bs at its disposal at Brandis and elsewhere. Subsequently Me 163s had only sporadic success, the scarcity of fuel and a high accident rate severely limiting operations. Production ended in February 1945, and in March and April the *Luftwaffe* high command disbanded two of JG400's *Gruppen* and reassigned their pilots to Me 262 jet units.

The *Komet* pilot was a breed apart. As well as the inherent danger of his steed, his experience of combat at more than twice the speed of his adversaries was unlike that of any other fighter pilot. The aircraft's very *modus operandi* was unique. It was towed to its take-off point and started by centrifugal pumps forcing *C-stoff* and *T-stoff* fuel at a prodigious but precise rate into the combustion chamber. Brakes off, the aircraft accelerated along the ground, teetering precariously on its dolly wheels.

After dropping the wheels from a height of about ten metres, the pilot rocketed into the sky at a 50-degree climb, and arrived at 30,000 ft—well above most Allied bomber formations—in just three minutes. The last few thousand feet were gained in an inertial glide with the engine idling. Continuing the glide the *Komet* came down out of the sun for a surprise sweep through the bombers, firing at any which presented themselves long enough to get his sights on them. Because of the cannon's limitations, a close approach was needed to ensure the minimum four or five hits considered necessary to bring down a bomber. Just as a collision seemed imminent, the *Komet* pilot broke off his attack, re-started the engine for a climb and, assuming his fuel held out, made another pass. If a bomber's gunners managed to score any hits it was largely by luck, as the rocket fighter typically flashed past much too swiftly to be properly tracked. But this speed—the aircraft's best defence—was also a liability, as the pilot had just seconds to line up a target. He could throttle back to increase his accuracy, but in the process exposed himself to more accurate return fire.

◄   ►

As it happened, insufficient numbers of Me 163s made it into the air to affect the course of the war. However, the Memorial's survivor remains a fascinating example of technology from the late war period when Germany, in retreat and with its industry being pounded into submission, was forced to press its most radical ideas into service.

The Japanese built their own version of the *Komet*, an interesting story in itself, although a detailed account is beyond the scope of this book. Even before US B-29 raids on the homeland began in 1944, Japan had acquired the manufacturing rights for the Me 163B, and when they began, its development was ordered and a unit formed to operate it. The Mitsubishi J8M1 (Navy designation) and Ki-200 (Army) development program, however, suffered numerous setbacks. German U-boats delivering pattern aircraft, blueprints and production engineers to Japan were either sunk or captured enroute. The aircraft's factory was bombed. Then, when the first of seven completed aircraft finally took off under power on 7 July 1945, just weeks before war's end, it suffered an engine failure and crashed.

TIME LINE—191907	
1944	(Dec?) Built
1945	(8 May) Captured at Husum, Germany and shipped to Royal Aircraft Establishment, RAF Farnborough, UK
1945	(8 Aug) To RAF Brize Norton
1946	(30 Apr) Crated at RAF Wroughton, UK, and shipped to RAAF Laverton Vic., with Bf 109G
1955	Transferred, still crated, to RAAF Tocumwal, then to AWM store, Duntroon ACT
1970	Loaned to RAAF Museum, Point Cook, Vic., and uncrated
1977–78	Repainted by RAAF
1981–82	Repainted in correct camouflage at Commonwealth Aircraft Corporation, Melbourne
1986	To AWM store, ACT
2001	Displayed in ANZAC Hall

DATA

Type	Me 163B-1a *Komet*
Design firm	Dr A. Lippisch, for Messerschmitt GmBH, Germany
Manufacturer	Final assembly by Junkers, Brandenberg-Briest
	Wings from Klemm, Böblingen
Role	Single-seat interceptor
No. built	Me 163B total 353 (including incomplete airframes)[41]
Type entered service	1944
Identity	*Werknummer* 191907
	UK Air Ministry serial no. AM222
Powerplant	Walter 109-509A rocket motor of 16.7 kN (1,700 kg) thrust
Fuel	Concentrated hydrogen peroxide with phosphate or oxyquinoline (*T-stoff*) and a catalyst of hydrazine-hydrate in methanol (*C-stoff*)
Armament	Two Rheinmetall-Borsig 30-mm MK-108 cannon with 60 rounds each
Wingspan	9.32 m
Length	5.69 m
Max. speed	960 km/h (Mach 0.82)
Powered endurance	8 min (4 min at full throttle)
Maximum take-off weight	4,309 kg

NOTES ON COLOUR SCHEME

While at the RAAF Museum, the aircraft, still in its original paint scheme, was unfortunately repainted in a non-original scheme, and the original paint stripped off the fuselage. The aircraft had, however, been photographed in detail before the repaint. These photos formed the basis of a second, more accurate camouflage application five years later, supervised by Memorial conservation staff and *Luftwaffe* paint expert Ken Merrick, at Commonwealth Aircraft Corporation. This was applied in nitrocellulose lacquer colours matched to original samples on the wings, in the following scheme: RLM81 *Braunviolett* (brown-violet) and RLM83 *Dunkelgrün* (dark green) upper camouflage in splinter pattern; RLM76 *Lichtblau* (light blue) lower surfaces and tail, with mottling of the upper colours on the tail. The original paint had been sealed in clear lacquer to reduce drag.

Accurate markings, less the detail stencilling, were applied prior to its display in ANZAC Hall in 2001, as follows: white outline crosses on fuselage; black and white crosses on upper and lower wing surfaces. *Werknummer* stencilled in black on tail, port side only. White outline swastika on both sides of tail. *C-stoff* (yellow square) and *T-stoff* (white disc) fuel markings on upper and lower fuselage sides. Lack of unit marking indicates that it had not yet been assigned to a unit when captured.

War in the Pacific
1941–1945

TIGER MOTH A17-704

Benalla aerodrome, north-east Victoria
MID-JANUARY, 1943

Without knowing the outcome, I carefully taxied a short distance on the grass airfield, checked my simple cockpit drill and slowly opened up the throttle to the full. After gaining speed, the tail came up and we were gently bumping along on the ground. I soon found that I was airborne!

I climbed quite correctly at 66 miles per hour, and at about 200 feet eased off the throttle, turned left when I reached 600 feet and climbed to 1,000 feet, throttling back, levelling off and rolling back the trim to take the pressure off the controls.

'All clear left' and I turned left 90 degrees. I was now flying in the opposite direction to my take-off path. Everything seemed to be perfectly in order.

The airfield was 1,000 feet down there to my left. Past the airfield I turned left 90 degrees again after carefully checking 'all clear left', no one behind me, altered the trim and again throttled back a little, turned left 90 degrees again and began the descent for landing. Soon I was down to 500 feet approaching the airfield at 66 miles per hour. I continued to ease the throttle back and was over the fence at about 200 feet, descending all the time. Almost all the power off, I hovered and sank slowly to the ground. I taxied up to [my instructor] Ian Johnson and he casually remarked, 'There you are, you silly bugger. I told you you could do it!'

I had 'gone solo'.[1]

◄ ►

Leading Aircraftman Richard Levy's first flight on his own in the slow, docile and forgiving de Havilland DH.82A Tiger Moth was an experience repeated thousands of times at airfields across Australia between 1939 and 1945. Although for the most part not dramatic, it was an event etched into the memory of those who trained with the vast British Commonwealth-wide program known as the Empire Air Training Scheme (EATS). Usually coming after about ten hours' dual instruction in the air, the first solo flight was a milestone in a pilot's road to an operational posting. Levy ended up in France piloting B-25 Mitchell bombers with the 2nd Tactical Air Force, RAF.

The EATS had its origins in a British proposal put forward in 1936. It was the outbreak of war in Europe in September 1939 which turned it into a reality, and indeed a necessity. At a conference in the Canadian capital, Ottawa, three months later, the scheme was formulated in detail. Britain recognised that from its population base alone, it could provide only less than half the trained aircrew required to man the projected numbers of RAF aircraft that would be needed for the defeat of Germany. EATS aimed to make up the shortfall from the dominion nations of Canada, Australia and New Zealand. As aircraft production was gearing up to meet wartime needs, so air force personnel intakes would need to be similarly raised. Australia agreed to provide, over three years, 28,000 trained aircrew—pilots, observers and wireless operators/air gunners—representing a fifth of the total required. Similar numbers of ground staff would also need to be trained. To satisfy the requirement for pilots alone, the RAAF would need to recruit nearly 500 pilot trainees every four weeks. Prime Minister Robert Menzies announced in March 1940 that Australia was embarking on a program of expansion of its air strength on an unprecedented scale: by a factor of seven in aircraft and 11 in manpower.[2]

In cooperation with the Allied Works Council, commonwealth and state departments and authorities, and shire councils, the RAAF began the mammoth task of establishing training schools and aerodromes. From Initial Training Schools (ITS), trainee pilots would disperse to Elementary Flying Training Schools (EFTS) to begin their flying

Workhorse of the Empire

Pre-flight engine run-up for Tiger Moths at Tamworth, NSW, in April 1941. AWM P00448.077

careers. By the time of Japan's attack on Pearl Harbor in December 1941, 12 far-flung schools were dotted around the Australian countryside. Each entailed a large construction program to provide not only airfield facilities, but also accommodation and infrastructure for what was in effect a self-contained community of up to a thousand personnel.

The workhorse for the elementary stage of flying instruction was the Tiger Moth, the chosen primary training aircraft in the 80-plus EFTS formed in Britain and its dominions. The RAAF operated a dozen of these schools in Australia (see table), each with an establishment of some 80 Tiger Moths. While each dominion set up elementary flying schools in its own country for its own nationals, for their next phase of flying training the pupils generally went to Canada (geographically closer to both the European war and to the US, the source of the majority of the advanced training aircraft) or to Southern Rhodesia (now Zimbabwe).

The Tiger Moth was simple in both construction and operation. Its fuselage was of tubular steel framework, the wings of timber with struts and wire bracing separating the two mainplanes in a single-bay design, and the whole aircraft fabric-covered. Its flying qualities and ease of handling allowed students ample room for error in most situations. Basic cockpit instrumentation and controls appeared in both the front and rear cockpits for the pupil and instructor: six 'blind flying' instruments, engine controls, joystick, and rudder pedals—and little else. There were no flaps, wheel brakes or undercarriage retraction for the student to worry about; flaps, in fact, were hardly necessary as the aircraft tended to 'float' near the ground and needed some coaxing to bring it down. Communication between instructor and pupil, as with the earlier Avro 504K, was via a Gosport speaking tube and acoustic headset.

Not all Tiger Moth flights began as smoothly as Richard Levy's. In late 1942 Flight Lieutenant James Swan, who had trained on Tiger Moths at Narromine, New South Wales, a year earlier, was serving as Operations Briefing Officer for the RAAF Catalina flying boat squadrons in north Queensland. With a Tiger Moth attached to the squadrons as a 'hack' for ferrying duties, he could once again enjoy the freedom and exhilaration of open-cockpit flying. The aircraft required two people to start: one to sit in the cockpit at the controls, while the other swung the propeller. On this particular flight, Swan had a sergeant passenger along for the ride.

Out on the grass field at Townsville's Garbutt airfield he chocked a wheel with his parachute, and then strapped his passenger into the front cockpit. A few flicks of switches prepared the controls, and he instructed the sergeant in the simple starting procedure: advance the throttle briefly when the engine fired up, then return it to idle. The man seemed a bit unsure of himself, so the instruction was repeated. Swan then walked up to the propeller, and pulled down on one of the two wooden blades to kick the engine over. What happened next gives substance to the assertion that instructing can be more hazardous than operational flying, as he recalls:

All went well up to the point when the engine decided to fire. It did, and he 'caught' it as instructed, then shoved the throttle full open. My movement away to the right took me clear of the prop so I was safe enough, but the aircraft jumped the improvised chock. I threw myself at the port wing leading edge and dug in my heels and all else, and hung on.

The aircraft proceeded to charge at high speed in a very tight circle. I was able to keep my end stationary, but all I could see was the world rapidly rotating round me with a terrified face peering at me from the cockpit. Every time I released the grip of one hand to signal to reduce power, the aircraft gained the upper hand and shoved me backwards a couple of feet. Scared to let go, I would grab again, recommence rotating and then once more try to get the message across. Finally the penny dropped, the power came off, we all stopped pretending to be whirling dervishes, and normal operations were resumed.[3]

Meanwhile at Parafield in Adelaide, 1 EFTS (the first RAAF flying school to be established after Point Cook) was sending its trainees through their paces. Cyril Francis was one young flyer who learned to fly there on Tiger Moths during August 1943, and as with many others, his graduation was not without incident. Approaching the airfield on his first solo landing, in full concentration, Francis was greeted with a barrage of warning flares as he touched down. Little did he know, until summoned to see the commanding officer, that he had been followed by a Lancaster bomber on final approach, and that it had had to abort its landing. The Lancaster, 'Queenie VI', was on a war bond tour and manned by a crew not long back from operations with 460 Squadron RAAF in England. Francis, after qualifying on Harvards in Canada the following year, would be posted to '460' just before war's end.

A day's flying on a typical EFTS aerodrome began pre-dawn before the wind picked up and, at the more remote locations in summer, before the heat built up. As a large base with four flights of Tiger Moths could become quite congested, most had satellite airstrips from which two or three of the flights flew each day. The aircraft used grass or dirt surfaces rather than runways, enabling them to take off and land into the wind. After a morning's flying, the afternoon would be spent in classroom instruction, often followed by night flying.

◄ ►

The Memorial's Tiger Moth, A17-704, was built at Mascot, Sydney, in 1943. It was part of a large order from Britain to supply 420 examples to training schools in South Africa and Southern Rhodesia. However, with Japan's entry into the war, exports of the aircraft ceased, and A17-704 was retained for the RAAF. When it joined 1 EFTS in June 1944, the unit had just moved to Tamworth, New South Wales. Taking their seat in the front cockpit, trainees went up with their instructors on familiarisation flights, gradually taking more control of the aircraft on successive flights. Each course was an intensive

Before its acquisition by the Memorial, A17-704 was displayed at Air World near Wangaratta, Vic. Courtesy of Martin Edwards

program lasting eight weeks or more, including an average of 60 hours in the air on Tiger Moths. Pilots learned to master basic aerial manoeuvres (see syllabus below) in addition to navigation, emergency landings, blind flying 'under the hood' using instruments only, and night flying. On the ground they were introduced to the Link trainer, a US-built flight simulator which replicated the experience of flying but in a safer environment.

By the time EATS effectively ended at the end of 1944, more than 38,000 RAAF aircrew students had received training, more than a quarter of them as pilots. Those who passed EFTS progressed to Service Flying Training Schools for advanced training on more powerful aircraft, generally the Harvard for those who went to Canada or the similar Wirraway for those remaining in Australia. Those destined for twin- or multi-engined squadrons went on to train on the Anson or Oxford, and ultimately on the aircraft they would fly operationally. Most were sent to the war against Germany and Italy, the majority of whom served in RAF squadrons and the remainder joining the 17 RAAF squadrons under RAF control.[4] From 1942 many graduates were retained for the war against Japan, and these were augmented by men returning from Europe or North Africa, having flown a tour there.

Whatever their subsequent service, many RAAF pilots retained a fondness throughout their flying days for the Tiger Moth, the little biplane in which they had first left the ground.

The Tiger Moth in context

The simple de Havilland DH.60 Moth, designed by Geoffrey de Havilland and first flown by him in 1925, revolutionised civil aviation in Australia and throughout the British Empire during the pre-war era. One of its variants, the DH.60T trainer, served as the basis for the DH.82 Tiger Moth which took to the air in 1931. By the outbreak of war, the DH.82 was the standard elementary trainer in Britain and in two dozen other nations, as well as being popular with civil aero clubs. The DH.82A variant, flying in RAF service as the Tiger Moth Mk II by 1935, introduced the more powerful Gipsy Major engine and plywood upper fuselage decking for strength. Small numbers of the aircraft joined Australian aero clubs, before being impressed into RAAF service after the outbreak of war.

The de Havilland company had established an Australian subsidiary in Melbourne in 1927. After four years it moved to Sydney's Mascot aerodrome, the site of Australia's first aircraft factory, established in 1919 by AFC airman Nigel Love (see Avro 504K chapter). Production began with wings for 20 imported fuselages in 1939, and in May that year the first example was delivered to the RAAF. In October the government approved funds in response to an Air Board submission to construct 350 aircraft, and work was stepped up almost immediately, the plan being to roll out one aircraft per working day. This rate was achieved, and in fact doubled from 1941. Imported Tiger Moths had begun joining elementary flying training schools around Australia before the first fully Australian-built example was delivered in May 1940. The Air Board and the Aircraft Production Commission realised that if Australia was going to meet its EATS obligations, the order with de Havilland would have to be raised to about 1,000 Tiger Moths, quite a challenge for Australia's nascent aircraft industry.

By war's end that figure would be exceeded, with 1,070 Tiger Moths built at Mascot—more than any other Australian-built aircraft. Of these 712,[5] in addition to 120 supplied from Britain, were for RAAF service, making it second only to the Avro Anson in number. The Anson provided the next step in pilot training for those going on to twin- or multi-engined aircraft; the majority of these pilots were initially destined for the RAF Bomber, Fighter, Coastal and Transport Commands in the war against Germany. With Japan's entry into the war, many graduate pilots stayed instead for service in the Pacific War.

Although built primarily to supply the EFTSs, numerous RAAF Tiger Moths saw service with non-training units, both in Australia and in New Guinea and the islands.

Cockpit of the Memorial's Tiger Moth. The cockpits for instructor and trainee were similar. Instruments in the panel include (left to right): air speed indicator, altimeter, rate of climb indicator, turn/bank indicator and engine rev counter, with the P8 compass mounted below centre. AWM REL28818

One of its roles, serving with 4 and 5 Squadrons RAAF, was army cooperation (see Wirraway chapter). After the war, Tiger Moths came onto the civilian market and were bought by aero clubs as they recommenced flying. The Tiger Moth became Australia's major leisure aircraft for many years, and performed roles as diverse as glider tug, aerial ambulance, and aerial top-dressing and crop-spraying for Australia's agricultural industry.

RAAF Elementary Flying Training Schools

(Airfield locations in November 1941)

1 EFTS	Parafield, SA
2 EFTS	Archerfield, Qld
3 EFTS	Essendon, Vic.
4 EFTS	Mascot, NSW
5 EFTS	Narromine, NSW
6 EFTS	Tamworth, NSW
7 EFTS	Western Junction, Tas.
8 EFTS	Narrandera, NSW
9 EFTS	Cunderdin, WA
10 EFTS	Temora, NSW
11 EFTS	Benalla, Vic.
12 EFTS	Bundaberg, Qld

Other categories of schools which trained EATS personnel in Australia

Initial Training Schools (6)
Service Flying Training Schools (8)
Air Observer Schools (3)
Bombing and Gunnery Schools (3)
Air Gunnery Schools (2)
Air Navigation Schools (2)
Wireless Air Gunnery Schools (3)
General Reconnaissance School (1)
Central Flying School (1)
Operational Training Units (8)

Additionally, civilian technical colleges, as well as seven RAAF Schools of Technical Training and an Engineering School, trained ground staff in engine, airframe and instrument fitting, armoury and other trades.

Elementary Flying Training School syllabus (8- to 12-week course)

The RAAF pilot training syllabus stipulated 12–14 weeks at Initial Training School, 8–12 weeks at Elementary Flying Training School, and 16–24 weeks at Service Flying Training School including two weeks of aerial gunnery. Additional postings might include General Reconnaissance School or Bombing and Gunnery School. Thus, a pilot could spend about a year in training before being posted to an operational area, where he would undergo final conversion training onto the type of aircraft he would fly to war.

a. Flying syllabus

1. Air experience; familiarity with cockpit layout
2. Effect of controls
3. Taxiing
4. Straight and level flight
5. Climbing, gliding and stalling
6. Medium turns
7. Taking off into wind
8. Powered approach and landing
9. Gliding approach and landing
10. Spinning
11. First solo
12. Sideslipping
13. Precautionary landing
14. Low flying (with instructor)
15. Steep turns
16. Climbing turns
17. Forced landings
18. Action in the event of fire (with instructor); abandoning aircraft
19. Instrument flying
20. Taking off and landing out of wind
21. Restarting engine in flight (with instructor)
22. Aerobatics (loop, slow roll, half flick, full flick, roll off top, Immelman, inverted flick, stall turn)

From memoirs of Rod Black, instructor with 5 EFTS (Narromine Aviation Museum collection)

b. Navigation air exercises

1. First dual cross country
2. Second dual cross country
3. Solo cross country
4. Night flying (minimum 5 hours, including 1 hour dual)
5. Out of wind landings and take off

c. Ground instruction syllabus

1. Airmanship (including engines, airframes, principles of flight, aircraft operation and regulations)—minimum 30 hours
2. Aircraft recognition—5 hours
3. Armament—17 hours
4. Drill—8 hours
   4a. Physical training and parachute drill—36 hours
5. Meteorology—8 hours
6. Navigation—34 hours
7. Signals—2 hours
8. Instrument flying (Link trainer)—12 hours
9. Discussions and debates—8 hours

From the RAAF's *Standard war syllabus of pilot training* (TD187/43)

'Keeping 'em flying': the ground staff's work

Tiger Moth inspections were done at 60, 120 and 180 flying hours, with a major overhaul at 240 hours when we'd pull the wings off, check the centre section for trueness, check all the flying and landing wires, put it all back together again and re-rig it. We'd jack it up level, unbolt the centre section, put the wheels on … We had a special jig to lay on the front spar with a spirit level, then tighten the wires to give the right dihedral, and another one for incidence.

I was in B Flight. We had to get the aircraft out of the hangar every morning, do the daily inspections on them, make sure the engine fitters did the oil and petrol, make sure there was no torn fabric, then wait for the trainee pilots to come out. It was our duty to help start them and taxi them out. Once they'd finished their detail (which might be an hour and a half) they'd come back in, and we'd grab the wingtip, as the Tiger Moth didn't have much in the way of steering. You had to help manoeuvre them into position. Airframe and engine fitters would refuel them to get ready for the next flight. We'd give them a visual check over, and they'd be ready for the next detail.

Keith Hayden
Airframe fitter, 5 EFTS Narromine

(From oral history interview, Narromine Aviation Museum collection)

NOTES ON COLOUR SCHEME

Overall trainer yellow. Blue and white roundels in standard six positions, and blue and white fin flashes. '04' in black on cowling sides. Serial number A17-704 in black under lower wings (large) and on rear fuselage (small). The aircraft was later overpainted in silver dope, and retained this scheme in civilian aero club service. The overall yellow scheme was later replicated.

TIMELINE—A17-704

1943	(Nov) Delivered to RAAF at Bankstown, NSW
1944	(Jun–Oct) Served with 1 Elementary Flying Training School, Tamworth, NSW
1944–51	Stored at Tamworth and Richmond, NSW
1951–57	Served with Base Squadron, RAAF Point Cook, Vic.
1956	(Aug) Damaged in collision with power lines at Little River, Vic.
1956	Ferried from Point Cook to Tocumwal, NSW, for disposal
1958	(Jun) Registered VH-ABF with Aero Club of Southern Tasmania
1967	Registered at Kerang, Vic.
1977	Purchased by Mr Malcolm Long. Displayed at Chewing Gum Field Air Museum, Qld, and later at Air World, Wangaratta, Vic.
2001	Purchased by AWM and stored at Treloar Technology Centre, ACT

DATA

Type	DH.82A Tiger Moth Mk II
Design firm	de Havilland, UK
Manufacturer	de Havilland Australia Ltd, Sydney, NSW
Role	Two-seat single-engined trainer
No. built	Approx. 7,200 worldwide including 1,070 in Australia
Type entered RAAF service	1940
Identity	A17-704 (RAAF) DX793 (RAF—originally built to UK order) Constructor's no. DHA836 VH-ABF (civil registration)
Crew	2 (instructor and student)
Powerplant	de Havilland Gipsy Major I inverted four-cylinder inline engine of 130 hp (licence-built by General Motors–Holden)
Armament	Nil (some Tiger Moths retrofitted with light bomb racks)
Wingspan	8.94 m
Length	7.29 m
Max. speed	175 km/h
Range	483 km
Loaded weight	830 kg

WAR IN THE PACIFIC **1941–1945**

Over Gona region, north-eastern Papua
1135 HOURS, 26 DECEMBER 1942

A lone Wirraway droned 1,000 ft over the coast on what had so far been an uneventful tactical reconnaissance flight. Pilot Officer Jack Archer and his observer Sergeant Les Coulston in the rear cockpit, both of Melbourne, looked down from the cockpit of A20-103 at the wreck of a Japanese transport ship. Beached a couple of kilometres offshore during the Japanese invasion of Buna, the wreck had now become a visible omen of the defeat of the Japanese in Papua. The enemy had been pushed back along the Kokoda Trail to defensive positions in the Gona–Buna–Sanananda area. Fighting in swampland with malaria rife, taking heavy casualties but inflicting more, Allied forces had finally captured Gona two weeks earlier. The thrust was now against Buna and Sanananda, and the Wirraways of 4 (Army Cooperation) Squadron RAAF were their eyes in the sky.

On the ground not far away, Australian troops of the 2/14th and 2/16th Battalions ran for cover as Japanese fighters came in at treetop height on a strafing attack. One of the Australian soldiers, Fred Myers, ran to a signaller to send Archer a warning, but there was no reply. 'We all decided he had been shot down,' recalls Myers. But the Wirraway was off at some distance and higher, and had not been noticed.

> ## Wirraways can't shoot down Zeros.
> *4 Squadron RAAF control officer*

Wirraway A20-103 at Berry airstrip on 16 January 1943. AWM P02885.001

Above: Pilot Officer Jack Archer (right) and Sergeant Les Coulston with Wirraway A20-103 a fortnight after their aerial victory. AWM 014032

Left: Roy Hodgkinson, *Extraordinary incident* (1943, gouache, 47.3 x 39.6 cm, AWM ART22743)

Archer was distracted when something caught his eye, ahead and below near ground level.[6] Banking and climbing to clear beach palms was what appeared to be another Wirraway. Coulston also saw it, but spotted the red insignia on its wings. He called to Archer, 'Hell, it's a Zero!' The Japanese pilot had apparently not seen the Wirraway, or perhaps had made Archer's initial assumption and mistaken it for a friendly fighter.

Archer's obvious course of action was to make a run for it: he knew as well as anyone that a Wirraway was a sitting duck for the nimble Zero. Instead, on impulse, the daring 22-year-old bore down for a front-quarter attack. He lined up his ring-and-bead gunsight, and at 200 m range pressed the trigger for a five-second burst from his two Vickers .303-in machine-guns. To his great astonishment and relief, his audacity paid off and the Japanese fighter went down, exploding on impact with the water 100 m offshore.

Archer had some convincing to do on return to his forward base at Popondetta, as his aircraft had no gun camera to record the event. Leaping from the cockpit, he ran to the control tent and exclaimed, gasping for air, 'Sir, I think I've shot down a Zero!' 'Don't be silly, Archer, Wirraways can't shoot down Zeros,' replied the control officer. But soon the phone was ringing, and the battalions confirmed that, yes, the improbable claim was true: several observers had seen a Japanese fighter strike the sea. A message was sent to 4 Squadron RAAF's commanding officer, Wing Commander Dallas Charlton, at Berry airstrip near Bomana, north of Port Moresby: 'ARCHER HAS SHOT DOWN ONE ZEKE[7] REPEAT ONE ZEKE. SEND SIX BOTTLES BEER.'

Beer was the most prized of canteen commodities in New Guinea and was not easy
to come by at the forward airstrips, but this was a special occasion. No other Wirraway
had shot down an enemy fighter. Soon one of the squadron aircraft was despatched
from Berry and crossed the treacherous Owen Stanley Range to Popondetta, carrying
a precious cargo of amber fluid. The beer was soon gone, and A20-103 was decorated
with a small painted Japanese flag, beside it the numerals '00'. Two days after the
victory, Australian soldiers went out to the submerged wreck of the fighter and found
that a single bullet had claimed the pilot, penetrating his head. Souvenirs of the aircraft
were salvaged: Archer ended up with the pilot's parachute, and Flying Officer John
Utber, whose log book attests to more than a hundred flights in A20-103, the joystick.
For 'doing the impossible—shooting down a Zero and bringing home his observer and
aircraft to tell the tale,' records the squadron Operations Record Book for 17 March,
Archer was awarded the US Silver Star by Brigadier General Whitehead, Commanding
General of the Allied Air Force in New Guinea. Coulston was Mentioned in Despatches.

Archer's enemy fighter was, in fact, possibly not a Zero but a Ki-43 *Hayabusa*,
codenamed Oscar (see Oscar chapter). The 11th *Sentai* (air group) of the Japanese
Army Air Force (JAAF) had just a week earlier moved to Vunakanau Airfield near
Rabaul in New Britain, which, ironically, had been a base for Wirraways at the time
of its occupation by the Japanese the previous January. By Boxing Day the Oscar had
operated over New Guinea for only a few days, and was thus unfamiliar to Australians.
Similar in appearance to the Zero from a distance, it was often mistaken for the more
famous fighter. If so, Archer's victim was probably the first JAAF aircraft to be shot
down by Australians in New Guinea; and one of the very same aircraft which had just

attacked Dobodura airfield 10 km to the south[8]—temporarily home to the Memorial's Hudson bomber (see Hudson chapter).

◄ ►

A20-103 had been in the initial batch of four Wirraways delivered from RAAF Laverton (Melbourne) to 4 Squadron at RAAF Richmond (Sydney) in September 1940, after the squadron had converted from Demon biplanes. It was at Richmond only a week before the squadron moved to RAAF Canberra. For two years the crews practised army cooperation methods and dive bombing, ground attack and photo-reconnaissance. This period laid the groundwork for the squadron's New Guinea deployment, which came in November 1942 with a move to Port Moresby. A20-103 arrived as a replacement on the 16th of the month. On the 26th, two detached flights were sent across the Owen Stanley Range for ground artillery support on the Buna–Gona–Sanananda front: one to Dobodura and the other to Popondetta, supporting Bullforce and Blackforce, respectively.[9] The squadron's army liaison officer briefed the crews for each flight, and both he and the artillery commanders were in radio contact with the aircraft when airborne.

The slow Wirraway was well suited for reconnaissance and ground support, but was also potentially an easy target for the enemy ground defences, and losses were high. Four days before Archer's victory, a Japanese anti-aircraft gun had claimed a Wirraway and crew, although the gun was soon located from the air and destroyed by artillery. Indeed, A20-103 had its own evidence of the danger of low flying: a bullet hole, discovered beneath its cockpit the day before its aerial victory. The bullet, jammed between a fuel tank and the cockpit floor, was not found and removed until the following year.

On New Year's Day 1943, Japanese resistance began to fail, and Buna fell the following day. Wirraways strafed and killed troops swimming or sailing in small craft for Sanananda, not far up the coastline.[10] A few weeks later Sanananda, too, fell to the Allies. A20-103 left 4 Squadron shortly afterwards for transfer back to Australia to 23 Squadron, which was operating both Wirraways and P-39 Airacobra fighters. Meanwhile, 4 Squadron stayed on in New Guinea. On 3 February an operation was flown which, in hindsight, was historic in pioneering the art of Forward Air Control[11] (FAC; see Bronco chapter). The Australian 2/6th Battalion and 2/5th Independent Company were involved in a firefight near Wau, and a plan was hatched for an accurate air attack. A Wirraway crew determined the Japanese and (with the help of flares lit by the troops) Australian positions, and then led three Beaufighters to the area and marked the enemy positions by firing machine-gun tracer rounds at them. The devastating firepower of the Beaufighters was brought to bear, and a new method of close air support had been invented. The technique was then regularly used by 4 Squadron's Wirraways and, from mid-1943, its Boomerang fighters, and similarly by 5 Squadron. FAC would evolve to become an invaluable aid to ground troops in conflicts to come.

Like the Wirraway, the Boomerang was deemed unsuitable for aerial combat against Japanese fighters, and supplemented the Wirraways in the army cooperation role. The squadron soon moved to Wau, and supported the Allied landings at Cape Gloucester before moving to Morotai and finally to Labuan (Borneo), where it was stationed at war's end.

A20-103's victorious few seconds off the Gona coast were a brief moment in its 18-year career with the RAAF, but it was that improbable achievement which led to its eventual selection for preservation by the Memorial. In the broader story, although it only spent less than two months in New Guinea, this unassuming aircraft was part of one of the most significant campaigns in Australian military history. The bloody battles to capture Buna, Gona and Sanananda culminated in major victories for the Allied forces, and 4 Squadron played no small part in the campaign. Several times a day, running the gauntlet of Japanese ground fire at tree-top height, the Wirraways went out on their vital sorties. Their bread-and-butter work was tactical reconnaissance and spotting for artillery, tasks pioneered by 3 Squadron AFC over the Western Front a quarter-century earlier (see Albatros chapter), but now in the age of modern communications with an AT5/AR8 voice radio set in place of the spark transmitter. As did 3 Squadron before them, they flew ground attack sorties, dropping 250-lb bombs and strafing enemy positions. Underwing stores canisters, including 'storepedoes' of ammunition and supplies, as well as messages, were also dropped in support of the ground forces.

The longer period of A20-103's career was spent as a trainer, during the war years with 5 Service Flying Training School (SFTS) at RAAF Uranquinty, New South Wales. As part of the Empire Air Training Scheme (EATS; see Tiger Moth chapter), 5 SFTS gave more advanced instruction to aircrew who made it through the high 'scrub' or failure rate of elementary flying training. The Wirraway trainee sat in the forward cockpit, the instructor in the rear with his own set of controls. Accidents were inevitable in training. In April 1944 a student taxied A20-103 into another Wirraway, causing extensive but repairable damage. Such an oversight was heavily punishable; even taxiing near another aircraft without a safety airman at each wingtip was rewarded with two weeks' field punishment for the pilot. Discipline in airmanship was a necessity born out of tragedy: in the three years to the end of 1944, for example, 5 SFTS alone lost 27 pupils and nine instructors killed in accidents.

At war's end, the Memorial looked to the RAAF for a Wirraway to enable it to preserve the memory of such an important chapter in Australian military aviation. Initially, interest focused not on A20-103 but on another historic Wirraway, A20-502. 'The Rocket', as it was known, had flown 953 operational sorties with 5 (Army Cooperation) Squadron. However, before a request for it had filtered through to the squadron, which was still overseas, 502 ended its days in flames on New Year's Eve 1945, when all forward units were ordered to destroy their Wirraways. In its place A20-3, the first Wirraway produced, came into the collection; but by 1954 it had deteriorated to such an extent that it was sold for scrap. When in 1957 A20-103 was finally retired from training duties at RAAF Point Cook, it was the sole remaining RAAF service aircraft with a Second World War operational history.

Prior to its display in Aircraft Hall in 1999, A20-103 underwent a thorough renovation and a return to its 1942 configuration. Today it serves as a reminder of two crucial aspects of Australia's war effort. In the trials and tribulations of establishing a military aircraft manufacturing industry, it is linked also to the Memorial's Tiger Moth, Beaufort and Mosquito, these four aircraft representing Australia's three wartime aircraft manufacturers (see second table below). In the tough fight for Buna, Gona and Sanananda at the end of the Kokoda campaign, it is linked to the Memorial's Hudson bomber, and also to the Kittyhawk fighter and the earlier fight for Milne Bay.

Movements of 4 Squadron RAAF

Date	Moved to
Sep 1940	Canberra (after converting from Demons at Richmond, NSW)
May 1942	Camden, NSW
Nov 1942	Port Moresby, Papua; forward base at Popondetta
Feb 1943	Wau, northern Papua
Sep 1943	Tsili-Tsili (detachment supporting Lae, Markham Valley and Ramu Valley operations)
Mar 1944	Nadzab (detachment to Gusap)
Oct–Nov 1944	Madang and Aitape (detachments)
Mar 1945	Morotai
Jun 1945	Labuan

The Wirraway in context

The Commonwealth Aircraft Corporation (CAC) Wirraway, its name an Aboriginal word meaning challenge, was the result of an ambitious attempt to supply the RAAF with a modern, locally produced aircraft for Australia's defence. With the worsening situation in Europe in the late 1930s, it appeared that Australia would no longer be able to rely solely on Britain for the supply of its warplanes. The Wirraway had its origins in an overseas mission in 1936 led by the chief of the newly formed CAC, Wing Commander Lawrence Wackett, to select an aircraft design to be built by the company at Fisherman's Bend, Melbourne. Though its stated role was 'general purpose', the intention was that it would also replace the Hawker Demon biplane in the fighter-bomber role. The chosen design, favoured for its relatively simple construction, was the North American Aviation NA-33 trainer. In 1938 an example of this and one of the earlier NA-16 were shipped to CAC and handed over to the RAAF for flight evaluation. In US production the NA-16 evolved into the Texan/Harvard, the standard advanced trainer for Britain's EATS. The design was modified by CAC, particularly in the wings and tail, and emerged as the Wirraway.

Left: The Wirraway displayed
in Aircraft Hall in 2002.
AWM PAIU2002/110.02

Right: Port side fabric panels
were removed to display the
complex interior. The nose art
includes Archer's victory flag,
three dive-bombing mission
symbols, and a *Man* magazine
illustration of a character from Hell.
AWM PAIU2002/110.05

Meanwhile, defence expenditure was doubled by the Lyons Government at the
start of 1938, and a generous £12.5 million for the air force paved the way for an
expansion program. That year Sir Edward Ellington, Inspector General of Britain's RAF,
was invited to visit Australia to report on the RAAF's state of readiness. While Ellington
believed that Australia's defence lay primarily with Britain, his report pointed to serious
deficiencies in the RAAF. Not least of these was the plan to rely on the defensive
capability of the Wirraway, which he considered suitable only as an advanced trainer.
The Air Board, for its part, disputed this and other aspects of the Ellington Report.

At year's end another £4 million in air force expenditure allowed for an expansion
of local aircraft manufacture, but the production of the Wirraway was now a foregone
conclusion. It was, indeed, Australia's most modern and advanced aircraft at the outbreak
of war in 1939, but there was little else in the RAAF inventory to compare it with. The
Wirraway did excel in some roles such as army cooperation and training, but in air-to-
air combat it was clear that it would easily be outclassed by modern fighters. In 1942
Kittyhawk and Spitfire fighters became available for Australia's defence, and the Wirraway
was released from this uncomfortable role to make its name as a versatile workhorse
for the RAAF. The following year the locally-designed CAC Boomerang, an 'emergency
fighter' offshoot of the Wirraway, entered squadron service. Its mediocre performance,
however, led to its use primarily in the same ground support roles as the Wirraway.

As Australia's first mass-produced aircraft, the Wirraway was a milestone for Australia's
fledgling aircraft industry. It proved the benefit of cooperation with major industrial
concerns such as BHP and General Motors-Holden. In displaying A20-103 in Aircraft
Hall, the technical achievements of the program were a major focus, with the aircraft's side
panels removed to display a complex interior. Wirraway production was grouped into
eight subtypes, A20-103 being the first CA-5 (the third variant) completed.

The first Wirraway built, A20-3, was test flown by Flight Lieutenant Ken Boss-Walker
(see Mosquito chapter) in March 1939. In July, two months before the outbreak of war,
the first delivery to the RAAF was made. Initial orders for 620 aircraft were completed by

June 1942, but more were ordered and eventually 755 Wirraways were built, making it the second most numerous Australian-built aircraft of the war, after the Tiger Moth.

Even before the Pacific war broke out, Wirraways were deployed overseas. In mid-1940, 21 Squadron went to Sembawang airfield at Singapore, although it had re-equipped with Buffalo fighters before Japan's entry into the war in December 1941. Meanwhile, 12 Squadron deployed to the new RAAF base at Darwin. At the start of the Pacific war, eight squadrons and three Service Flying Training Schools were equipped with Wirraways. One, 24 Squadron, went to Rabaul to defend New Britain. On 20 January 1942, the squadron was decimated when its eight Wirraways valiantly attempted to defend the island against a hundred Japanese bombers and Zero fighters. With just two Wirraways and a Hudson bomber left, the commanding officer, Wing Commander John Lerew, received orders from Australia to remain and defend the aerodrome. His reply, *Nos morituri te salutamus* ('We who are about to die, salute you'), the ancient Roman gladiatorial salutation, has become part of air force folklore. But the Hudson evacuated a number of wounded personnel before the Japanese invasion came; the remaining squadron personnel made their way through the jungle on foot, and were rescued by flying boats.

A month later, on 19 February, the Wirraways of 12 Squadron were at Darwin when the town and air base were attacked and their hangar destroyed. With the disaster of the Rabaul raid still in recent memory, it was wisely decided not to send them up against the raiders. After moving to nearby airfields mid-year, the squadron re-equipped with a specialist dive-bombing aircraft, the American Vengeance.

Apart from its army cooperation duties, the Wirraway's main wartime role was as a trainer for service flying and operational training schools, and as a liaison/communications aircraft. In the latter role, it served with most of the RAAF squadrons in Australia. After the war, the Wirraway soldiered on in these roles for nearly 15 years before being replaced by another CAC design, the Winjeel.

Pilot's cockpit of the Memorial's Wirraway in 2008; note the ring gun-sight above the instrument panel. AWM RELAWM31891.001

AUSTRALIAN AIRCRAFT PRODUCTION 1939–45

Type	Role	Built by	No. delivered
Wirraway	general purpose/trainer/ army cooperation	CAC	755*
Wackett	trainer	CAC	202
Boomerang	fighter/army cooperation	CAC	250
Woomera	strike, reconnaissance	CAC	2
Mustang	fighter	CAC	200*
Tiger Moth	trainer	DHA	1,085
Mosquito	fighter-bomber, photo-reconnaissance	DHA	212*
Beaufighter	strike fighter	DAP	364
Beaufort	medium/torpedo bomber	DAP	701

CAC = Commonwealth Aircraft Corporation
DHA = de Havilland Australia
DAP = Department of Aircraft Production
* Includes post-war deliveries

TIMELINE—A20-103

1940	(Sep) Delivered to RAAF Laverton, Vic., and to 4 Squadron, RAAF Richmond, NSW
1940–42	Served with 4 Squadron at Richmond; Canberra; Camden, NSW; and Kingaroy, Qld
1942	(Sep) Retrofitted with dive-bombing flaps by Clyde Engineering
1942–43	Served with 4 Squadron, based at Berry (Bomana), Papua New Guinea (Nov 1942–Jan 1943)
1943	(Jan–Jun) Served with 23 Squadron RAAF, Lowood, Qld
1943–45	Served with 5 Service Flying Training School, Uranquinty, NSW; damaged in ground accident (Oct 1944)
1945	Served with 3 Communications Unit, Mascot, NSW. Refurbished by Clyde Engineering, including replacement of wings
1945–50	Stored at 7 Aircraft Depot, RAAF Tocumwal, NSW
1951–57	Served as a trainer with 1 Advanced Flying Training School, RAAF Point Cook, Vic. Forced landing, 1954
1959	Trucked from Tocumwal to AWM store, Duntroon, ACT
c. 1968–70	Refurbished by Australian Society for Aero-historical Preservation for display in Aeroplane Hall
c. 1981	Replaced on display by RAAF Museum's Boomerang; to storage
1997	Conserved, refurbished and repainted to 1942 configuration
1999	Displayed in Aircraft Hall

DATA

Type	CA-5 Wirraway Mk II
Design firm	Commonwealth Aircraft Corporation
Manufacturer	Commonwealth Aircraft Corporation, Melbourne
Role	General purpose/trainer
No. built	32 (Wirraway total 755)
Type entered service	1939
Identity	A20-103
	CAC constructor's number 103
Crew	2 (pilot and observer)
Powerplant	CAC-built Pratt & Whitney R-1340-S1H1-G Wasp 9-cylinder radial engine of 600 hp
Armament	Two Vickers .303-in Mk V machine-guns in nose and one or two Vickers gas-operated machine-guns in rear cockpit; two 250-lb GP bombs on wing racks
Wingspan	13.10 m
Length	8.48 m
Max speed	354 km/h
Range	1,160 km
Max take-off weight	2,990 kg

NOTES ON COLOUR SCHEME

In 4 Squadron RAAF service in New Guinea: RAAF foliage green/earth brown camouflage on upper surfaces, sky blue undersides. Blue and white roundels in standard six positions, and blue and white fin flash (red in roundels and flash was overpainted prior to PNG deployment). Squadron letter 'D' 36 in (90 cm) high, and serial number A20-103, both in medium sea grey, on each fuselage side. '03' repeated on tip of rudder. The character painted on the port side of the nose is from a cartoon of Hell appearing in *Man* magazine of September 1942, chosen by A20-103's usual pilot FO Utber and painted by squadron artist Sgt Joe Booker. Joining the character are three yellow bomb symbols denoting dive-bombing attacks on Gona and Buna, and (following the 26 December 1942 victory) a small Japanese flag with '00' alongside.

At the time of its transfer to the Memorial, A20-103 was in a training scheme of overall aluminium paint with black anti-glare panel, chromate yellow fuselage band and large black '103' on fuselage sides, the full serial number also in black on the rear fuselage sides.

While on display in Aeroplane Hall until its replacement by the RAAF Museum's Boomerang in the early 1980s, the aircraft bore an inaccurate paint scheme and insignia which had been based on unclear photographs. This was rectified during its 1996–97 refurbishment, with colours being matched spectroscopically to original samples. The replacement cartoon character was traced by projecting a slide of the original onto the aircraft; it was left in black and white as the original colours are not known.

BEAUFORT A9-557

Over Elimi village, northern New Guinea
1045 HOURS, 20 JANUARY 1945

Twenty thousand soldiers of the Japanese Eighteenth Army, occupying the region of
the northern New Guinea coastline between Aitape and Wewak, were cut off from
supplies and were starving. For the preceding six months, relentless attacks on their
positions, depots, sea routes and airfields had effectively destroyed their supply lines
and their ability to conduct an offensive. All they could do now in their weakened state
was to attempt to defend critical positions, as they retreated against the offensive being
mounted by the 6th Australian Division. Key air support for the offensive came from the
Beaufort bomber force of 71 Wing RAAF, which was concentrating on enemy supply
depots in and around Wewak.

Over the village of Elimi near Wewak, six Beauforts of the wing's 100 Squadron
unloaded their bomb loads on fuel and ammunition dumps. The anti-aircraft fire
was fiercely accurate, and Beaufort A9-557, carrying 6th Division air liaison officer
Captain Cyril Nancarrow, came away with several holes in its fuselage. Its pilot,
Flight Lieutenant Jack Fowler, then found himself with a serious dilemma: a 40-lb
fragmentation bomb had initially failed to release, and was now lying loose and live in

> *On Beau bloody bombers we're all qualified.*
> *We're off to the war in the DAP's pride.*
>
> *7 Squadron RAAF song*

The final flight of A9-557 (at left) as Beauforts of 100 Squadron head for the Wewak area, 20 January 1945.
AWM OG3362

the bomb bay. A landing would be risky, as the jolt of touch-down could dislodge and detonate the bomb. Fowler tried a series of sharp dives to dislodge it over the sea, to no avail. After conferring with his crew—Flying Officers Geoff Waite, Frank Smith and Jack Shipman—he decided to land with the bomb on board rather than bale his crew out and lose a valuable aircraft. He would leave the Beaufort's landing flaps undeployed: a flaps-free landing, though faster, would reduce bounce on contact with the runway.

Fowler radioed base at Tadji airfield about his predicament. He was instructed to open his bomb bay doors, which it was hoped would hold the bomb in the fold of the doors so it could not dislodge. As the Beaufort approached the runway, a fire truck was waiting in readiness. At 11.36 am, travelling at well over the usual landing speed of 95 knots, it touched down smoothly. Unbeknown to the crew the pneumatic wheel brake lines had been hit over Elimi, and the brakes had little effect as the bomber sped down the runway. As the eastern end of the runway loomed with alarming speed, Fowler executed a sliding broadside as he attempted a left turn into a taxiway. The Beaufort careened through the motor transport revetment, demolishing several jeeps.[12] Finally the bomber came to a stop, its nose poking through the side of a shed. No explosion came, and the shaken crew sat silent for a minute before emerging unhurt. In a final twist, the bomb dropped onto the seat of a jeep, but still failed to explode.

Thus the flying career of Beaufort A9-557, a veteran of 103 operations, came to an end. Over a relatively short but intensive period of seven months, it had been flown by 19 different crews and dropped 146,000 lb of bombs on Japanese positions in and around New Guinea.

Tragically, Jack Fowler and his three crewmen were killed by another errant bomb on 13 March, less than two months after their lucky escape. Over Maprik West near the Torricelli Ranges of northern New Guinea, their Beaufort, A9-650, blew up over the target. A faulty bomb fuse was believed to have caused the explosion of the 1,400-lb bomb load, which threw fragments of the bomber over a wide area. The remains of the four crewmen were recovered six months later.

The month before its crash landing, A9-557 had in fact become a composite aircraft with the grafting of a replacement nose section. The Repair and Servicing Unit[13] at Tadji, 12 RSU, carried out such operations in trying conditions, with minimal equipment in almost intolerable heat and humidity, and regular torrential rain. It was such work that allowed 71 Wing to maintain its high rate of operations.

A9-557's new nose unit had originally belonged to Beaufort A9-461 of 7 Squadron RAAF, this aircraft itself a veteran of 47 operations. Perhaps its most notable, and controversial, exploit was its role in secret chemical warfare trials: the dropping of mustard gas cylinders among volunteer human guinea pigs on North Brook Island, off the coast of Queensland. Like 557, 461 had come to grief in a crash landing. On 12 November 1944, Flying Officer Smylie was landing in rain at Tadji with one engine dead, when it skidded off the steel plank runway and ran into a ditch, collapsing the undercarriage.

Right: Crewmen who flew Beaufort A9-557 on 34 missions, all killed on 13 March 1945. Left to right: Flying Officer J.W. Shipman, Flight Lieutenant Harry John 'Jack' Fowler, Flying Officer F.O. Smith and Flying Officer A.G. Waite.
AWM P02067.001

Below: Result of the crash-landing of A9-557 on 20 January 1945, showing the wrecked jeeps.
AWM P02589.001

After its spectacular final landing, A9-557 was pulled away to provide much-needed parts for the other well-worn Beauforts of 71 Wing, and left with others on the side of the airfield. The jungle grew around them, and for 30 years these former workhorses of the RAAF were largely forgotten. Then in 1974, a determined team recovered several of the airframes and took 557 to a Victorian property. It was acquired by the Memorial in 1992; from 1997 it underwent one of the most complex and thorough aircraft restorations ever undertaken in Australia. Made up of parts salvaged from around Australia, from the United States and from Tadji and Goodenough Island during 2000–

Above: This Beaufort earmarked for the Memorial during the war, A9-580, had flown 120 operations with 8 Squadron RAAF against the Japanese. In 1945 it accompanied Lancaster 'G for George' on the Third Victory Loan tour in Australia.
AWM P02948.097

Left: The Memorial's Beaufort in ANZAC Hall, March 2003.
AWM PAIU2003/012.06

01, put together with the skills of volunteers and contractors, A9-557 is at the time of writing the most authentic and complete Beaufort in existence.

The Beaufort in context

The Memorial's Beaufort is almost unique in representing the RAAF's primary bomber type of the Pacific war. Specifically, it commemorates the final New Guinea campaign in the Wewak area with which it is so closely associated. More widely, it commemorates the 505[14] RAAF personnel who died in Beaufort units. It also represents a prodigious wartime Australian production effort.

Australia's Beaufort production program had its roots in both Britain's and Australia's defence needs during the late 1930s, brought about by the worsening Asian and European political climate. Australia's need was for large numbers of aircraft capable of searching its vast coastline for an invasion fleet and attacking it. The aircraft chosen, the Beaufort, was a British light bomber capable of carrying a torpedo designed by Bristol and first flown in October 1938. Early the following year Britain's Air Ministry, conscious that the nation's aircraft production capacity would be stretched in the event of war, negotiated for the Beaufort to be produced in Australia, with the aim that it would supplement Britain's Beaufort output as well as fulfill Australia's requirement. The initial plan was for Australia's output to be evenly split between the two nations, although the pressing needs of the Pacific war changed this. Also, the design was extensively modified in Australia and incorporated a number of improvements.

At the outbreak of war, Australia had relatively little industry and few skilled metal workers. Beaufort construction, under the Beaufort Division of the Department of Aircraft Production (DAP) at Fisherman's Bend, Victoria, was thus a massive undertaking. It involved the coordination of seven factories in three states, 40 companies, and some 600 subcontractors. Following the flight of the first locally-built Beaufort in August 1941, Beaufort Division employees alone numbered 8,500, more than a third of them women. To these must be added many thousands working for the firms which helped to make and assemble the 39,000 parts required for each aircraft.

Unfortunately, the Beaufort's reputation in Australia was marred by a seemingly minor subassembly: the aircraft's elevator trim[15] actuating system. The cause of a number of mysterious fatal crashes was traced to the failure of this mechanism, while other incidents were thought to be to the result of carbon monoxide seepage into the cabin, causing the pilot to pass out. With these concerns, and the aircraft's reputation of being difficult to fly and requiring constant vigilance, airmen greeted a posting to Beaufort training with apprehension. In action, however, most crews found it to be an effective warplane. Apart from its poor single-engine performance (that is, with one engine out), it had no major vices in its handling and was agile for a bomber. Surprisingly, it could out-turn a Kittyhawk fighter.

NOTES ON COLOUR SCHEME

Original scheme was RAAF dark green and dark earth camouflage on upper surfaces, with sky blue (a very light bluish grey) undersides, blue and white roundels in six positions, blue and white fin flash, and white 100 Squadron aircraft identification 'QH-L' on fuselage sides. By the time of A9-557's crash landing in January 1945, it had been overpainted in overall dark green, with no codes. Serial number was retained, stenciled on rear fuselage in light grey. When recovered in 1974, the dark green paint had weathered down to the earlier scheme.

TIMELINE—A9-557

1943	(Nov–Dec) Assembled by Department of Aircraft Production
1944	(Jan) Received at RAAF Laverton, Vic.
	(Jul) Joined 100 Squadron RAAF at Tadji airfield, Papua New Guinea
1945	(Jan) Approved for conversion to components, following crash landing at Tadji
1974	Relocated from Tadji to Romsey, Vic., by Ian Whitney
1991	Acquired by R. Greinert, transported to Sydney
1992	Acquired in an exchange by AWM
1997–2002	Restored
2003	(28 Mar) Unveiled during veterans' reunion for short-term display in ANZAC Hall, before returning to storage

DATA

Type	Beaufort Mk VIII
Design firm	Bristol, UK
Manufacturer	Department of Aircraft Production (Beaufort Division), Melbourne
Role	General reconnaissance bomber/torpedo bomber
No. built	520 (2,129 all marks, including 700 in Australia)
Type entered service	1941
Identity	A9-557; A9-461 (nose section)
Crew	4 (pilot, navigator/bomb aimer and two wireless operator/air gunners)
Powerplant	Two Pratt & Whitney Twin Wasp R-1830-S3C4-G 14-cylinder radial engines of 1,200 hp each, with two-speed superchargers
Armament	2,000-lb bomb load (internal and external) or torpedo
	Six .303-in machine-guns in nose, beam, dorsal and turret positions; two wing-mounted 0.5-in machine-guns
Wingspan	17.63 m
Length	13.49 m
Max. speed	430 km/h
Range	2,333 km with auxiliary fuel
Max. take-off weight	10,206 kg

KITTYHAWK A29-133

'Fall River' (No. 1 airstrip), Milne Bay, eastern Papua
0630 HOURS, 26 AUGUST 1942

Twenty-two-year-old Pilot Officer Bruce 'Buster' Brown hung on as the utility truck splashed through mud and rain, and skidded to a halt at the P-40E Kittyhawk fighter with the name 'Polly' painted on its nose. He bolted out the back of the truck, then leapt up onto the wing and into the cockpit. His ground crew passed his parachute harness over, and he quickly but surely clipped it on, buckled his seat harness, and donned his helmet and throat microphone. He pulled the canopy closed to keep out the rain and began flicking the panel switches, mentally going through the pre-take-off checklist. Fuel. Boost pump. Battery switch. Energise. Engine cooling gills open. He wound up the flywheel for ignition. His hands were on the mixture control and throttle as the 1,150-hp Allison V-12 engine coughed noisily into life.

Brakes released, the wheels began rolling through muddy rainwater covering a steel matting taxiway. Brown surveyed the scene in the dawn light as other Kittyhawks made their way towards the runway, zigzagging slightly so they could see forward past

> *[The RAAF Kittyhawk squadrons'] incessant attacks over three successive days proved the decisive factor.*
>
> *Lieutenant General Cyril Clowes CBE DSO MC*
> *Commander, Milne Force, 1942*

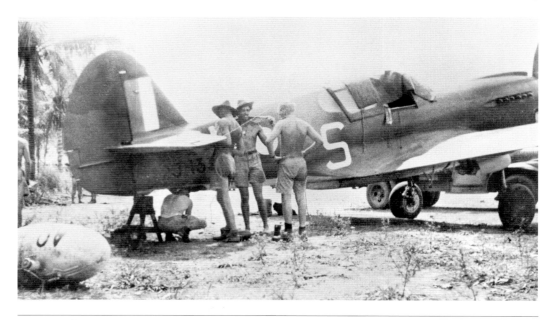

Ground staff of 75 Squadron RAAF at Milne Bay work on A29-133, 1942. AWM P02821.004

the aircraft's high nose. Already they were searching for enemy aircraft above. Unlike Britain—a world away in every sense—where Brown had begun his war service in Spitfires, Milne Bay had no proper fighter control system, although three weeks earlier a radar station had become operational. There was no time to relax: the take-off run and climb would be the worst time to be caught by enemy fighters. Today, however, it was Brown and his fellow pilots of 75 and 76 Squadrons RAAF who would catch the Japanese by surprise as they attempted to land an amphibious invasion force at Milne Bay.

Squadron Leader Les Jackson led the flight of six Kittyhawks. Jackson had replaced his brother John as 75 Squadron's commanding officer in April, after John was reported missing in action during the defence of Port Moresby. Jackson, Brown and their four fellow pilots were now on a mission to locate and attack the landing barges and stores which had begun to make landfall just after midnight. Ground attack was a role for which the P-40 was well suited, although the weather was against them, with rain and low misty cloud reducing visibility to a few hundred metres.

It was a devastatingly successful mission. The pilots located a dozen steel landing barges full of troops and made numerous strafing passes, each pilot firing his entire ammunition supply of 1,500 rounds. The carnage was repeated during the course of the day as flight after flight returned to the barge landing sites to repel the invasion. George Odgers, an official RAAF historian, later wrote how

> *all day long the frequent explosions, bursts of cannon and machine-gun fire, as well as the roar of the aircraft engines, could be heard on the sodden runway from which the RAAF fighters operated. The Japanese landing barges were ripped open and sunk by bombs and cannon fire; the enemy troops were strafed; an ammunition truck was blown up. Ground crews of the RAAF worked with their clothes and bodies splashed with mud and sodden with rain.*[16]

◄ ►

Only the previous month, the US Army's 46th Engineering Regiment had finished constructing Milne Bay's No. 1 airstrip. Allied fighters could now both cover the sea route to Port Moresby and launch attacks on enemy positions along the north coast of New Guinea. The Japanese navy, however, was determined to take Milne Bay. Following the defeat of Japan's seaborne attack force in the battle of the Coral Sea in May, the base was needed in its quest for Port Moresby. Thus, Milne Bay became a linchpin in the whole New Guinea campaign.

It was an urgent situation requiring the immediate deployment of new fighters. Within two weeks of arrival in Australia on 8 June 1942, Kittyhawk A29-133 was re-allocated from the fighter training unit, 2 Operational Training Unit, to an operational assignment: it was to go to 75 Squadron. One of the squadron pilots, John Pettett, took off from Bankstown in Sydney, overflew his wife in their house at Mosman, and continued on to Kingaroy, Queensland. There, 75 was re-equipping after an intensive

Flight Lieutenant Bruce 'Buster' Brown DFC and Bar (right) with Leading Aircraftman Alex Farthing, a flight rigger with 75 Squadron RAAF, on Kittyhawk A29-133 at Milne Bay. AWM P02821.003

six weeks defending Port Moresby from Japanese aerial onslaughts. That action had secured Moresby and its airfields, for the time being at least; and against losses of 12 Australian pilots and 24 Kittyhawks, it brought claims of 60 Japanese aircraft destroyed (33 confirmed).[17] Some of the pilots now regrouping at Kingaroy, including Pettett, were veterans of that action, while others such as Brown had flown Spitfires over Europe. Brown took A29-133 as his steed almost from his first day in Kittyhawks. He named it 'Polly'—his nickname for his fiancée, Olga, whom he had known since his school days. After a period of training at Lowood, Les Jackson led his 20 Kittyhawk pilots to Moresby. On 25 July, the first of the fighters touched down on the newly constructed No. 1 airstrip at Milne Bay.

Both 75 and 76 Squadrons were soon in action. On 4 August Japanese Zero fighters strafed some of the Kittyhawks on the ground, destroying one, while others engaged the enemy and shot down a dive-bomber. A few days later, Brown was piloting 'Polly' when it was attacked and damaged by two Zeros. The squadron then searched out and destroyed a Japanese float-plane base. In between these moments of excitement long hours were spent on shipping patrols, searching for the Japanese convoy which, intelligence sources had established, was coming their way. The second Japanese air raid on 11 August had bittersweet results for the two squadrons. While intercepting the incoming formation of a dozen Zeros, four of the 22 Australian pilots airborne were killed by the more experienced Japanese, against claims of four Zeros probably destroyed. 'Polly' damaged another.

In preparation for meeting the invasion force, the Kittyhawks were modified to carry bombs; like their equivalents flying with the two RAAF fighter squadrons in North Africa, they were now 'Kittybombers'. A landing force was spotted on 24 August, and the following day the P-40s attacked barges ashore at Goodenough Island. With a low cloud base, level bombing rather than dive bombing was carried out. That night, Brown was the pilot on duty when the enemy convoy entered Milne Bay and landing barges full of troops and equipment started coming ashore. He recalled 50 years later, in 1992, that around midnight the Japanese began shelling inland from the base. Brown called Les Jackson and in the dawn light they took off. 'Polly' was in the first wave of the attack on the barges as the Kittyhawks bombed and strafed them, in company with Hudson bombers of 6 and 32 Squadrons RAAF, also based at Milne Bay. Meanwhile out at sea, B-17 Flying Fortresses of the 19th Bombardment Group based at Mareeba, Queensland, bombed the convoy after it left the bay.

Bruce Brown was in the midst of the fighting. Over the course of the Milne Bay battle, 'Polly' was hit three times by Zeros and another four times by ground fire. And, with rudimentary equipment and in constant rain, the hard-pressed ground crews re-fuelled, re-armed, maintained and repaired the Kittyhawks time after time, and even got involved in the fighting. They replaced 300 0.5 in machine-gun barrels and re-stocked some 200,000 rounds of ammunition in the wings. It was a hot, muddy quagmire, and the threat of tropical diseases was all around. It was said that Milne Bay would have been a hell-hole even without the enemy to contend with.

In between defending their airfield against air raids, for ten days the Kittyhawk squadrons attacked targets in support of the hard-pressed troops of the 7th and 18th Australian Infantry Brigades. By 5 September the 2,400-strong invasion force had been overwhelmed by a totally unexpected force of some 9,500 Australian army, RAAF and American men,[18] and the Japanese finally began withdrawing. The area was littered with the bodies of nearly 800 dead, 161 of them Australian, lying among scattered equipment and bogged tanks. Major General Cyril Clowes, commanding Milne Force, later commented that in particular 75 and 76 Squadrons' 'incessant attacks over [the first] three successive days proved the decisive factor in the decision to re-embark what was left of the [Japanese invasion] force'.[19] Milne Bay entered the history books as Japan's first major defeat on land. It was largely an Australian victory, and one in which the RAAF squadrons had played a crucial part. Japanese hopes for securing Port Moresby now lay with a weakened overland force moving along the Kokoda Trail. Within weeks, however, within sight of its goal, that force too was turned back by constant resistance and lack of supplies.

In the desperate Milne Bay battle, 45 enemy aircraft were claimed destroyed but seven of the Australian fighter pilots had been lost, including 76 Squadron's commanding officer, Squadron Leader Peter Turnbull. On 27 August, while diving to attack a troop detachment, his Kittyhawk was seen to flick upside down and crash into the jungle. He was succeeded by Squadron Leader Keith 'Bluey' Truscott (see Spitfire chapter), and was honoured by the naming of Milne Bay's No. 3 airstrip after him.

Pilot Officer Bruce Brown's enemy contacts in Kittyhawk A29-133, Milne Bay, 1942

(Notes from pilot's log book)

2 August	Shot up and burned a bomber on Duboyne Island. Scramble. Caught by Zeros. Plenty of holes.
11 August	Scramble. Zero and dive-bombers intercepted. Credited with probable Zero destroyed, then Geoff Atherton and Hugh Shield shot one off my tail. We lost FO Sheldon & WO Shelley (75 Squadron), and PO McLeod & Sgt Ingster (76 Squadron).
23 August	Scramble. Nil sightings (lull before the storm).
24 August	Patrol over base. Barge load of Japanese destroyed. Scramble—jumped from above over Goodenough Bay. Damage to some.
25 August	Sea patrol. Sighted Japanese convoy heading for Milne Bay. Strafed destroyer and troop transports. FO Whetters missing.
26 August	Shelled by Japanese cruisers. Troops landed about 2 am. Off at dawn strafing enemy troops, stores, barges and dive-bombing.
27 August	Reconnaissance. Sqn Ldr Turnbull (76 Squadron) and Sgt Munro (75 Squadron) missing.
28 August	Strafing army front line then told to proceed to Moresby to get new barrels for our 6 guns. Return to Milne Bay. Strafing Japanese troops.
31 August	Strafing Japanese front line. PO Davis killed.

◄   ►

At the end of September, 75 and 76 Squadrons were relieved by American units and moved back to Cairns. Brown was hospitalised with malaria, and when recovered received another Kittyhawk, A29-126, which he also named 'Polly'. In March 1943 this second of Olga's namesakes was passed on to Flight Sergeant Dennis Wilson, but a name change was called for, as Dr Wilson related in 1992:

> *I inherited 'Polly' from my flight commander Buster Brown after my previous aircraft came to a sticky end. As 'Polly' was Buster's very new wife I obviously had to change the name; so not having much imagination (or a girl friend) I had them paint out the 'P' and she became 'Olly'.*[20]

Wilson's association with 'Olly' lasted six months and included surviving an engine failure that forced him to bring it in for a 'dead stick' landing at Milne Bay; in September he flew it to Moresby to pick up a new Kittyhawk.

Meanwhile, A29-133 had not seen the last of Milne Bay. It too returned in March 1943 with 75 Squadron, now under the command of 23-year-old Squadron Leader Wilf

Arthur DFC. Arthur was a P-40 veteran of 3 Squadron RAAF in North Africa, with ten aerial victories. He now took A29-133 as his personal aircraft. On 14 April, he led the squadron into action against a force of nearly 100 Japanese aircraft heading for Milne Bay at high altitude—it was Japan's 24th and largest air attack on this target. His action won him the Distinguished Service Order.

The bombers reached the area just after midday. More than 8 km up in the stratosphere, Arthur in his newly re-engined 133 led two head-on attacks in line abreast against the leading formation of Betty (Mitsubish G4M) bombers. He pressed the firing button; nothing happened. The guns were jammed. He radioed a request for permission to land but then, while diving across the bay toward the airstrip, saw six Val (Aichi D3A) dive-bombers escorted by two fighters. Guns or not, and with his fuel running out, he decided to press on. Feigning an attack on one Val he spotted two more flying low over the water, and almost managed to force the rear aircraft into the sea. The Kittyhawks of 75 and 77 Squadrons claimed six Betty bombers, a Val and three Zeros destroyed. American Lightnings and anti-aircraft fire added another four enemy aircraft, including a Betty claimed by the famous ace Captain Dick Bong (see the Oscar chapter). Comparatively light damage was done to the harbour and shipping. Arthur had clocked up his 1,000th hour of flying: 'What a way!' he wrote in his log book. It was the last major Japanese attack on Milne Bay.

Bruce Brown went on to command 77 Squadron, reaching the rank of wing commander, and was awarded the DFC and Bar. Wilf Arthur DSO DFC survived a mid-air collision in November 1943, and later as the 24-year-old commander of 81 Wing was the RAAF's youngest group captain. In April 1945 he was involved in the 'Morotai Mutiny' when he, with Australia's most successful fighter ace, Group Captain Clive Caldwell DSO DFC and Bar, and six other senior RAAF officers, protested the apparently ineffectual employment, at that time, of the RAAF fighter squadrons in the ground attack role.

Later variants of the Kittyhawk continued to see front-line RAAF service in the gradually northward-moving island campaign until war's end. But in the postwar years, as the RAAF equipped with Australian-built Mustangs, the type had become obsolete and was scrapped by the hundreds at Oakey in Queensland, Werribee in Victoria and other locations. A few were publicly sold off at Laverton near Melbourne, and the derelict hulks of several machines ended up in civilian hands. Within a few years even these survivors had been destroyed—with one exception. In about 1947, A29-133, minus its engine, was bought from the scrap dealers by some racing car enthusiasts who cannibalised its prolific supply of nuts, bolts and almost everything else they could use.

One January day in 1960, fruiterer Nelson Wilson was doing his rounds in the outer Melbourne suburb of Burwood, when he noticed a derelict aircraft fuselage lying in the grass behind a house. Faintly visible under the tailplane was the serial number A29-133. 'Polly's' owner had been offered £50 by a scrap metal dealer, but by July the following year Wilson had come up with enough money to match the offer,

In 1999 the Memorial's Kittyhawk was displayed in a Milne Bay set-piece in Aircraft Hall, showing armourers working on its machine-guns. Suspended above is its old adversary, the Zero. AWM PAIU2001/122.15

and retrieved it in 1962. It was the beginning of a 25-year effort by Wilson, his son Greg and a team of helpers to get the Kittyhawk back into the air. The project never quite reached its goal, and early in 1992, after complex negotiations, a contract was signed for the sale of the substantially restored aircraft, at the time the only ex-RAAF Kittyhawk in Australia, to the Memorial.

In two semi-trailer loads, the fuselage and wings were transported from Wandin and Yering near Melbourne to the Memorial's conservation annexe at Mitchell, ACT. Ten intensive weeks were spent on its assembly and preparation for display. With just two days to go before its big day, Memorial staff, volunteers and RAAF personnel finally had 'Polly' back in one piece and looking as it did when it first joined 75 Squadron. On 26 August 1992, 50 years to the day after Polly's decisive missions at Milne Bay, Brown, Arthur and a host of other former 75 and 76 Squadron pilots were guests at the Memorial's Aeroplane Hall for the fighter's unveiling by Prime Minister Paul Keating.

Displayed in a set-piece representing a Milne Bay dispersal, 'Polly' was again on public view for the re-opening of the Memorial's Bradbury Aircraft Hall. In the words of 'Buster' Brown at the 1992 gathering, it stands as 'one of the aircraft which, in conjunction with the army in the Milne Bay show, did help save Australia

In 2000 Wing Commander Bruce Brown DFC and Bar and his wife Olga ('Polly') viewed his old Kittyhawk in its new setting. AWM PAIU2000/090.06

from a foe contemplating invasion ... She will be a fine memorial to a lot of guys who lost their lives flying Kittyhawks.' There were many who did: 75 Squadron alone lost 44 men in and around New Guinea during the war.

The Kittyhawk in context

Simply put, the American P-40 Kittyhawk (known as the Warhawk in US service) was Australia's most significant fighter of the Second World War. Over three-and-a-half years, 841 were delivered to the RAAF, the first 163 of which were the P-40E subtype. In addition, 67 examples were ordered by the RAAF for 120 NEI (Netherlands East Indies) Squadron based at Canberra. The P-40 was available in such large numbers because it was considered obsolescent, with types such as the P-38 Lightning, P-47 Thunderbolt and P-51 Mustang out-performing it in US Army Air Force service, particularly at high altitudes.

Developed in 1938 from the radial-engined P-36 Mohawk, the Curtiss P-40 introduced an Allison liquid-cooled engine. Initial production (the P-40B and C subtypes) went into RAF service as Tomahawks; 3 Squadron RAAF in Palestine equipped with them in mid-1941 and supported the 7th Australian Division in operations against the Vichy French in Syria. At year's end the squadron re-equipped with the P-40E (the Kittyhawk Mk IA in RAAF nomenclature), when it and 450 Squadron RAAF became fighter-bomber units in the war against Italian forces and Rommel's *Afrika Korps* in North Africa. Clive Caldwell destroyed some 22 enemy aircraft while flying P-40s with RAF squadrons. His victims included not just the slow Ju 87 Stuka dive-bomber (of which he destroyed five in one day) but ten Messerschmitt Bf 109s. This demonstrates that when it was flown by a skilled pilot who could utilise its advantages, the P-40 could equal the best of its opponents. In the Middle East and North African campaigns, the majority of 3 Squadron's claims of over 200 enemy aircraft destroyed, and 450 Squadron's claims of 39, were with the P-40. From mid-1942, the Kittyhawk became the 'Kittybomber' when it was adapted for bombing, and its role largely changed to ground attack. The following year, 3 and 450 Squadrons flew it in the Mediterranean campaign over Italy and Yugoslavia.

On the other side of the world from parched desert and sandstorms was the sweltering Pacific theatre of war. From early 1942, the American 49th Fighter Group's P-40 squadrons defended Darwin from Japanese air attacks. The RAAF itself received Kittyhawks only after repeated requests to the US government. Prime Minister John Curtin had turned to Churchill in January 1942 with a plea for some of Britain's allocation of American-built aircraft to be diverted to Australia. It was essential, he argued, to bolster the RAAF's 'extremely limited' aerial striking and defence force. In the event, from March 1942 both US and British allocations were diverted to Australia. In the precarious year of 1942 it was the RAAF's only modern fighter, and Australia's most effective aerial defence. Though inferior in manoeuvrability to the Japanese Zero, the P-40 was nevertheless a ruggedly built and stable fighter with respectable power, speed and armament. While 75 and 76 Squadrons flew in action in New Guinea, 77 Squadron's Kittyhawks defended northern Australia

Cockpit of the Memorial's Kittyhawk, which was considered roomy by wartime fighter standards. AWM REL/20242

from when they replaced the 49th Fighter Group in August 1942, until early the following year when 77 Squadron also moved to New Guinea. During 1943 and 1944, RAAF Kittyhawks bore the brunt of the war in New Guinea in attacking ground targets, intercepting enemy bombers and fighters, and escorting both RAAF and US Army Air Force bombers in raids against the airfields and installations along New Guinea's north coast (see Oscar chapter for more about these raids).

The Kittyhawk was the RAAF's most widely used combat aircraft of the war; it equipped eight squadrons in the war against Japan and two against Germany, Italy and the Vichy French, and it flew until the last day of the Pacific war. By early 1944 the majority of examples in Pacific war service were P-40N (Kittyhawk Mk IV) models, with additional examples of the P-40K and M (Kittyhawk Mk III). The squadrons followed the war's progress north, based at Noemfoor Island off north-west Dutch New Guinea by mid-year, then to Morotai at year's end as part of the 1st Tactical Air Force, from where they attacked targets in northern New Guinea while the Americans staged north to the Philippines. Moving on to Tarakan in Borneo, they ended the war at Balikpapan with the rest of the RAAF's front-line forces.

TIMELINE—A29-133	
1942	Built to an RAF order but diverted to RAAF; received at 2 Aircraft Depot, RAAF Richmond, NSW
1942–43	Served with 75 Squadron RAAF at Kingaroy, Qld, and Milne Bay, Horn Island, and Cairns, Qld
1943	To 82 Squadron, Bankstown, NSW
1944	To 1 Engineering School for instructional purposes
c. 1947	Disposed of by Dept of Aircraft Production, probably at Laverton, Vic.
1949	Airframe minus engine and propeller sold to an insurance assessor
1961	Purchased by Nelson Wilson of Lilydale, Vic., who with his family restored the aircraft over the next 25 years with the intention of flying it
1991	Discussions between Wilson family and AWM for purchase begun
1992	Purchased by AWM and delivered by road to AWM annexe, Mitchell, ACT. Restoration completed, and unveiled in Aircraft Hall
1999	Incorporated into a ground maintenance set-piece in refurbished Aircraft Hall

DATA

Type	P-40E-1 (Kittyhawk Mk IA)
Design firm	Curtiss, USA
Manufacturer	Curtiss, Buffalo, New York, USA
Role	Single-seat fighter/fighter bomber
No. built	1,500 (P-40E total 2,320; P-40 total 13,738)
No. in RAAF service	163 (P-40 total 848)
Type entered RAAF service	1941
Identity	A29-133 (RAAF)
	41-36084 (USAAF)
Powerplant	Allison V-1710-39, V-12 liquid-cooled supercharged engine of 1,150 hp
Armament	Six wing-mounted 0.5-in Colt Browning M2 machine-guns; provision for a 500-lb (227-kg) bomb or auxiliary fuel tank
Wingspan	11.37 m
Length	9.68 m
Max. speed	580 km/h at 15,000 ft
Range	1,448 km with drop tank
Max. take-off weight	4,131 kg

NOTES ON COLOUR SCHEME

1942-period 75 Squadron RAAF scheme: US factory-applied upper surface disruptive camouflage of dark green and light earth/middle stone, with sky undersides. Blue and white roundels in six positions. Blue and white fin flashes. White aircraft identification letter 'S' on mid-fuselage, both sides. Serial number stencilled in black on rear fuselage sides. Stylised 'Polly' in white on starboard side of nose.

HUDSON A16-105

Dobodura airfield, eastern Papua
1050 HOURS, 26 DECEMBER 1942

Eleven Ki-43 *Hayabusa* fighters, known as Oscars, of the 11th *Sentai*, Japanese Army Air Force,[21] headed south-east at 13,000 ft. The flight had left its forward airfield near Lae an hour earlier on this, one of the unit's first missions in the Papua New Guinea theatre, and now the pilots sighted the Allied airfield complex which was their target. Their mission was to attack the base to disrupt the aerial supply chain for the Buna campaign.

If the Australians at Dobodura had thought this newly constructed base was still unknown to the enemy, they were under no illusions now. The Oscars came down for the attack. In several strafing runs they fired on three consecutive Hudson transports taking off from one of the grass airstrips, damaging two. Japanese hopes for an unhindered attack, however, were thwarted by three flights of US P-40E Warhawks of

> *For fifteen men in jungle green rose from the kunai grass*
> *And came towards the plane*
> *My men in silence watched them pass.*
>
> Wing Commander David Campbell, DFC and Bar, 'Men in green'

Hudson Mk I bombers of 1 Operational Training Unit. In December 1942 the foreground aircraft, A16-34, joined A16-105 in the Detached Flight in New Guinea, where both were flown by Flight Lieutenant David Campbell. AWM 006878

of the 9th Squadron, 49th Fighter Group. Two of the Americans made a pass through the Oscars just as they arrived. Lieutenants John Landers and Jim Watkins downed two before Landers himself was shot down. RAAF Hudson A16-105 was one of the lucky ones which was spared the attacks.

But Squadron Leader Neville Hemsworth DFC in Hudson A16-3, with wounded soldiers aboard, was faced with a dilemma: should he run the gauntlet and try to get away, or stay on the ground and sit out the attack? He chose to go, heading for low cloud. Immediately, the fighters homed in on his Hudson.

His turret gunner, Flight Sergeant Henry Stephens, was grievously wounded but still kept firing at the attackers. Hemsworth banked at 400 ft over the coast, heading for a friendly corvette, as bullets from the Oscars tore through the floor and ricocheted off his armoured seat. The Hudson was now on fire. As it crossed the coast, American

US Lodestars (a transport equivalent of the Hudson) helped to bring some 3,000 troops to Wanigela, New Guinea, for the Allied coastal advance on Buna in late 1942. A makeshift runway had been prepared by the 2/10th Australian Infantry Battalion. AWM 027395

anti-aircraft gunners mistook it for an enemy bomber, and opened fire. Hemsworth's options were rapidly diminishing. His best chance to extinguish the flames was to ditch the crippled bomber in the bay. Though severely burnt and lacerated, Hemsworth, his observer and wireless operator survived the water landing. Two of the wounded soldiers aboard died from bullet wounds or drowned in the sea; Stephens was rescued with the crew, but died in hospital.

◄ ►

Three months earlier, after advancing along the Kokoda Trail almost as far as Port Moresby, the Japanese South Seas Force was ordered to withdraw to Buna, Gona and Sanananda on the Papuan north coast to establish a stronghold. Numerous factors continued to weaken the force. Intense ground fighting and attacks by Allied aircraft were relentless, and while the Allies had the advantage of air deliveries, the Japanese had to supply their troops overland from the north coast. Also, heavy Japanese losses sustained at Guadalcanal and Milne Bay drastically reduced reinforcements. Soon the Allied ground troops and artillery crews, though hard-pressed themselves, were pushing the Japanese further back towards the beach positions.

In November the Japanese army's 6th Air Division had been committed to the New Guinea area of operations, and on 18 December 60 Oscars of the 11th *Sentai* arrived at Rabaul in New Britain.[22] A week later, on the day of their first attack on Dobodura—in fact, just half an hour later—the Memorial's Wirraway A20-103, flying from nearby Popondetta, had its famous victory over a Japanese fighter. Thus an intriguing link was formed between A20-103 and the Memorial's Hudson A16-105: the latter was flying out of Dobodura, just a few kilometres away, after bringing in US troops to support the same campaign at the very same time. A20-103's victim was quite possibly one of the Oscars returning from Dobodura.

Joining the land battle were Australian gunners of the 2/1st Field Regiment, veterans of the North Africa and Greece campaigns. Adequate supplies would be crucial to their success. US General George Kenney, commander of the Allied Air Forces in the South-West Pacific Area, had urgently requested aircraft to bring in ammunition, supplies and fresh troops for battle. A US Army Air Force transport group provided a constant stream of C-47s for the half-hour trip from Port Moresby, over the Owen Stanley Range, to the Popondetta and Dobodura airfields just a few kilometres from the north coast. Skimming over the jungle treetops they landed only long enough for their precious cargo to be unloaded, engines still running in case of Japanese air attack, before leaving for another load.

The Australian Minister for Air, Arthur Drakeford, promised a RAAF response to Kenney's call. Douglas DC-2s of 36 Squadron helped out on the Townsville to Port Moresby supply leg, but still there were not enough aircraft or crews to get the supplies to where they were needed. In the absence of sufficient transports, nine Hudson bombers from 6 Squadron at Port Moresby were pressed into service to air drop ammunition and supplies directly to the Buna area.

Finally, the general reconnaissance training school, 1 Operational Training Unit (OTU) at Bairnsdale, Victoria, was called upon. Here at 1 OTU, after initial training on Wirraways and twin-engined Ansons or Oxfords, future bomber crews converted onto Hudsons and Beauforts during a course lasting up to six weeks. Following the attack on Sydney Harbour by Japanese midget submarines on the night of 31 May–1 June 1942, 1 OTU had been making daily sea reconnaissance flights off Australia's south-east coast. Now they were about to get closer to the enemy. After an all-night maintenance effort on the aircraft, a dozen Hudsons and 108 officers and airmen departed Bairnsdale on 10 December, leaving only five Hudsons and postponing two training courses. At Ward's aerodrome near Moresby, the flight, called simply 1 OTU Detached Flight and led by Squadron Leader Oliver Hall, joined a motley collection of civilian aircraft. For their new role, the Hudsons were stripped of non-essential equipment and each had a Vickers gas-operated machine-gun installed in place of the roof hatch.

Collectively, the hurriedly assembled group was given the name RAAF Special Transport Flight. While the OTU crews included trainees, their pilots were not green; most, in fact, were instructors with a good deal of operational experience. On 14 December the flight made its first deliveries, air-dropping ammunition and other supplies at Soputa along the road to Sanananda. The crews were back there the following day, only to suffer their biggest blow: the loss to ground fire of Squadron Leader 'Pedro' Pedrina DFC, commander of Beaufort training at 1 OTU, and two of his crew. The low and slow approach required for air-dropping was risky, and Pedrina had been at just 200 ft and on his third run over the drop zone. The risks were hard to justify when it was found that the stores were being damaged on impact with the ground. Instead the Hudsons would land, unloading their cargo while wounded soldiers waited to board for the return trip to Moresby.

Flying A16-105 was Flight Lieutenant David Campbell DFC, with his crew Pilot Officer Dent (navigator), Flight Sergeant Allen and Sergeant Brewin (wireless/air gunners). Campbell was a veteran of the defence of Port Moresby and missions to Rabaul earlier in the war, before being posted to Bairnsdale as an instructor. One of his pupils there was Ray Kelly, whose first Hudson flight had been in A16-105; Kelly, coincidentally, was now with the 6 Squadron detachment in New Guinea on the same supply task. Campbell, who later commanded 1, 2 and 32 Squadrons RAAF, and as a wing commander earned a Bar to his Distinguished Flying Cross, is now best known as a poet. His most famous poem, 'Men in green', contrasts the fresh troops he flew into battle with the wounded he brought back to Moresby, and makes reference to a Hudson that is most likely A16-105.

Above: Ray Kelly, a former pilot of the Memorial's Hudson, casts his mind back 60 years as he sits in its cockpit in October 2002. Ray visited with his wife and two grandsons, who were intrigued to hear that he once had to escape through the canopy hatch above him. AWM PAIU2002/162.04

Top: A RAAF Hudson lands at Port Moresby, 11 July 1942. AWM 025897

The detached flight had been in action for nearly a month when, on 11 January, it returned to 1 OTU at Bairnsdale. In 645 sorties over the Owen Stanley Range the men had delivered some 800 t of supplies from Port Moresby to the Dobodura and Soputa region, providing a crucial link in the chain that led to Allied victory in Papua New Guinea. A16-105 had played its part with 28 flights, including a welcome special delivery of a tonne of Christmas turkeys for the troops at Milne Bay. On New Year's Day it was ferried to Townsville because it was using too much oil.

A16-105's fortnight with Special Transport Flight was its most significant period of service. However, it also serves to represent the aircraft type in which the majority of Australian bomber crews trained during the early war years, and commemorates those crewmen who died both on Hudson operations and in training accidents. Some 170 airmen were killed while flying with 1 OTU at Nhill, Bairnsdale and East Sale in Victoria. A16-105 served with the unit for three years and three months, the second longest period of any Hudson, before departing for a major overhaul when the last course had been completed.[23]

Under the ownership of aircraft collector Malcolm Long, from whom the Memorial purchased it, A16-105 and sister Hudson A16-112 were the world's last remaining airworthy examples of this rare warplane. The latter continued to make flying appearances at airshows, initially as part of Long's 'Wings of Yesterday' flying air museum and, from 2004, with the Temora Aviation Museum.

The Hudson in context

Lockheed's twin-engined designs progressed from the sleek L-10 Electra airliner of 1934 to the L-14 Super Electra, of which the Hudson was a military version initiated by a British order. It first flew in 1938 and, in response to the Ellington Report which was highly critical of the RAAF's obsolescent equipment, was ordered for Australia in November that year. The first hundred Hudsons were purchased in early 1940, while later Hudsons were supplied 'lend-lease' after the Lend Lease Bill was passed by the US Congress in March 1941. By August 1940 two squadrons were in Malaya (under RAF command), and eventually Hudsons were to equip 13 RAAF squadrons. They were Australia's primary bomber until gradually replaced in that role by the Beaufort.

As a bombing trainer, up to 25 aircraft made up the Hudson strength of 1 OTU. Pilots newly trained on twin-engined aircraft converted onto the Hudson over a four- to six-week course. They began dual flying with an instructor, and continued as second pilot, then solo, before graduating to instrument and night flying. Meanwhile, navigators and wireless air gunners trained on Oxfords and Ansons. During a second month of training the pilot, navigator/bomb aimer, two wireless air gunners and a turret gunner came together in the Hudson to meld into an effective aircrew. Bombing, gunnery, reconnaissance, navigation, fighter affiliation and other tasks which made up the curriculum were all exercises in close teamwork.

Apart from the importance of its training work with 1 OTU, A16-105 represents more generally the 247 Hudsons delivered to the RAAF, many of which saw active service. At the start of the Pacific war the first 90 or so, together with a dozen Catalina flying boats, represented the entire long-range offensive capability of the RAAF.[24] The Hudsons of 1 and 8 Squadrons at Kota Bharu in Malaya were in action from the first day. Shortly after 2 am on 8 December 1941 (local time), just before the Pearl Harbor attack, they took off to bomb the Japanese invasion force off the Malayan coast. Two relic engines recovered from the sea, and now in the Memorial's collection, are all that has been found of the first two Hudsons shot down during the attack.

The following year, on the other side of the world, 459 Squadron RAAF took the Hudson to war against the German shipping and U-boats in the Mediterranean that were supporting the campaigns in North Africa. As with other aircraft types flown by the RAF, a scattering of Australians also served in RAF Hudson squadrons.

After the war the Hudson was gradually phased out of RAAF service. However, it soon returned to its airliner roots, finding a new lease of life in civilian service. Small airlines bought and converted numerous examples, and these soldiered on well into the 1960s. Adastra Aerial Surveys bought seven, including A16-105, and continued the photographic and geophysical surveys around Australia that the RAAF Survey Flight had earlier begun. As is the case with many aircraft types, it is thanks to postwar use that a Hudson has survived in the National Collection.

TIMELINE—A16-105

1941	(Dec) Received ex-USA at RAAF Richmond, NSW, and was the third aircraft delivered to 1 Operational Training Unit RAAF, East Sale, Vic.
1942	(Jul) Crash landed at Western Junction, Tas. (Sep) Fitted with Boulton & Paul gun turret (Dec) On secondment to RAAF Special Transport Flight, New Guinea
1945	Left 1 OTU; stored at RAAF Richmond NSW
1947	Sold for £200 to European Air Transport (NSW) and converted for civil charter use including the addition of a nose door
1949	Sold to Curtis Madsen Airlines registered as VH-BKY, transferred to East-West Airlines (NSW) registered as VH-EWS. Also registered variously as SMO (c. 1960s) and AGP for passenger and freight services
1962–66	Sold to Herald Flying Services (NSW) of John Fairfax & Sons and leased to Adastra Aerial Surveys for photographic and geophysical survey flights, with camera fitted in cabin
1966–71	Sold to Sepal Pty Ltd for Adastra; continued survey work
1976	Purchased with A16-112 by Malcolm Long and restored to airworthiness and Second World War paint scheme; new nose reportedly fitted
1981	Displayed at Chewing Gum Field Museum, Coolangatta, Qld
1985	Displayed at Air World, Wangaratta, Vic.
1987	Last flown
2001	Purchased by AWM; trucked from Wangaratta to AWM and displayed briefly in ANZAC Hall

(Sources for service 1947–71 include timeline at www.adastron.com)

NOTES ON COLOUR SCHEME

Hudson Mk IVAs were factory painted by Lockheed in US equivalents of the RAF Temperate Land Scheme of dark green and dark earth camouflage with sky undersides. Many were later repainted in RAAF foliage green and earth brown camouflage with sky blue undersides, as necessary. During its New Guinea service with 1 OTU Detached Flight, A16-105 retained its camouflage.

Markings: blue/white/red roundels in standard six positions, and fin flashes. Fuselage roundels probably had yellow surrounds, which were later painted out. In about September 1942 the red was overpainted in white. The OTU identification '05' possibly appeared in white or yellow on the rear fuselage sides. RAAF serial number in medium sea grey on rear fuselage. US airframe number '6034' was in small yellow stenciling on the nose tip.

Following its purchase by Malcolm Long, and at the time of delivery to the Memorial, the aircraft was repainted in camouflage and markings of Hudson A16-129 of 6 Squadron RAAF, with white code letters 'FX-F' on rear fuselage, and a nose art caricature of the squadron commanding officer. Its correct serial number, A16-105, however, was painted in black on the rear fuselage. Prior to being briefly displayed in ANZAC Hall, the aircraft's squadron code letters were overpainted.

DATA

Type	Hudson Mk IVA (US designation: A-28-LO)
Design firm	Lockheed, USA
Manufacturer	Lockheed, Burbank, California, USA
Role	General reconnaissance/bomber
No. built	52 (Mk IVA) 2,642 (all variants)
Type entered RAAF service	1940
Identity	A16-105 (RAAF) 6034 (US airframe number) 41-23175 (USAAC serial number) VH-BKY, EWS, SMO, AGP (civil registrations; see timeline)
Crew	5 (pilot, navigator/bomb aimer, two wireless/air gunners, air gunner)
Powerplant	Two Pratt & Whitney R-1830-45 (SC3G) Twin Wasp 14-cylinder radial engines, each of 1,050 hp
Armament	Offensive: 635 kg of bombs
	Defensive: four .303-in Browning machine-guns (in nose and Boulton & Paul dorsal turret); four .303-in Vickers gas-operated machine-guns in beam, ventral and roof hatch positions.
Wingspan	19.96 m
Length	13.51 m
Max. speed	443 km/h
Range	3,476 km
Max. take-off weight	8,391 kg (an average of 1,100 kg of freight or personnel per flight was carried during service with Special Transport Flight)

DAKOTA A65-71 (VH-CIN)

Canberra

EARLY MORNING, 6 JULY 1945

Prime Minister John Curtin had led Australia through the worst of the Second World War. Now his body lay in a wooden casket on the back of a converted Portee gun truck, a four-man military guard accompanying it as it slowly made its way through eastern Canberra. From the memorial service at Parliament House, the procession drove to RAAF Base Canberra, past the aircraft hangars, and out along the tarmac. Preceding the truck was the RAAF band, and following it a guard of eight men.

The crowd of dignitaries paid their last respects outside a C-47 Dakota transport plane. A cinematographer, perched on the roof of a car, filmed as the casket was unloaded and carried into the aircraft's open rear doorway; the footage would be shown in Cinesound news items around Australia over the next few days. Soon the aircraft was

> ## *No glamour ... just a hard slog for aircrew and ground crew alike.*
>
> *Flight Lieutenant Alan Randall, 37 Squadron RAAF*

Prime Minister John Curtin's coffin is loaded into Dakota A65-71 at RAAF Canberra, on 6 July 1945, for the flight to Perth. AWM P01378.004

taxiing along the tarmac, and at 1612 hours it took off, then circled Canberra with an escort of 12 Boomerang and Kittyhawk fighters. After a low pass of Parliament House and the Prime Minister's Lodge, the Dakota made for Adelaide and on to Perth, Curtin's home city, where he was laid to rest.

◄ ►

The Prime Ministerial assignment was a distinguished moment in the long history of Dakota A65-71. However, there is far more to this aircraft's significance. Its flying career was to span a remarkable 50 years, supporting Australian forces in conflicts from the Second World War to Vietnam, and finally in the public relations role, taking RAAF heritage to the public.

During 1939–41 the RAAF received deliveries of small numbers of Douglas DC-2s and DC-3 Dakotas, procured or on loan from civil airlines. In 1943, the US Army Air Force made a loan of two dozen military Dakotas to 36 Squadron at Townsville. As the first of these were arriving, in February 1943 the RAAF began taking delivery of

Dakota A65-71 in 37 Squadron service, c. 1945. AWM P01627.001

124 lend-leased C-47 military Dakotas to eventually equip all its transport squadrons operating in Australia and New Guinea. As well as courier and mail runs around Australia, they made deliveries and aerial supply drops to the troops in New Guinea who were fighting the Japanese in the struggle to secure the Kokoda Trail. Here, the jungle terrain made delivery of supplies and personnel by the 'biscuit bombers' an essential part of the Allied war effort. Their regular flights over the Owen Stanley Range were fraught with danger in weather that was often described as atrocious; airstrips too were makeshift and minimally prepared. The Dakotas carried freight ranging from

ammunition and food to aircraft engines and vehicles, and also dropped paratroops and their supplies into the jungle.

When 37 (Transport) Squadron RAAF at Essendon, Victoria, began converting from the Lockheed Lodestar to the C-47B Dakota in February 1945, among its initial deliveries was A65-71. The squadron soon established detachments at Parafield, South Australia, and at Morotai in the Halmahera Islands in support of the final Australian campaigns of the war in Borneo. After the war, A65-71 joined 38 Squadron of 86 (Transport) Wing, based at Schofields, New South Wales, and was sent on detachment to Darwin. In support of the British Commonwealth Occupation Force it also flew the courier run to Iwakuni, Japan. This task was shared between the squadrons of the wing until 26 December 1947, when Squadron Leader John Balfe AFC flew this Dakota on the last such flight by a RAAF aircraft before the service was chartered to Qantas Empire Airways.

That year, 38 Squadron was awarded the Duke of Gloucester Cup for the most proficient service unit, and A65-71 played its part with VIP flights to and from Batavia in October for the Department of External Affairs. At RAAF Williamtown near Newcastle it took paratroops aloft on exercises for the School of Air Portability, and in 1950 delivered relief supplies to civilians devastated by the New South Wales floods.

In June that year, 38 Squadron moved to Changi, Singapore, for two and a half years in support of the fight against communist insurgency in Malaya, the Malayan Emergency (1950–1960). After joining the squadron in February 1951 with a courier run to Iwakuni in support of Australian forces in Korea, A65-71 flew at least 126 missions during the early period of the Emergency. The flights from Changi and Kuala Lumpur included air supply drops to Federated Malay Police and Gurkha units, paratroop drops, ambulance flights, leaflet drops, and freight deliveries. RAAF Historian Chris Clark describes the importance of the Dakotas:

> *Transport planes were an essential part of the strategy adopted to defeat the communist insurrection, which required that police and army patrols occupied jungle and village areas throughout the Malay Peninsula on a semi-permanent basis. It was aircraft which positioned these patrols, with their equipment, and then kept them resupplied. RAAF airlift crews also flew leaflet-dropping missions urging the Communist Terrorists to surrender, a tactic which was reportedly very successful. By the time the remaining Dakotas and crews were withdrawn in November 1952, the squadron had flown more than two million kilometres, carried more than 17,000 passengers along with some 2,000 tonnes of freight, dropped about 800 tonnes of stores, and evacuated 326 wounded men.* [25]

In 1963, when the Indonesian Confrontation began following the creation of Malaysia, the aircraft was stationed at Butterworth with the Canberra bombers of 2 Squadron.

With Australia's involvement in the Vietnam War, RAAF Dakotas delivered supplies almost from the start, and a small number of medical evacuation flights were made in 1965 before the Dakota was replaced in this role by the C-130 Hercules. In March 1968, A65-71 joined the RAAF Transport Support Flight at Butterworth to provide transport for diplomats, passengers and freight to locations throughout South-East Asia, including Vung Tau in South Vietnam. By 1981, with the phasing out of most Dakotas from the transport role, it was one of only four left flying in RAAF service. Prior to its transfer to the Memorial that year it was repainted in the original wartime 37 Squadron scheme, and flew in the RAAF's Diamond Jubilee celebrations.

Four years later the old workhorse was back in the air, the RAAF operating it on the Memorial's behalf. The public were able to see this historic veteran in the air, and occasionally even fly in it, during its service on publicity tours, at airshows and as a film prop. Its most important post-operational work was during the 1988 bicentennial celebrations, when it spent several weeks flying around outback Australia for a RAAF heritage tour.

Its service with numerous RAAF transport units through conflicts from 1945 to 1972 formed the rationale for A65-71's selection for preservation. Nevertheless, the most often quoted incident involving the aircraft occurred far from the trouble spots of South-East Asia. It happened on 15 May 1956 on a 36 Squadron courier service from Richmond to Williamtown. Its pilot was exuberant at the prospect of being reunited with his wife and child in Canberra, where he was based and would shortly be returning. Aboard were five

crewmen, two RAAF passengers, and a full load of cargo. At 7.30 am while off the coast of Swansea the pilot saw a ship heading south, and decided to celebrate by 'beating it up' at mast-top height, just 20 m above water. The sea was rough with a 5-m swell, and as the stern of the collier M.V. *Hexham Bank* rose up, he pulled back hard on the control wheel to clear its rear mast. It was too late. The tip of the steel mast hit the aircraft, bending the mast back and knocking off part of the yardarm, an aerial and a beacon lamp.

The damage to the aircraft was more serious. The mast ripped a 4-m long gash down A65-71's fuselage, showering the ship's deck with aluminium debris, and the tail wheel was hit. Of more immediate concern to the crew, though, was that a blade of the port propeller had hit the yardarm and been bent back at right angles. The resulting vibration threatened to shake the aircraft apart before the engine was shut down. No one was injured, and the aircraft managed to limp 20 km to RAAF Williamtown. On landing, the two shaken passengers bolted from the aircraft and the pilot was placed under open arrest. Although repairs costing £5,000 were made at RAAF Parafield, pilots reported unusual vibrations in the aircraft for years afterwards.

Thus, A65-71 is among the few RAAF aircraft to have survived a collision with a ship's mast. Another was a wartime Beaufighter, which returned with the beacon from a German vessel embedded in it; the beacon was later displayed in the Memorial's Aircraft Hall.

The Dakota in context

'The DC-3 groaned,' writes Mike Jerram, quoting a former co-pilot, 'it protested, it rattled, it leaked oil, it ran hot, it ran cold, it ran rough, it staggered along on hot days and scared you half to death, its wings flexed and twisted in a horrifying manner, it sank back to earth with a great sigh of relief—but it flew and flew and flew.'[26] Far from implying any fault with the aircraft, such descriptions indicate the extremes to which the Dakota was pushed. It was a well engineered, structurally sound and reliable aircraft which many claim has never been equalled before or since. More than 70 years after its first flight in 1935, meticulously maintained DC-3s still take passengers up for a nostalgic first-hand experience of how flying used to be.

By the start of the Second World War, the DC-3 had already earned its place as one of the world's great passenger aircraft. With the success of its predecessor, the DC-2, in the 1934 London-to-Melbourne Centenary Air Race, it was clear that Douglas had produced a winning design in every respect: reliability, speed, endurance and practicality.

The C-47 military version came into service in early 1942. Nearly 10,000 were built, and incorporated the necessities of a military cargo plane: large doors in the port side, and strengthened metal flooring with tie-down points. The C-47B variant of 1944 featured two-stage superchargers for high-altitude performance.

Cockpit of the Memorial's Dakota while the aircraft was stored at the Treloar Technology Centre in 2008. AWM REL/02368.001

The ubiquitous Dakota soldiered on in the RAAF for over 50 years, an unprecedented record. It served during the Second World War, the Malayan Emergency, the Indonesian Confrontation and the Vietnam War. In addition, during 1948–49, 36 and 38 Squadrons provided ten crews to fly RAF Dakotas in the Berlin Airlift. RAAF Dakotas also saw extensive use during the Korean War with 30 Transport Unit (later 36 Squadron), 90 (Composite) Wing at Iwakuni, Japan, in logistical support for Australian forces and for medical evacuation flights.

TIMELINE—A65-71

1944	Built by Douglas at Oklahoma City, Oklahoma, USA
1945	(Feb) Flown to RAAF Amberley, Qld, and served with 37 Squadron RAAF, Schofields, NSW, and Essendon, Vic.; (Apr–May) to Morotai
1947	With 36 Squadron and 38 Squadron (86 Wing Queen's Flight), Schofields, NSW
1951	(Feb–Nov); flew from Singapore and Kuala Lumpur with 38 Squadron (90 Wing) during Malayan Emergency, and on courier flights to Japan during Korean War
1952	(May) Re-issued to 38 Squadron (90 Wing); (Dec) to 86 Wing
1952–63	With 36 and 38 Squadrons RAAF, Richmond, NSW, and Fairbairn, ACT
1963–67	With C Flight of 2 Squadron RAAF, Butterworth, Malaysia
1967	With 10 (Maritime Reconnaissance) Squadron RAAF, Townsville, Qld, as 'squadron hack'
1968–80	With RAAF Transport Support Flight, Butterworth, Malaysia
1980	Taken out of service at RAAF Richmond, on retirement of type, and transferred to AWM
1981	Repainted in approximate 37 Squadron scheme of 1945; flew in RAAF Diamond Jubilee before being towed to storage at AWM store, Duntroon, ACT
1985	Towed to RAAF Fairbairn for return to flying status
1988	Conducted Bicentennial RAAF heritage outback tour; operated by 486 (Maintenance) Squadron on behalf of the AWM for airshow appearances and publicity
c.1996	Repainted in accurate 37 Squadron paint scheme of 1945
1997	Last flight from RAAF Richmond to RAAF Fairbairn
2000	Towed from RAAF Fairbairn to AWM Treloar Technology Centre, ACT, for storage

NOTES ON COLOUR SCHEME

At the time of its retirement from RAAF service, A65-71 was natural metal with a white upper fuselage and kangaroo roundels in six positions. In 1981 it was repainted in an approximation of its 1945 paint scheme in 37 Squadron RAAF markings, and repainted more accurately in the late 1990s as follows: USAAF olive drab (upper) and neutral grey (lower). Squadron code 'OM-N' stencilled in white either side of RAAF roundel on both sides. Blue and white roundels in six positions. Civil registration 'VH-CIN' in white on fin and rudder, with blue and white fin flash below, on both sides. Serial number stencilled in black below tailplane.

DATA

Type	C-47B-20-DK (Dakota Mk IV)
Design firm	Douglas Aircraft Company, USA
Manufacturer	Douglas, Oklahoma City, Oklahoma, USA
Role	Transport
No. built	3,364 (C-47B)
	10,655 (DC-3 and C-47 total)
No. in RAAF service	65 (C-47B); 124 (C-47 total)
Type entered RAAF service	1943
Identity	A65-71 (RAAF)
	VH-CIN (civil, 1945-48)
	43-49870 (USAAF)
	15686/27131 (US Construction No.)
Powerplant	Two Pratt & Whitney R-1830-90C 14-cylinder Twin Wasp radial engines, each of 1,200 hp
Crew	Up to 4 (captain, co-pilot, navigator, wireless operator)
Armament	None fixed (window ports for small arms)
Wingspan	29 m
Length	19.7 m
Max. speed	368 km/h
Range	2,414 km
Loaded weight	13,290 kg
Max. payload	3,400 kg, or 28 troops, or 18 stretchers

MOSQUITO A52-319

31,000 ft over Surabaya naval base, Netherlands East Indies
25 JUNE 1944

Flying Officer Ken 'Baldy' Boss-Walker and his navigator, Pilot Officer Jeff Love, had ferried the first operational Australian-built Mosquito, A52-2, from Bankstown in Sydney to a bush base called Coomalie Creek, south of Darwin, the previous month. There it had joined the RAAF photographic reconnaissance unit, 1 PRU. Mosquito A52-2 had started life as an FB.40 fighter-bomber before being converted to a PR.40 version for photo-reconnaissance (PR) work. In addition to a large F-52 camera with a 50-cm focal length in the rear fuselage, two F-24 cameras replaced the usual forward armament of four .303-in machine-guns and four 20-mm cannon. The protruding lenses broke the otherwise clean, streamlined profile of the nose. In addition to

> *It was reliable, powerful, sleek and elegant—a machine of legendary versatility, the scourge of the Luftwaffe—and it was ours!*
> *Pilot Officer Colin King DFM, 87 Squadron RAAF (1953)*

A PR.41 Mosquito of 87 (Survey) Squadron at Alice Springs, 1950. Note the bulged camera port on the nose underside. AWM P05193.002

underwing fuel tanks, extra tanks were fitted in the bomb bay, which was not required for bombs.

Boss-Walker and Love were now on their longest PR mission so far. The Japanese naval base at Surabaya in Java was the largest and most important outside Japan, and Allied intelligence needed to know of any enemy ships in dock. To extend the aircraft's already respectable range, the crew had flown it to a forward base at Broome in north-west Western Australia the previous day and refuelled.

Over Surabaya, the left engine of A52-2 spluttered and died. The 1,500 km return trip, over water and with one engine out, was not a pleasant prospect, but the remarkable Mosquito could, if handled properly, maintain height even on half power. After more than ten hours in the air it made it back to Broome, landing with empty fuel tanks but carrying perfect negatives of the Surabaya docks which showed that the Japanese fleet was elsewhere.

On this occasion the two men had reason both to curse and to praise the aircraft, but overall the Mosquito rarely let its crews down. The fast and agile Mosquitos of 1 PRU, which became 87 (Photographic Reconnaissance) Squadron in September 1944, were well-liked and suited to their role. There was, in fact, hardly a role for which the 'wooden wonder' was not suited.

◄ ►

The PR Mosquito carried no armament, as it was considered that this would only weigh it down while it was evading enemy aircraft. The theory had been proven many times in Europe, and, on 6 April 1945, in the Pacific War as well. On that day one of 87 Squadron's British-built PR.XVI Mosquitos was at 21,000 ft, tracking Japanese warships in the Flores Sea. The light cruiser *Isuzu* and its three escort vessels had left Surabaya two days earlier, and had then transported an army detachment from Timor to Sumbawa Island. From below the Mosquito came two Japanese Oscar fighters; the Australians accelerated to 640 km/h and left them behind. Returning to the convoy later, the Mosquito crew watched as the *Isuzu* was bombed by RAAF Liberators, two of which were shot down by the Oscars. They photographed the cruiser again. Back at base, the developed prints revealed three direct bomb strikes. The following day, the *Isuzu* was sunk by US submarines.

The Japanese naval base at Surabaya, Java, taken with the Mosquito's F-52 camera from 31,000 ft on 25 June 1944. Flying Officer Ken Boss-Walker was awarded a Distinguished Flying Cross for the flight. AWM P03430.002

The squadron saw widespread service during the final year of the war, living up to its motto *Videmus militamus* (we see and we fight)—though with unarmed aircraft, the fighting was indirect. From Coomalie Creek, and from a detachment that had been sent to Labuan in Borneo, the Mosquitos and a few P-43 Lancers and P-38 Lightnings provided the PR support for the Allied air forces based in Australia's North-West Area. The films they brought back were quickly developed and printed in an iron-roofed hut in the bush, the photographic staff working in shifts day and night under primitive conditions. Good, clear photographs were highly prized by intelligence staff. They examined the prints in detail to identify the latest developments, potential targets and troop movements in Japanese-held territory.

In peacetime, a civil application was found for the squadron. The Mosquitos were flown in October 1945 to Parkes, New South Wales, from where a detachment briefly returned to Labuan for aerial mapping photography in January. As RAAF Parkes closed down, the unit, now known as RAAF Survey Flight, moved to Canberra from May 1946. The following year it swapped its PR.XVIs for postwar Australian production PR.41 Mosquitos specially configured for photographic survey work. Painted in silver dope to reflect heat in the harsh Australian sun, they had two-stage, two-speed supercharged Merlin engines for high-altitude performance, pressurised cockpits and extra fuel capacity in bomb bay and underwing tanks. The flight, soon to be renamed yet again as 87 (Survey) Squadron, was now set a task that would occupy it for the next six years: to produce the first comprehensive photographic coverage of Australia. In an early example of a RAAF unit 'paying its way', funding came from the Department of National Development's Central Mapping Authority. Using 1:50,000 scale prints made from negatives exposed at 25,000 ft, topographical maps were to be produced by the Commonwealth Survey Committee and the National Mapping Council. Part of the impetus for the program was to identify likely sources of oil and minerals.

Detachments of the squadron were sent to remote airfields around Australia, where the men lived in primitive conditions and supplemented their meagre rations by hunting and fishing. In the air, cramped in a cold cockpit for hours and breathing from oxygen masks, the two crewmen worked as a team during the image exposure runs: the pilot keeping to a precise course, speed and altitude without the aid of an autopilot, the navigator to his right rear crouched over the camera sight. Their primary navigation aid was a G-3 gyro-magnetic compass. Up to five cameras were mounted in the aircraft—three aimed straight down (one in the nose and two in the rear fuselage) and two aimed obliquely in the rear—to give horizon-to-horizon coverage of the vast expanse of land below. In addition to the British F-52, the primary camera used in this work was the American K-17, an all-purpose aerial camera employed extensively during the war for reconnaissance and bomb damage assessment. It used 9-in (23-cm) square film in 200-exposure magazines, and a choice of lenses up to a massive 24-in (61-cm) focal length.

For its first year of survey work the squadron won the 1948 Duke of Gloucester Cup, an award for the most proficient RAAF unit. By the end of the program, two thirds of the continent, as well as parts of New Guinea and Fiji, had been covered by its eyes in the sky. For the final coverage of the Great Sandy Desert in Western Australia, in May 1953 a detachment of four PR.41s arrived at the red gravel airstrip of Port Hedland. More remote still was Noonkanbah airfield, a satellite base near Broome from where the detachment covered the northern extremes of the desert. Pilot Col King had recently returned to Australia after flying Meteor jets in Korea, and recalls the living conditions as tent accommodation with dirt floors 'which crawled with the biggest, nastiest centipedes I had ever seen'.[27] The 150 personnel which made up the detachment approximately doubled the local town population.

In August 1953 the detachment farewelled Port Hedland in style with a formation flypast 'on the deck' and returned to Canberra before ferrying them to Tocumwal, New South Wales, for storage. Col King made what was probably the RAAF's last Mosquito flight, barrel-rolling and thundering over Tocumwal before landing it 'to become fodder for the chainsaw'. The Mosquito had finished its service with the RAAF, and 87 Squadron disbanded.[28]

The 'bouncing bomb' down under

In addition to the 23 photo-reconnaissance Mosquito PR.XVIs in RAAF service, another three modified examples accompanied a top-secret RAF squadron which was sent to Australia aboard aircraft carriers in late 1944. The bulk of the Mosquitos of 618 Squadron, RAF Coastal Command, were B.IV bombers specially modified to carry a pair of Highball mines, or 'bouncing bombs', designed by Dr Barnes Wallis of Dambusters fame. The intended task of the PR.XVIs was to photograph Japanese shipping to aid in planning an attack.

Originally, 618 Squadron had been formed to attack the German battleship *Tirpitz* in the fjords of Norway, but the weapons were not ready in time and the squadron was instead deployed to the Pacific War theatre. Arriving at Narromine in central New South Wales in February 1945, the squadron awaited orders to embark on British aircraft carriers at Sydney and sail into the Pacific in search of Japanese capital ships to attack. Had it done so, the crews would have carried out their dangerous mission at a height of less than 20 m above the sea, at full speed, dropping their spinning spherical mines onto the water to skip for up to 2 km to their target.

Some preparations were made for the squadron to move to Manus Island in the Admiralties. However, the mission never went ahead, owing both to American resistance to the mission and to a lack of potential shipping targets by this late stage of the war. The squadron disbanded in July 1945. However, a legacy of 618 Squadron remains: parts of its 36 remaining Mosquitos, which were bought by local farmers in 1947 for their valuable timber, components and fuel. It is planned that these salvaged parts will contribute to an ambitious restoration project. This would add to the Camden Museum of Aviation's ex–618 Squadron FB.VI, the RAAF Museum's ex–87 Squadron PR.XVI, and the Memorial's PR.41, as Australia's fourth Mosquito rebuild.

◄ ►

The Memorial's PR.41 Mosquito was completed as FB.40 fighter bomber A52-210 initially. Because of gluing problems its wings were condemned, and the aircraft was soon converted to a PR version in response to changing RAAF requirements, gaining the replacement serial number A52-319 (in line with the 300-series serial block allocated for the PR.41). Little of interest is recorded of its short life with the air force, apart from an electrical fire in the cockpit (duly extinguished by the pilot) during a ferry flight from Richmond, New South Wales, to Archerfield, Queensland, in March 1948. Apart from occasional flights from Archerfield, the last being in November 1949, it was stored until 1953.

Half of the PR.41s that were built served with 87 Squadron. A52-319 was one of about a dozen that were evidently surplus to requirements, and did not join the unit. The story of its survival is (as is often the case) a convoluted one involving the efforts of a diverse range of people, starting with a veteran First World War pilot and aviation pioneer. Captain Jimmy Woods operated two Avro Ansons on tourist flights from Perth to Rottnest Island in the postwar years. He bought the Mosquito for £450 with another venture in mind: to fly in the 1953 England-to-New Zealand air race. Carrying the civil

AIR POWER IN THE PACIFIC

This dramatic view of the Mosquito greets visitors as they enter Aircraft Hall. AWM PAIU2001/127.15

registration VH-WAD and the name 'The Quokka' on its nose (named after the small marsupials prevalent on Rottnest), the former A52-319 had just 40 flying hours logged when Woods ferried it to Perth. It turned out to be its last flight, as he was forced to pull out of the race through lack of sponsorship.

The aircraft sat at Perth's Guildford airport, hangared until in 1962 it was placed outside in a wire compound. For company it had the Lancaster owned by the Western Australian branch of the RAAF Association. Both suffered badly from exposure, but particularly the wooden Mosquito. The association wanted to acquire it, too, but did not have the funds to repay Woods for its years of hangarage. In 1967 the Department of Civil Aviation, viewing it as an eyesore, moved it to a secluded corner of the airport, where vandals did more damage. Eventually it was bought by American air enthusiast David Kubista, who had it shipped to Melbourne in 1972, bound for the United States to be restored as a racer. But this venture too fell through, and 'The Quokka', its fuselage by now broken in two, again deteriorated in the open at Port Melbourne wharf. 'It now appears to be beyond salvage,' noted the RAAF.

Nevertheless, the aircraft was put up for sale in 1979. The Memorial's Director successfully bid for the aircraft at auction, and had it trucked to Hawker de Havilland at Bankstown, its place of origin, for restoration. Over several years the wooden structure was rebuilt by apprentices, and in 1994 a comprehensive set of restoration guidelines was drawn up by Memorial conservation staff for its completion. Some timber had to be replaced, but it was found by conservation staff that many areas could be preserved and strengthened by a combination of consolidation and repair with epoxy resin. By then the Memorial had its own large workshop facility, and the aircraft was trucked to Canberra for completion, including fabric covering and painting, by Memorial staff and volunteers. The project was completed in time for its display as a physical centrepiece of the Memorial's revitalised Aircraft Hall in 1999.

The Mosquito in context

When de Havilland first proposed its Mosquito design in 1938, the concept of an unarmed bomber was quite radical. One measure of the influence that it would have is the fact that in the postwar jet era, this radical concept become the norm in British bomber design.

But before (and for the most part, during) the war, it was generally believed that bombers would always be vulnerable to enemy fighters and therefore needed defensive armament. The Mosquito, de Havilland argued, had a better defence: its speed. With a lightweight airframe of balsa, plywood and spruce—'non strategic' materials which, de Havilland argued, would utilise the woodworking skills base in wartime, putting less demand on metalworking facilities—and unencumbered with the weight and drag of guns and turrets, the unloaded Mosquito proved to be faster than the Spitfire fighter. At the time of its first flight in November 1940, in fact, it was among the fastest aircraft in the world. No enemy fighter then in production would be able to catch it. Nevertheless, Britain's Air Ministry still had trouble accepting that an unarmed bomber would 'get through', and when it finally agreed to de Havilland's proposal, it was on the grounds that it would make a more suitable PR aircraft.

From the start, de Havilland saw that the Mosquito was adaptable not only to this role but to that of fighter as well. The first three prototypes, in fact, were bomber, fighter and PR types respectively. In the latter role, a lack of bombs and armament allowed for performance that was second to none. It was a PR version which made the Mosquito's operational debut over Paris in September 1941—the start of what became regular flights over enemy-occupied cities and installations.

Following the type's outstanding early successes in the war against Germany, it was decided in 1942 that de Havilland (Australia) would build Mosquitos at Bankstown. It had the lowest loss rate of any British bomber. RAAF aircrews with the RAF in Europe attested to its performance, and later two UK-based RAAF squadrons converted to it.

Mosquito fighter-bombers of
1 Squadron Detachment RAAF
based at Amberley, Brisbane, peel
off for a practice attack dive in July
1945. AWM NEA0666

In December 1942, 456 Squadron began replacing its Beaufighters with Mosquitos for
night fighter, fighter intruder and ground attack duties. From July 1944 the squadron's
targets included V-1 flying bombs, of which it accounted for 24 of the 600 destroyed
by Mosquitos, in addition to 39 aircraft confirmed destroyed.[29] In August 1943, 464
Squadron swapped its Ventura bombers for Mosquitos and achieved fame for a series
of spectacular raids on special targets: Amiens prison in February 1944 to free French
Resistance prisoners; the SS barracks at Bonneuil-Matours in July 1944; and Gestapo

headquarters in Denmark. In support of the Allied invasion, it also attacked V-1 launch sites and German transport.

In the war against Japan, 1 (Attack) Squadron RAAF based at Labuan, Borneo, used British-built Mosquitos against ground targets during the last weeks of the war. Another unit, 94 Squadron based at Sydney, received locally-built examples too late to see action. Thus, the only Australian-built Mosquitos to see war service were 87 Squadron's six PR.40s. Part of the significance of A52-319 is in representing this often overlooked but important role, the one which Britain's Air Ministry first envisaged for the Mosquito and in which the type first operated with the RAF. Equally importantly, it is the sole surviving example of Australia's unprecedented, albeit problematic, wartime foray into the production of a modern wooden military aircraft.

Building the Mosquito was a complex business, and required production techniques quite different from those employed for more conventional aluminium aircraft. The fuselage was formed in two longitudinal half-shells made of balsa sheet sandwiched between plywood, each formed around a concrete mould and glued together with the help of steel bands. There were few internal formers, the shell itself providing structural integrity. Each half was then fitted out with most internal equipment before the two were joined like a model kit. The wings were constructed around laminated spruce spars and ribs, and skinned with plywood. As with Beaufort bomber production, hundreds of subcontractors around Australia and overseas produced components. Women were fully integrated into the production force, performing a variety of roles including doping, painting, electrical work and assembly.

A fortnight before Ken Boss-Walker's hair-raising return flight from Java in June 1944, his brother Hubert, a de Havilland test pilot, had been killed when the wings of Mosquito A52-12 came apart in the air over Bankstown. All Mosquito mainplanes were inspected, and the type was grounded during July. Seventeen mainplanes produced by General Motors-Holden at Pagewood in Sydney were found to be faulty. Another crash in January 1945, at the operational training unit at Williamtown near Newcastle, was also owing to wing failure. The problem, poor glue adhesion in the joining of the upper surface plywood skin to the wing spars, was then revealed in another 25 aircraft. The crashes and subsequent findings were a severe blow to the Australian Mosquito production program. With the wing problems and others, deliveries were so delayed that only a handful of Australian-built examples were in service before war's end. By the time the last Mosquitos were delivered from the Bankstown assembly plant in 1948, the rate of production had slowed further in order to keep the workforce occupied and on hand while waiting for the impending Vampire jet production program.

Mosquito variants in RAAF service

(Numbers delivered are shown in brackets. Note wartime use of Roman numerals, postwar use of Arabic numerals.)

	British-built	Australian-built
Fighter	F.II (1) pattern	
Fighter-bomber	FB.VI (38)[30]	FB.40 (153)[31]
Photo-reconnaissance	PR.XVI (23)	PR.40 (6)
		PR.41 (28)
Trainer	T.III (14)	T.43 (22)
(Total numbers)	(76)	(209)

Key to variants

FB.40: Australian-built version of FB.VI (A52-1 to 200 serials)

PR.40: Solid-nose, unarmed PR conversion from FB.40 (A52-2, 4, 6, 7, 9, 26)

PR.41: As above; US and British cameras fitted (A52-300 serials)

FB.VI: Fighter-bomber armed with four 20-mm cannon and four .303-in machine-guns (A52-500 serials)

PR.XVI: Glazed-nose, unarmed PR variant (A52-600 serials)

T.III: Dual-control unarmed trainer (A52-1000 serials)

T.43: Australian-built T.III, converted from FB.40 (A52-1000 serials)

TIMELINE—A52-319

1946	Constructed as fighter-bomber (FB.40) A52-210
1947	(Nov) Converted to PR (PR.41) version
1948	(Jan) Test flown by de Havilland test pilot Brian 'Blackjack' Walker before delivered to RAAF. Stored at RAAF Richmond, NSW, and RAAF Archerfield, Qld
1949	Made occasional flights from Archerfield and placed in long term storage there
1953	(Jul) Purchased by Captain Jimmy Woods, civil registered and last flown (to Perth)
1961	Moved into secure open storage at Guildford airport, Perth
1967	Moved to insecure open storage at Guildford
1968	Sold to James Harwood & Co of WA, fuselage badly damaged during removal
1971	Sold to David Kubista of USA
1972	Shipped to Melbourne
1979	Purchased at auction by the AWM and relocated to Bankstown, NSW, for restoration
1999	Restoration completed by the AWM; displayed in Aircraft Hall

DATA

Type	DH.98 Mosquito PR.41
Design firm	de Havilland
Manufacturer	de Havilland (Australia), Bankstown, NSW
Role	Photo-reconnaissance
No. built	28 (Mosquito total 7,781, including 212 in Australia)
Type entered service	1944
Identity	A52-319 (RAAF) (originally completed as A52-210) VH-WAD (Australian civil register)
Crew	2 (pilot and navigator)
Powerplant	Two supercharged Packard Merlin 69 V-12 liquid-cooled engines of 1,710 hp (1,274 kW) each
Armament	Nil
Wingspan	16.51 m
Length	12.45 m
Max. speed	684 km/h
Range	5,633 km (with underwing and bomb bay fuel tanks)
Max take-off weight	11,567 kg

NOTES ON COLOUR SCHEME

Repainted during conservation in postwar RAAF scheme: Overall silver dope. Red/white/blue roundels (in six standard positions) and fin flashes. Serial number in black on rear fuselage sides. Propeller spinners were originally black, but have been painted in the red/white/blue stripes applicable to 87 Squadron RAAF, the unit which flew the PR.41 Mosquito.

When civil registered as 'VH-WAD' in 1953, the aircraft retained its overall silver, with roundels and fin flash removed. The registration was painted in small black lettering on the fin, and larger on underside of port wing and upper surface of starboard wing. Name 'The Quokka' on right side of nose. Propeller spinners were red.

MUSTANG A68-648

Mildura, Victoria
20 MAY 1945

After a frustrating four-month delay, the instructors and students of 2 Operational Training Unit (2 OTU) were elated: the first of the long-awaited North American P-51 Mustangs had arrived. The new US-built fighters had been flown up from the RAAF aircraft depot at Laverton near Melbourne, where they had been assembled after their sea voyage from America; although the Commonwealth Aircraft Corporation (CAC) in Melbourne was now building Mustangs, the first locally-produced example was still two weeks away from delivery to the RAAF. The shiny, bare-metal fighters would supplement, and eventually replace, the unit's Curtiss P-40 Kittyhawks which were 'rather weary from old age',[32] a description particularly apt for the old P-40Es, now in their third year of service. The men looked forward to trying out for themselves the fighter that had become a legend in every theatre of war since the Merlin-engined Mustang's combat debut 18 months earlier.

There was little doubt that the Mustang was a better all-round fighter than the Curtiss Kittyhawk, even in its final P-40N version which now made up a good proportion of 2 OTU's complement. The Mustang, built by North American Aviation in 1940, had first flown two years after the Kittyhawk, and incorporated the latest

State of the art.

Running up the Merlin engine of an RAAF Mustang. AWM 128013

innovations (some of which, it turns out, were developed by Curtiss for a fighter intended to replace its famous forebear). In its smaller turning circle alone the Kittyhawk had a slight advantage, but in all other manoeuvres and performance attributes, the Mustang was superior. Its greatest asset in this wide-ranging war was its seven-league boots: with a range of 3,350 km, thanks in part to prodigious internal fuel capacity and underwing drop tanks, it could fly further than any other Allied fighter. On long-range missions lasting up to eight hours, the only limiting factors were its supply of ammunition and the endurance of its pilot. On US bomber escort duties in Europe and the Pacific, and on deep penetration ground attack sorties in the China–Burma–India war theatre, such long range ability was potentially war-winning.

Since 1942, 2 OTU had been converting pilots onto the RAAF's limited inventory of fighters: Kittyhawks, Spitfires and CAC Boomerangs. It was a large unit, with over a thousand personnel at any one time. As was true of many country towns which hosted RAAF stations, the people of Mildura and the surrounding Sunraysia region invited the men into their homes, and long-lasting friendships, and even marital bonds, were formed. They did not, however, forget the purpose for which they were there: to learn to fight in the air. The course syllabus followed standard operational instruction, building on the experience gained by pupil pilots in their elementary and service flying training. Familiarisation with the aircraft type was gained on the ground before the pupil's first flight in a fighter, which was necessarily solo as there were no two-seat training fighters on hand. This summary of the P-51D pilot's checklist gives an idea of the complexity of fighters built towards the end of the war:

- Ignition off; mixture to idle cut-off
- Generator and battery on; throttle to start position
- Propeller control to full increase; supercharger to auto
- Oil and coolant radiator air controls to auto
- Carburettor air control to 'ram air'
- Fuel shutoff valve on; select fuel tank
- Fuel booster pump on; check pressure
- Hand prime and electric prime
- Ignition switch to 'both'; engage starter
- As engine starts, move mixture to auto rich or run; warm up engine at 1,300 rpm
- Check oil pressure, coolant and oil temperature, suction, hydraulic pressure
- Check fuel tank selector switch, fuel levels, manifold pressure regulator, flap operation
- Check magnetos and supercharger operation in high-blower setting
- Check movement of flying controls; trim rudder 5 degrees right
- Propeller control to full increase; fuel booster pump on
- Set flaps down 15–20 degrees; lock tailwheel
- Lock canopy; put emergency canopy release handle to safe position
- Move throttle control to gate (61-inch mercury at 3,000 rpm)

Circuits and landings were followed by aerobatics, cross-country exercises by day and night, flying by instruments, and formation flying. The single-seat fighter pilot was also a navigator, his aids consisting of a map case and a Dalton computer strapped to his leg. Depending on the area of operations he was sent to, he might also have the help of radio navigation beacons. Then, of course, there were the aircraft's military applications to master: dogfight simulations, dive bombing, skip bombing, air-to-ground gunnery, rocket firing, and formation attacks.[33]

By war's end, 2 OTU had trained 1,247 pilots. The cost was high: 52 lives lost, together with many aircraft written off in accidents.[34] Just two of these training fatalities were in Mustangs. A fortnight after the aircraft's arrival, on 5 June 1945, Flying Officer Kenneth Chester was taking Mustang A68-507 on a familiarisation flight over the Gol Gol bombing and gunnery range near Mildura when a propeller blade broke away, cutting off half the starboard wing. The aircraft disintegrated and crashed. Then on 13 September, Flight Sergeant Ronald Milledge in A68-636 crashed during a battle climb exercise at a property 30 km north-east of the base. Both men were buried at Mildura cemetery.

The unit's low fatality figure with the Mustang was partly due to the relatively short time it was in service before the war ended, but it also undoubtedly reflects on the ease with which pilots were able to make the transition to the aircraft. It was almost viceless. One of its few foibles, common to most powerful single-engined fighters of the day, was a tendency to veer left due to the considerable propeller torque during take-off. This was easily countered, but nevertheless caused a number of accidents and near misses among the many Australians who would fly the Mustang over its 15-year service life.

A week after 2 OTU got its first Mustangs, 84 Squadron RAAF at Ross River airfield near Townsville began re-equipping when pilots from Mildura ferried in its first few examples of the new fighter. Their slow arrival meant that it was the end of July before the squadron had built up to its establishment of 24, its pilots all the while eager for transfer to the combat zone. It was not to be. Hostilities had already ceased when, on 30 August, six Mustangs of 84 Squadron finally flew to Labuan, Borneo, to join the 1st Tactical Air Force. At the end of July a second Townsville-based unit, 86 Squadron at Bohle River, had begun conversion training on P-51K Mustangs, but this squadron was not required in the forward areas. Both units had been flying Kittyhawks on patrols in the Torres Strait region, and had feared disbandment before the impending arrival of their new mounts was announced. They were given a reprieve, but only a brief one that did not take them into action.

After the war, more RAAF units at Labuan converted to Mustangs. When 76, 77 and 82 Squadrons had reached their complements in early 1946, they left for Japan as part of the British Commonwealth Air Force (BCAIR), the air element of the occupation forces. After two years in Japan, all but 77 Squadron disbanded at Iwakuni at the end of 1948.

The hundred US-built Mustangs in the serial range A68-600 to 699 were shipped from the United States covered in a removable sprayed-on anti-corrosion material called Plastiphane, arriving at Laverton for assembly, modifications and air testing. They were destined not to join active squadrons; a third of them went to 2 OTU, A68-648 being issued on 29 July 1945, just a fortnight before the cessation of hostilities. By this time the unit had 25 Mustangs on hand. Over the next 18 months, new fighter pilots took to the air in the final stage of their flight training, while others converted from older fighters. Although too late for these men to take the Mustang into action against the Japanese, deliveries to 2 OTU continued after the war, with 33 on strength at the end of August. The unit disbanded in March 1947. A68-648 spent just three months with the unit before Flight Lieutenant Keith Kildey DFM ferried it back to Laverton, where it spent two years as a testbed with 1 Aircraft Performance Unit (later Aircraft Research and Development Unit).

◄ ►

Australians had, in fact, already seen a good deal of action with Mustangs in the war against Germany. At Fano in Italy, 3 Squadron RAAF swapped its Kittyhawks for Mustang Mk IIIs, IVs and IVas (P-51Cs, Ds and Ks in US nomenclature) in November 1944 and proudly painted the Southern Cross insignia on their blue rudders. After just five days of conversion training the men recommenced operations under the umbrella of 239 Wing RAF, seeing intensive action in bombing and reconnaissance operations over Italy and in support of Tito's partisan forces in Yugoslavia. Messerschmitt Bf 109s were

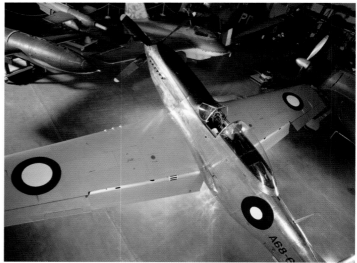

occasionally encountered, but the squadron's targets were primarily on the ground: the enemy's rail, road and water transport system, and (in the war's final weeks) retreating German columns.

In 1948, after re-forming as a tactical reconnaissance unit from the defunct 4 Squadron at Canberra, 3 Squadron again flew Mustangs—now Australian-built examples fitted with aerial cameras. Interestingly, the squadron was pitted against another aircraft type in the Memorial's collection, the RAN's Sea Fury, during exercises in July 1949.

In the jet age the Mustang's days as Australia's front-line fighter were numbered, but it still had one more war to fight. On 23 June 1950 the Mustangs of 77 Squadron, by now the RAAF's sole fighter unit with the occupation forces in Japan, made their last flight before being readied for shipping back to Australia. The following night, the men had a farewell party to remember their four years in the country. It was still in progress the next morning when a phone call put the squadron on immediate standby: North Korean forces had crossed the 38th Parallel and invaded South Korea.

During the first nine months of the Korean War, the squadron's Mustangs flew 3,800 sorties against North Korean and Chinese forces. Armed with bombs, napalm tanks or up to ten 60-lb rockets in addition to its six 0.5-in machine-guns, the Mustang made a formidable ground attack and close support weapon. The squadron also flew escort for B-29 Superfortress bomber formations. During its Mustang period the squadron lost eight pilots and 18 aircraft in action, before converting to Meteor jets in April 1951.

In Australia, the Citizen Air Force (CAF) squadrons (numbered 21 to 25) had equipped with Mustangs just after the war. These were the last RAAF units to fly piston-engined fighters, finally making the transition to jets in 1959. By then the RAAF's Mustang had, in addition to these five CAF squadrons, served with ten fighter squadrons, a tactical reconnaissance squadron and 14 miscellaneous units.

Mustang A68-648 did not leave Australia; its service was in training pilots who did. However, as a US-built P-51D it is representative of many of the Mustangs which saw action in Italy with 3 Squadron during 1944–45, and of the majority of those in Korea with 77 Squadron during 1950–51.

Cockpit of the Memorial's Mustang.
AWM P06429.003

The Mustang in context

It is one of the ironies of aviation in the Second World War that America's best all-round fighter was originally designed and built for the Anglo–French Purchasing Commission. The RAF introduced the Mustang into the European war in mid-1942, three years before it was brought on strength at Mildura—a long time in war, with technology advancing so fast that many designs are obsolescent soon after entering service. But in all-round performance, the Mustang could still hold its own against any piston-engined fighter in 1945.

The aircraft was the remarkable outcome of just four months of development, from signing the contract to the first flight of the NA-73X prototype in October 1940. The design and technical staff at North American Aviation worked 16 hours a day, seven days a week on the project to rush it through to fruition. But they also had a head start, in the form of design and wind tunnel data from the Curtiss XP-46 fighter project. North American incorporated fuselage design features from this aircraft, and added its own wing design. The distinctive underslung radiator inlet/outlet concept was retained and refined until it actually produced a small amount of additional thrust. The resulting airframe was so aerodynamically clean that in a dive from high altitude, numerous Mustang pilots encountered the phenomenon of compressibility—a near-uncontrollable state as the aircraft approached the speed of sound.

Much of the Mustang's wartime success lay in two developments. The first was a 'laminar flow' wing utilising a National Advisory Committee for Aeronautics (NACA, later NASA) airfoil section, with its thickest point two-thirds back from the leading edge. The result was an aerodynamic drag, or air resistance, coefficient of just 0.003.[35] The second factor was the reliable Merlin engine (introduced on the P-51B variant) with its two-stage supercharger, which at high altitude gave superior acceleration, climb rate and speed to most other piston-engined fighters.

The cockpit was more comfortable and roomy than in many single-seat fighters, and the teardrop-shaped canopy of the P-51D, K and Australian-built models (the CA-17 and CA-18) afforded excellent visibility. The only visibility problem was on the ground, when taxiing: the pilot's forward view was blocked by the engine cowlings, necessitating a zig-zag pattern during taxiing. On the take-off run, the aircraft's generous acceleration down the runway quickly raised the tail and lowered the obstructing nose for a clearer view.

Any fighter is simply a means of bringing armament to bear on the enemy. The later Mustangs carried the same punch as the Kittyhawk, with six 0.5 in machineguns sighted by the pilot using a sophistocated K-14[36] computing gunsight. Pitted by American pilots against the latest version of the Japanese Zero (the Zeke 52) it was found that the Mustang, with superior acceleration, speed and zoom climb, could stay on the offensive in a dogfight and break off combat at will. However, at lower speeds the Zeke 52 was markedly superior in manoeuvrability and turn radius, prompting US authorities to advise pilots to avoid attempting to follow the Zeke in turns and to instead use the Mustang's speed advantage in hit-and-run tactics. Japan's best fighters,[37] which Australian Mustang pilots might have encountered had the war continued, roughly matched the Mustang except in maximum speed and range.

The Mustang also represents a milestone in Australia's aviation industry: the local production of this, the Allies' best all-round fighter of the war. Selected in April 1944 partly because CAC already had ties with North American through the production of the Wirraway, the Mustang was seen as a superior high-altitude fighter to the other main contender for the contract, the Spitfire Mk VIII. With limited resources, CAC became the only firm outside the United States to build the Mustang, and produced 200 examples between 1945 and 1951, to bring the RAAF's total Mustang deliveries to almost 500. Although the first Australian-built examples rolled off the assembly lines too late to see action during the Second World War, they served as Australia's primary peacetime fighter until the arrival of Meteor and Vampire jets. A few saw action in Korea, joining the US-built examples with 77 Squadron. As a postscript to the CAC production story, the company also produced an aircraft arguably superior to the Mustang. The outstanding CA-15, though, did not fly until six months after the war. Stillborn, it was a victim of the jet age.

TIMELINE—A68-648

1945	(Jun) Received ex-USA at 1 Aircraft Depot (1 AD), RAAF Laverton, Vic. (Jul) To 2 Operational Training Unit, RAAF Mildura, Vic. (Nov) To 1 AD
1946	(Jun) To 1 Aircraft Performance Unit, RAAF Laverton for trials including deterioration filter on mainplanes
1948	(Jun) To RAAF Point Cook, Vic., for Category 'B' storage
1950	(Jun) Airframe transferred to Melbourne Technical College (later RMIT) for apprentice instruction; outer wings later removed
1983	Purchased from RMIT by the AWM with engine, propeller and components. Restoration begun by Bob Eastgate and Bob Jones at RAAF Point Cook. Wings supplied by Aeronautical Research Laboratories
1992	Restoration completed; disassembled for transport by road to AWM and assembled at AWM annexe, Mitchell, ACT
1999	Displayed in Aircraft Hall

DATA

Type	P-51D-20-NT Mustang
Design firm	North American Aviation (NAA)
Manufacturer	NAA, Dallas, Texas, USA
Role	Single-seat fighter
No. built	7,965 P-51Ds (Mustang total 15,875)
Type entered service	1944
Identity	111-36389 (construction no.) 44-13106 (USAAF) A68-648 (RAAF)
Powerplant	Packard V-1650-7 Merlin V-12 engine of 1,720 hp
Armament	Six 0.50-in Browning M2 machine-guns
	Two 500- or 1,000-lb bombs or up to ten 5-in rockets
Wingspan	11.29 m
Length	9.81 m
Max. speed	703 km/h
Range	3,350 km
Max. take-off weight	5,200 kg

NOTES ON COLOUR SCHEME

1945-period RAAF scheme: fuselage overall bare aluminium, wings painted dull silver. Markings on OTU Mustangs were minimal, as follows: Blue and white roundels in six positions. Blue and white fin flashes. Black anti-glare panel forward of windscreen. RAAF serial number stencilled in black on rear fuselage sides.

A6M ZERO 5784

Over Buna, north coast of Papua
1400 HOURS, 22 JULY 1942

Chief Petty Officer Saburo Sakai set his propeller pitch, mixture and throttle levers for maximum power, and mentally planned his attack as he led the eight Zeros of his *shotai* (section) in behind their prey. The speck in the distance slowly grew to reveal itself as an Australian Lockheed Hudson bomber that was shadowing a Japanese cruiser force in the Huon Gulf off Buna. It had little chance of escape.

The Zeros were out on a combat air patrol, and had first been alerted to the presence of an Allied aircraft by the concussion of bomb blasts around Japanese supply dumps on the shore. As the nimble fighters closed in, Pilot Officer Warren Cowan[38] in the cockpit of Hudson A16-201 of 32 Squadron RAAF opened up the throttles, pushed the control column forward, and dived away with an impressive turn of speed. Sakai dropped his auxiliary fuel tank and pushed the throttle to maximum boost to catch up with the bomber. Then, while still several hundred metres away, he fired his two 20-mm cannon and 7.7-mm machine-guns.

> *The Zero excited me as nothing else had ever done before.*
>
> *Saburo Sakai, Japanese fighter ace*

After 30 years, the elements had taken their toll on the Zero at Gasmata airstrip. AWM P02821.002

What happened next was startling. No sooner had I fired than the Hudson went up in a steep climbing turn to the right, rolled quickly, and roared back with full speed directly at me. I was so surprised that for several moments I sat motionless in the cockpit. The next second every forward-firing gun in the Hudson opened up in a withering barrage.[39]

The Zeros scattered. Sakai turned out of the stream of bullets and the Hudson heeled over in a snap roll, the fastest one he had ever seen a bomber execute. During the desperate ten-minute battle that followed, Sakai made at least four firing passes, but did not manage to score a hit; nor did Hiroyoshi Nishizawa, an equally skilled pilot. These were no novice pilots: their unit was the feared Tainan[40] *Kokutai* (air corps) of the Imperial Japanese Naval Air Force (IJNAF). The Rabaul-based Tainan group's Zeros operated mainly from the forward base at Lae, which had been occupied by the Japanese since March. From May to July under Lieutenant Junichi Sasai, the unit's fighters claimed some 300 US and Australian aircraft destroyed—more than any other Japanese unit—for the loss of 20 Zeros.[41] Nishizawa was destined to become Japan's greatest fighter ace, and Sakai ranked not far behind him. Sakai continues:

Finally a heavy burst caught the rear turret; I saw the gunner throw his hands up and collapse. Without the interfering stream of bullets from the turret, I closed in to twenty yards and held the gun trigger down, aiming for the right wing. Seconds later flame streamed out, then spread to the left wing. The pilot stayed with the ship; it was too low for him or the crew to bale out. The Hudson lost speed rapidly and glided in toward the jungle. Trees sheared off the two flaming wings and the fuselage, also trailing great sheets of flame, burst into the dense growth like a giant sliver of burning steel. There was a sudden explosion, and smoke boiled upward.[42]

Sergeant Lauri Sheard in the Hudson's shattered turret was most likely dead before the aircraft crashed near Popondetta, east of Kokoda. The rest of the crew, Cowan and Sergeant Russell Polack in the cockpit and Pilot Officer David Taylor in the navigator's station, were killed on impact. In June 1945 their remains were located and buried at nearby Soputa war cemetery, and later re-buried at Bomana, north of Port Moresby.

◄ ►

On the night of 6 January 1943, a Catalina flying boat of 11 Squadron RAAF lumbered over Gasmata airstrip on the south coast of New Britain. After dropping flares, Flight Lieutenant David Vernon and his crew caught sight of three Japanese fighters parked near the north-west end of the runway. From 2,000 ft up, the big Cat's gunners strafed the fighters in six passes, and on three more passes incendiary bombs were dropped. Anti-aircraft fire opened up during the second pass, but was silenced by the attacks. Soon a raging fire had taken hold in the grass around the fighters, and the Catalina droned off into the night.

It is interesting to speculate on a common link between these two seemingly unconnected events: that the Zero which shot down Hudson A16-201 was just possibly one of the fighters strafed by Vernon. That Zero may be the one now suspended from the ceiling of the Memorial's Aircraft Hall.

The grass airstrip at Gasmata was boggy in the wet, although crushed coral paved its inland portion. A take-off run towards the sea ended in a sheer cliff. Originally created before the war by an Australian civilian contractor for aircraft flying in and out of the adjacent plantation,[45] it was upgraded by the IJNAF after the Japanese invasion of the island in February 1942. It was soon a 3,200-ft (960-m) strip with taxiways and anti-aircraft defences, and was used as a staging base and an emergency field for aircraft in trouble. G3M (Nell) bombers, Ki-46 (Dinah) reconnaissance aircraft, and the Zeros of Tainan *Kokutai*, among others, used it.[44] Hidden among palm trees were drums of fuel and basic maintenance equipment, tended by the sparse local population. When needed, maintenance staff were flown in from the main base at Vunakanau airfield at Rabaul, squeezed into the back of a Zero.

From the time of its Japanese occupation, Gasmata and its airfield were regularly bombed by the US Fifth Air Force. In March 1943 the IJNAF used it as a staging base in the battle of the Bismarck Sea, but two months later the bombardment had severely hampered operations. In late July and August a series of RAAF bombing and strafing attacks on the airfield by 30 Squadron (Beaufighters), 22 Squadron (Bostons) and 77 Squadron (Kittyhawks) attracted only light anti-aircraft fire, and Gasmata was soon abandoned. In March 1944 it was recaptured by the Australian army.

In 1973, Japanese aircraft wrecks including Zeros, Nells, Dinahs and B5N Kate torpedo bombers could still be seen scattered about Gasmata airport. One badly deteriorated but relatively intact Zero sat on the grass by the strip, having at some time been pushed into the open by locals. Bullet holes indicated that it had been attacked from the air, and repairs to previous battle damage were evident. Faintly visible on the fuselage were the serial number 5784 and a faded blue diagonal stripe: a *shōtai* leader's marking. That year, a nearby bomb-damaged Aichi D3A Val dive-bomber was salvaged, with RAAF help, and shipped to the Admiral Nimitz Museum in Texas. An attempt to salvage the Zero involved cutting its engine mounts and wings off with gas torches for transport (as the Zero's wings were constructed in one mainplane for strength and lightness, and do not separate), and other damage was done before it made its way to Port Moresby. There the Papua New Guinea government impounded it.

In 1976, arguing against a PNG government clampdown on the removal of national cultural property, the Australian High Commissioner negotiated its release for the Memorial, and the Zero was flown by C-130 Hercules transport to RAAF Point Cook, Victoria. Joining it were the remains of another A6M2 Model 22, serial 3618, recovered from Kahili on Bougainville. Six years later the two made their way to RAAF Forest

Hill at Wagga Wagga, New South Wales. A third Zero, also recovered during the early 1970s and flown by RAAF transport aircraft to Australia, joined them. This was an A6M5 Model 52, serial 4043 (tail number 3-108 of the 12th *Kokutai*[45]), which had been surrendered by its pilot to the Royal New Zealand Air Force at Jacquinot Bay, New Britain, in 1945. As an apprentice training project with a difference, and as a volunteer 'spare time' project for other personnel, the RAAF at Forest Hill planned to produce one restored aircraft from the three and present it to the Memorial.

The markings of 5784, indicating an aircraft of a *shotai* leader, made an easy decision of which was the more historically significant example for restoration, despite 4043 being in the best state. The other two airframes would serve as sources of parts. Heading the RAAF team were Warrant Officer Dennis Doggett and Flight Lieutenant Wayne Scholz. It was a monumental task. All three airframes had suffered severe corrosion in the tropical conditions. The dissimilar metals and reactive duralumin alloys with magnesium in their structure, especially the Extra Super Duralumin alloy used in the airframe and wing spar caps, had accelerated the process. These materials had been chosen by Mitsubishi for their light weight and strength, not for longevity. The result was that many items had to be refabricated, including the spar caps (courtesy of Hawker de Havilland) and most of the metal fuselage skin, making this primarily a restoration rather than a conservation project. Among the many surprising finds during the restoration was a 1939 German production stamping on the metal of a wing rib, physical evidence that Germany supplied Japan with some of its war matériel. In 1988, after five years and an estimated 20,000 man-hours of work, the aircraft was completed in time for display at the Bicentennial Airshow at RAAF Richmond near Sydney.

Discovering the history of 5784 was a somewhat convoluted process. The stencilled serial number was still visible on the fuselage, but it was the tail code that could provide the clues to its unit. New Zealand aviation historian Dr Charles Darby had first recorded the aircraft's tail marking as V-173.[46] 'V' indicated the Tainan *Kokutai*. In 1983 the Memorial wrote to Saburo Sakai, as he was the leading surviving Japanese fighter ace and one of the few contactable veterans of the unit. Sakai was asked if its identity meant anything to him. Jaws dropped when he wrote back with the news that 'V-173 was my plane in June and July 1942'. This particular Zero had outstanding performance, he wrote, and it was only because V-173 went in for a major 200-hourly overhaul that he changed to another Zero, V-128, for the operations over Guadalcanal and lost track of his former mount. The period Sakai flew V-173 encompasses not only intensive operations in New Guinea, but also numerous raids on the Darwin area, as well as the later raids on the airfield on Horn Island, in the Torres Strait, in which Zeros took part.

Chief Petty Officer Saburo Sakai

Sakai first went into action in Type 96 fighters with the 12th *Kokutai* in the war against China in 1938. In June 1941 Petty Officer Sakai joined the Tainan *Kokutai*, which from December flew Zeros against US aircraft in the Philippines, where he shot down the first fighter lost on the first day of the campaign. The *Kokutai* also flew in the Netherlands East Indies, where Sakai encountered Dutch as well as US aircraft. In April 1942 the Tainan *Kokutai* moved to Rabaul, New Britain, using Lae as a forward base in the New Guinea campaign. Over the next four months he shot down numerous US P-39 and P-40 fighters and B-17, B-25 and B-26 bombers, as well as RAAF aircraft. By 7 August 1942 he was Japan's most successful fighter ace. On that day he shot down a US Navy F4F Wildcat, the first aircraft to be lost over Guadalcanal, but was badly wounded by a bullet from a US Navy SBD Dauntless dive-bomber and permanently blinded in one eye. Ten months later, however, he was back in the cockpit, flying in the defence of the Japanese home islands. In one combat with US Navy F6F Hellcats, his unit, the Yokosuka *Kokutai*, lost 23 Zeros. His unit was almost destroyed in the defence of Iwo Jima. His last flight was on 17 August 1945, two days after the Japanese surrender, to intercept four B-32 Dominator bombers on a photographic mission over Tokyo. The bombers returned with slight damage.

Saburo Sakai. AWM P02865.002

Sakai survived some 200 aerial combats, partly because his keen eyesight allowed him to spot the enemy first and, therefore, often to dictate the terms of combat. He estimated that he destroyed or damaged over 60 aircraft (Japanese researchers have estimated 32 destroyed) during his seven years as a fighter pilot. After the war he often expressed admiration for his former foes, and fostered family and friendship ties with America. Before his death in 2000, he advocated that the gallant Hudson crew he had shot down should be awarded posthumous medals. 'We all did our best for our respective countries,' he reflected.[47]

Other aces who flew A6M2s with Tainan *Kokutai*

(Total claimed number of aerial victories are in brackets, and may include shared or probable claims.)

† PO1 Shizuo Ishii (26)
† WO Hiroyoshi Nishizawa (87)
† PO1 Toshio Ohta (34)
  WO Hiroshi Okano (19)
† Lt(jg) Junichi Sasai (27)
† NAP2/c Kazushi Uto (19)

† Denotes died in service

Source: Shores, *Air aces*, pp. 147–48

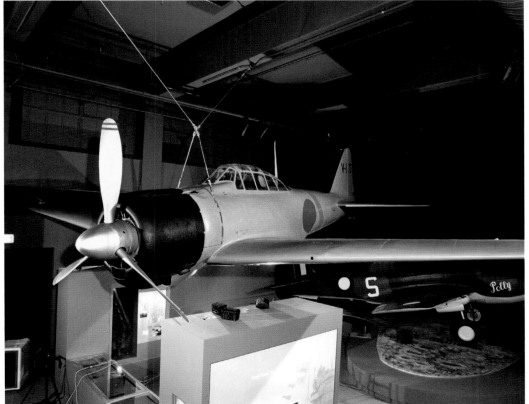

Two views of the restored Zero suspended in Aircraft Hall in 2001. AWM PAIU2001/121.18; PAIU2001/121.14

The Japanese naval air contribution in New Guinea

By March 1942, Japan's first stage of operations was complete, focusing on the Netherlands East Indies and the capture of Rabaul on New Britain as a base for mounting operations against Port Moresby. After an invasion of Australia had been ruled out as being beyond Japan's capacity, High Command then planned for the second stage, a major offensive aimed at far-reaching and long-term security of occupation to force Britain and finally the United States out of the war. The advance in the Solomons and New Guinea was continued, the aim being to cut off supplies between the United States and Australia. Lae and Salamaua on the north-eastern New Guinea coast were occupied on 8 March; the former was established as the primary advance base, and the Tainan *Kokutai* sent 11 Zeros there.

During V-173's period with Tainan *Kokutai*, prior to August 1942, the Rabaul-based naval air units operating from Lae flew bomber escort, fighter sweeps and ground attack against Moresby and other Allied bases. At the same time they defended their bases against the onslaught of Allied bombing. Heavy losses were suffered by both sides which, in the long run, only the Allies could afford to sustain. In November the Japanese army, after rejecting the first request, agreed to commit its 6th Air Division to bolster the navy's depleted air strength in New Guinea, and army fighters began operations from Rabaul in December (see Oscar chapter). Soon 164 army aircraft and 190 navy were based in the Rabaul area. Initially the army aircraft provided air defence for ground operations and defended their airfields, the navy taking care of other operations in New Guinea and the Solomons.

On 1 November, the Tainan *Kokutai* was renamed the 251st *Kokutai* and remained at Rabaul until mid-1943. Following defeat at Guadalcanal and in the Bismarck Sea in February and March, the army elected to concentrate its air forces on the New Guinea campaign. A year later, the last of the navy's aircraft at Rabaul were flown to Truk, ending naval air presence in the New Guinea–Solomons area. The army air units did not last much longer, with relentless Allied bombing of their airfields.

With reference to Hiroyuki Shindo, *Japanese air operations over New Guinea during the Second World War* (see http://ajrp.awm.gov.au)

The Zero in context

The brainchild of Mitsubishi designer Jiro Horikoshi, the A6M (navy designation: Type 0 Carrier Fighter) first flew in April 1939, and entered service the following year—Japanese year 2600, hence the type number. It was unofficially referred to as *Reisen*, a contraction of *Rei Sentoki* (Zero fighter), or the Zero-sen. Under the American system of codenames for Japanese aircraft (adopted also by Australia), it was known as Zeke. From its exceptional performance it was evident from the start that this was to be Japan's most-produced fighter aircraft, and it remained in production until the end of the war.

A6M2 Zeros on the aircraft carrier *Akagi* prepare to attack Pearl Harbor, Hawaii, on 7 December 1941. AWM P03172.001

The A6M2 model, first flown in January 1940, was the initial production variant. Before it had even been fully tested, a pre-production batch of 15 examples was sent to the war in China during the summer for combat evaluation. In their first meeting with China's air force (Russian-built Polikarpov I-15 biplanes and I-16 monoplane fighters) in September, all 27 enemy aircraft were destroyed for the loss of no Zeros.[48] Over the ensuing year the Zero enjoyed complete air superiority, the force losing just two aircraft to anti-aircraft fire. Despite a report on its capabilities being sent to US Army Air Force Headquarters by General Claire Chennault, US adviser to the Chinese Air Force and leader of the famed Flying Tigers volunteer group, the warning was ignored or treated as fanciful. At Pearl Harbor on 7 December 1941 and for the next six months, the Zero totally shattered America's belief in the inferiority of Japanese technology. Worse, the Zero was designed as a carrier-borne fighter (a role which traditionally had placed restraints on performance) and still out-performed all land-based fighters.

In light of subsequent events, it is difficult to appreciate the air of invincibility enjoyed by the Zero during those first months of the Pacific war, and the dread felt by the Australian airmen who came up against it flying inadequate aircraft. It was 25 per cent faster and had almost twice the range of the fighter it replaced, the Type 96 (A5M, codenamed Claude) of 1937 with its fixed undercarriage and open cockpit. Although most pilots agreed that the Type 96 was a better dogfighter than the Zero, the latter was still very responsive to control and could both out-manoeuvre and out-climb every Allied aircraft. Its light construction, sleek design and large, effective control surfaces allowed all this with a much less powerful engine than those of its opponents. Its propeller torque gave it a particularly tight left turn. Importantly, its raised cockpit canopy afforded good all-round visibility.

But like many myths, the invincibility of the Zero was gradually dispelled: firstly after the capture and analysis of intact Zeros in 1942, and then by the introduction into service of US fighters which could deal with it. Even then, few fighters could actually out-turn the Zero, relying instead on heavier armament, more power, speed and greater ability to absorb damage.

The Zero's agility and long range arose largely from its light weight, but this came at a price. The A6M2's Achilles' heel was its lack of armour and self-sealing fuel tanks, both standard features in Allied aircraft but considered unnecessary among Japanese pilots. If hit by anti-aircraft or machine-gun fire, the A6M2 was highly susceptible to structural damage and catching fire. The aircraft, and indeed its pilot, was considered expendable. The 925-hp engine, although giving it a good climb rate, did not give it a particularly good level or diving speed. In any case, above 400 km/h the controls became stiff as resistance on the large control surfaces, which were a big advantage at lower speeds, increased; and until later models were developed, its thin wing skin could not withstand high speeds.

Several other factors worked against the Zero. One was difficulty of production. Its design did not lend itself well to mass production techniques. Had this not been the case, many more Zeros might have been built to counter America's vast production capacity.[49] Also, Japanese pilots could not be trained effectively in sufficient numbers to replace the combat losses of the hardened veterans of the China war. The little they were taught concentrated on individual fighting skills in air-to-air combat, at the expense of teamwork skills. Saburo Sakai believed that American pilots learned their sense of teamwork from football. They were also able to send messages over the radio, whereas the Japanese aircraft radios were next to useless. Sakai, in fact, had his removed to save weight.

The A6M3 model featured a more powerful engine with two-stage supercharger, and thicker skin on the wings to withstand the higher diving speeds which were by then considered essential in combat. It introduced shortened 'clipped' wings, and the changed appearance prompted US and Australian airmen to give it a new codename, Hamp. Its disadvantage was reduced range, and it was largely a failure in the Solomons campaign. The major production version of the Zero was the A6M5 which introduced still more power, some armour and heavier armament. The A6M7 was a specialised dive-bomber that was instead used for *kamikaze* suicide attacks, although earlier models predominated in this last-ditch effort in the defence of the Philippines, Okinawa and Iwo Jima in the final nine months of war. The planned ultimate Zero variant, the A6M8 mounting a powerful 1,560-hp Kinsei engine and featuring all self-sealing fuel tanks, would have been an effective fighter and an answer to the American Hellcat, had it been put into production.

Cockpit of the Memorial's Zero after completion in 1988. AWM P06429.004

TIMELINE—5784

1942	(Mid-year) Built by Mitsubishi at Suzuka near Nagoya, Japan Flown with Tainan *Kokutai* and abandoned at Gasmata, New Guinea
1973	Wings cut off; impounded at Port Moresby by government of Papua New Guinea; donated to AWM
1976	Shipped to Australia and stored at RAAF Point Cook, Vic.
1983–88	Restored for AWM, using components from two other Zeros, by apprentices at RAAF Forest Hill, Wagga Wagga, NSW
1988	Restoration completed; displayed at Bicentennial Airshow, Richmond, NSW
2000	Displayed in Aircraft Hall

DATA

Type	Navy Type 0 carrier fighter (*Reisen*) A6M2 Model 21
Design firm	Mitsubishi Jukogyo KK (Mitsubishi Heavy Industries Co Ltd), Japan
Manufacturer	Mitsubishi, Japan
Role	Single-seat carrier- and land-based fighter
No. built	10,449 (estimated total Mitsubishi and Nakajima A6M production) 1,552 (estimated total A6M2 Model 21)
Type entered service	1940
Identity	5784 (constructor's number) V-173 (tail number)
Powerplant	Nakajima NK1C Sakae 12 14-cylinder radial engine of 925 hp
Armament	Two wing-mounted 20-mm Type 99 Mk I cannon Two nose-mounted 7.7-mm Type 97 machine-guns
Wingspan	12 m
Length	9.06 m
Max. speed	534 km/h
Range	3,110 km (8 hours' endurance) with auxiliary tank
Max. take-off weight	2,796 kg

NOTES ON COLOUR SCHEME

Type 05 overall light grey (N9) scheme with black engine cowling and six standard all-red *hinomaru* national insignia. Propeller blades are bare metal (front) and brown (rear) with double red tip stripes. Bare metal spinner. Manufacturer's data panel stencilled in black on rear port fuselage side. Blue diagonal fuselage band aft of *hinomaru*. Tail code 'V-173' in black on both sides of tail. Main undercarriage leg covers have '73' in white above yellow and red stripes midway up; '173' in black on drop tank pylon.

KI-43 OSCAR 5465

7,000 ft over Sumbawa Island, Netherlands East Indies
22 MARCH 1945

Group Captain Deryck Kingwell's 11-man B-24 Liberator crew was concentrating on the task of bombing two Japanese 'sugar dog' supply vessels. Suddenly the bombardier, Flying Officer A.G. Worley, was distracted when two enemy fighters appeared 2,000 ft below. He identified them as an Oscar and a Zeke (Allied code for a Zero) before losing them. Five minutes later they re-appeared 1,000 ft above and ahead, and the Zeke approached. Four small cylindrical objects, possibly phosphorous bombs, fell from it and flashed past just 15 m off the left wing.

Then the Oscar came in for a head-on firing pass. It broke away at 300 m, its pilot evidently wary of the Liberator's ten 0.5-in machine-guns. In a second pass the Liberator's aileron cable was cut and the tailplane, rudder and two engines hit.

エンジンの音轟々と
隼は征く雲の果て

*(With a roar of its engine
The Hayabusa flies beyond the clouds)*

*Major Tateo Kato's Falcon Corps song
(64th Sentai)*

A Ki-43 *Hayabusa* in flight. AWM 129705

A shell caused havoc in the nose compartment, cutting electrical lines and exploding at Kingwell's rudder pedals. Both he and Worley were wounded, and the autopilot damaged. But the attacks had only just begun. The Oscar turned and came in again from ahead and below, this time passing just 100 m below the bomber. While these attacks took the crew's attention, from somewhere above—presumably from the Zeke—dropped a most unusual weapon. It was a 1-m long heavy metal chain, which smashed the front turret perspex and wounded gunner Flight Sergeant J.S. Thompson, who nevertheless kept firing until the turret quit. Its hydraulic oil sprayed under the fuselage onto the ventral ball turret, effectively putting it out of action as well.

The fourth pass was made by the Zeke from the 3 o'clock position and 150 m above, and the fifth by the Oscar from ahead. Four more passes were made, but the Liberator had by then, 40 minutes after the first attack, passed into the safety of broken cloud. On the return trip, while engineer Flight Sergeant W.J. Wignal tied the severed control cable together, another fighter was sighted near Timor. It sat 2 km away for five minutes before turning away, and the Liberator continued on its route back to base at Fenton airfield, south of Darwin.

Two weeks later, on 6 April, Worley, Thompson, Wignal and four others in this crew again met with fighters identified as Oscars and Zekes. Flying 12,000 ft above the Flores Sea, several attacked a formation of nine RAAF Liberators which were bombing the Japanese light cruiser *Isuzu*. Homing in on the third element of bombers from the front left quarter, in line astern they nearly rammed Flying Officer McDonald's bomber, breaking away just 15 m from it. The colours and markings were clearly visible: dark-green and brown camouflage, with orange lightning flashes marking their tails. The attackers were evidently experienced and determined, and broke up the bomber formation. One Liberator was hit in the flight deck by cannon fire, setting its bomb bay fuel tanks on fire. It went down into the sea. During a 12-minute parachute descent, a surviving crewman watched as a second bomber was shot down. Sitting in another Liberator, the squadron gunnery leader had one of the fighters in his sights and was about to shoot when, to his horror, Flight Lieutenant Ford's burning Liberator streaked past before his eyes. The Japanese fighter was claimed as shot down by the gunners, but of the 22 crewmen aboard the two Liberators, only three survived.

◄ ►

The Nakajima Army Type 1 Fighter or Ki-43 *Hayabusa* (peregrine falcon), known to the Allies as the Oscar, was flown by the Japanese army, and the A6M Zero or Zeke by the navy. The two services were not known for their cooperation, but regularly coordinated attacks such as in these actions against the Liberators. An early attempt by the two services to coordinate operations had come in November 1942 when they signed a *Central agreement on operations in the South Pacific Area*, defining their areas of responsibility. In the New Guinea region, the army's air arm, the Imperial Japanese Army Air Force (IJAAF), would conduct the bulk of air operations. Firstly it committed its 6th Air Division to the region, and in December sent the 11th *Sentai* with 60 Ki-43 fighters to Rabaul in New Britain for air defence. From there, they also flew against targets on mainland Papua New Guinea, starting with an attack on Buna on Christmas day when they claimed six fighters shot down for two losses (see also Hudson chapter). In January, they were relieved by the 1st *Sentai*.

Earlier in 1942, Japan's forces had taken the Allied airfields along the north coast of New Guinea. In 1943, these were upgraded and new ones constructed, with the complex at Wewak being developed into the IJAAF's principal air base in New Guinea. Initially, these bases were to be used for operations against Port Moresby in preparation for its capture. Although this aim was effectively abandoned by March, the New Guinea campaign was still considered important and several army *sentai* were operating from the new and upgraded bases by mid-year.

By the end of 1943, the situation for Japan had deteriorated markedly. In the few months from December to the following March the weakened IJAAF in New Guinea was decimated. In preparation for landing assaults, the Allied air forces relentlessly raided Wewak and the other airfield complexes, including Madang and nearby Alexishafen along the northern coastline. In January alone, more than 400 Liberators, Mitchells and Marauders of the US Army's Fifth Air Force dropped 1,100 t of bombs on these and neighbouring targets.

As forward bases for Wewak-based aircraft, Alexishafen's two airfields (Sek and Danip) were only basic, each with a single unsealed runway. They had been constructed in February 1943 by the Japanese with the help of conscripted local labour. With little by way of construction machinery, the airfields were cleared and built largely by hand. It was difficult work and tediously slow.

By mid-January 1944, with constant pounding from Allied air attacks, the Japanese were no longer able to maintain Alexishafen and its airstrips as the important supply and distribution centre that it had been. But there were still large numbers of apparently serviceable aircraft there, and the attacks were stepped up in February, now in support of General MacArthur's thrust into the Admiralty Islands to the north. RAAF Vengeance dive bombers and Kittyhawks made harassing raids, while American Bostons, Mitchells and other types delivered increasing bomb tonnages. Particularly effective against aircraft on the ground were 'parafrags', small bombs dropped at low level by parachute so they would fall over a wider area and, on detonation, spread fragments of shrapnel far and wide. By mid-January the airfields at Alexishafen were so heavily bomb-cratered that they could not be used, and Japanese documents report that by the end of February they were finally out of commission.

Wewak and Hollandia to its west in Dutch New Guinea had been heavily hit since their Japanese occupation. One raid on Wewak in August 1943 had destroyed over a hundred aircraft on the ground, reducing the 4th Air Army to just 30 operational aircraft.[50] Though weary from constant air attacks and a near-starvation diet, the pilots of several *sentai* flew Ki-43s against this onslaught. By early 1944 these included the 33rd, 63rd and 77th.

Japanese fighter losses were unsustainable. Of the reinforcements that arrived at Wewak in February 1944, virtually all the aircraft and a third of the pilots had been lost a month later.[51] On 30 and 31 March over Hollandia, just a fortnight after the 4th Air Army had withdrawn there from Wewak, 47 serviceable fighters climbed into the air to attack two mass raids by US Fifth Air Force Liberators and their escorts of Lightnings and Thunderbolts. Only two Oscars were shot down, but some 130 Japanese aircraft of all types were destroyed on the ground. The 63rd *Sentai* was almost destroyed, only eight Oscars surviving. Australians were among the Liberator crews of the 65th Squadron, 43rd Bombardment Group, which led two other B-24 groups of the US Army Air Force (USAAF) over the target. This group of five RAAF crews under Wing Commander John Hampshire was finishing an operational posting to the unit to gain experience on the B-24 prior to the type's acquisition by the RAAF. It is interesting to speculate that their Liberators may have been attacked by fighters of the 63rd *Sentai*, the unit with which the Memorial's Oscar served.

The 63rd *Sentai*

The 63rd was formed in February 1943 in northern Honshu from elements of other units, and spent the rest of the year in Japan. Leaving from snow-covered Hokkaido, the men arrived in the humid jungle environment of Hollandia and Wewak in January and February 1944. Commanding the unit's 3rd *Chutai* (squadron), with which the Memorial's Ki-43 served, were Captain Shichiro Watanabe and, following in February, Lieutenant Hiroshi Endo. With a complement of 38 Ki-43-II fighters, the 63rd was one of several new *sentai* arriving in New Guinea at the time, including two other fighter units at Hollandia (the 33rd and 77th).

The 63rd was destined for a short but intense four months of service. It got off to a bad start, losing five aircraft in its first action over the US airfield complex at Nadzab. However, on 18 January the commander of the unit's 2nd *Chutai*, Captain Tomio Matsumoto, shot down three US Lightning fighters before being killed when he rammed a fourth. The whole unit soon consolidated at Wewak to join the other *sentai* defending the airfield complex there.

The pilots had several successes. On 8 March, for example, 1st Lieutenant Toshimasa Ueki destroyed two Liberators during a US bombing raid. A week, later, the 63rd returned to Hollandia when all units at Wewak withdrew there. Its last interception before the Allied landing at Hollandia was made on 21 April by six remaining Ki-43-IIs; thereafter, the unit effectively ceased to exist and was disbanded in July.

63rd *Sentai* pilots killed in action (1944)

16 Jan	1st Lt Kiyoshi Hasegawa (Saidor)
16 Jan	Sgt Maj Tadashi Oishi (Saidor)
16 Jan	Cpl Mitsuhiro Kono (Saidor)
16 Jan	Sgt Maj Isao Iwamitsu (Madang)
18 Jan	Capt Tomio Matsumoto (Wewak)
17 Feb	Sgt Maj Tatsuichiro Katagiri (Mindanao)
13 Mar	1st Lt Takeshi Hamasuna (Wewak)
13 Mar	Cpl Takamitsu Yamamoto (Wewak)
15 Mar	1st Lt Yasuji Ogi (Wewak)
15 Mar	Lt Shigekatsu Shimoura (Wewak)

Information from Hata, Izawa and Shores, *Japanese Army Air Force fighter units and their aces 1931–1945*

A third, even more devastating raid three days later attracted 30–40 Oscars and Ki-61 Tonys into the air to combat more than 200 bombers. The Japanese pilots were up against some of the USAAF's most experienced pilots, flying its best available fighter, the P-38 Lightning, and were outnumbered. Eleven fighters were shot down. One of the Oscars was the 25th victim claimed by Lightning ace Major Dick Bong. On 12 April, in the last large-scale combat over Hollandia, Bong claimed another three Oscars to become America's leading fighter ace.

The US landings in April resulted in the recapture of Hollandia, with its hundreds of damaged Japanese aircraft left for the men of 75 Squadron RAAF to examine when they moved there in August. The 33rd and 77th *Sentai*, meanwhile, had given their remaining aircraft to the 63rd, but it, too, effectively ceased to exist. The men began a retreat on foot through the jungle towards Sarmi, during which most would die. Meanwhile, an intact Oscar had been recovered from Hollandia by the Americans. Repaired, it was flown in combat trials against P-40N Warhawks and, reportedly, generally came out ahead. It was sent to the Allied Technical Air Intelligence Unit (ATAIU) at Eagle Farm airfield in Brisbane for further evaluation.

At the end of April, the Australian 30th Battalion moved into Alexishafen. The damage they discovered was not all the result of Allied attacks: the Japanese had set off bombs on the runway, probably damaged any intact aircraft, and booby-trapped the surrounds, which created a job for bomb disposal teams. The ATAIU visited in June looking for any Japanese army aircraft that might be found relatively intact. Instead they counted the broken remains of 36 Oscars, Tonys, Dinahs, Lilys, Helens and others, remnants of the bombing and strafing. The scene was just part of what one Japanese serviceman later described as 'the annihilation of our Army Air Force in New Guinea'.

◄　►

Apart from the incursion of vegetation, little changed at Alexishafen over the next 30 years. Local residents showed visitors the aircraft wrecks and other sights, and Japanese visitors would occasionally come to honour the dead by burning incense and leaving gifts for the ancestor spirits.[52] During the late 1970s, many of the wrecks were taken by recovery teams or by scrap metal dealers. However, the remains of several Oscars were left sitting among towering kunai grass near the fighter strip. Like the Zero, its navy counterpart, the Oscar was lightly constructed using thin sheet metal of alloy which corroded and holed easily. The airframes therefore suffered greatly from exposure to dampness, rotting vegetation, grass fires, and the local people who found that pieces of its metal skin could be put to all sorts of uses. Nevertheless, some were still salvageable, but to do so was easier said than done. The ever-present threat of snakes, water-filled bomb craters, and even live bombs just metres from the aircraft made the job of hand-clearing and bulldozing a path to them even more of a trial.

In 1984, a recovery team of Australian War Memorial staff and others made the trip to Alexishafen to select Oscar airframes and components for use in a restoration project. One Ki-43-II in particular, its serial number 5465 still visible below the tailplane, was found to be relatively intact. A RAAF Iroquois helicopter was called in, and lifted the underslung fighter from its resting place. Unfortunately, downblast from the rotor started the Oscar spinning and it was dropped and damaged, putting an end to that idea. The team settled on the safer option: a more traditional method of aircraft salvage, using a crane and low-loader truck. The vehicles were driven in, the bulldozer driver earning his keep as they became bogged in the sodden ground. After some effort, Oscar 5465 was lifted and driven away.

The Memorial already had the fuselage of a Ki-43-II that had been brought to Australia for assessment after the war, and was being restored by a volunteer group in Sydney. The plan was to rebuild a complete aircraft. The government of Papua New

Hayabusa, or Oscar, No. 5465 as recovered in 1984 at Alexishafen, Papua New Guinea. AWM P02821.001

Guinea, after consultation with the National Museum and Art Gallery at Port Moresby, granted export permits for the finds at Alexishafen. The Bishop of Madang was also consulted, as the land was owned by a Catholic mission. It wasn't long before the airframe of 5465, together with the mainplanes of two Ki-43s (numbered 4700 and 6023), two engines and an assortment of components, were steam-cleaned and loaded aboard HMAS *Tarakan* for shipment to Australia. Joining them on the ship were two Douglas Boston bombers, destined to be fully restored by the RAAF.

After their arrival in Australia, one of the first jobs was to try to piece together the history of 5465. To this end, traces of its painted markings were closely examined. On the rear fuselage, the white *senchi hyoshiki* combat band, applied only to front-line service aircraft, was faintly visible. The key to its former unit came from traces of its distinctive tail marking: a yellow chevron, thinly outlined in red. This was the marking of the 63rd *Sentai*, the yellow colour normally identifying the third *chutai* within a *sentai*. Other evidence of the aircraft's past came from its damaged state. The underside of the airframe showed the scraping damage consistent with a heavy landing. The skin was extensively holed all over. Some holes had been punched to aid in fumigation on arrival in Australia, but most were from battle damage. The unmistakable puncture holes from parafrag bomb shrapnel and machine-gun bullets, presumably made during the Allied raids of 1944, peppered the fuselage. Later, a couple of spent American 0.5-in machine-gun cartridge cases were found in the cockpit. One can only speculate about how they got there.

The only Ki-43 units listed as having been actually based at Alexishafen were the 248th *Sentai* and a detachment of the 77th.[53] The presence of what appeared to be a 63rd *Sentai* Oscar there can probably be explained by the underside damage: it would seem that 5465 crash-landed there, presumably after suffering combat damage or mechanical failure.

The remains of the three salvaged Oscars were taken to the Memorial's Duntroon store. After some years, with only the rear fuselage of the Memorial's original Ki-43-II having been worked on, it was decided not to continue with restoration. The Memorial would instead retain the basically complete airframe of 5465, unrestored and preserved as a relic, and exchange the remaining sections. The preservation task involved immersing the components in an electrochemical bath of citric acid and sodium hydroxide added to the water of a small above-ground swimming pool. Over a month-long period, this solution gradually extracted corrosive salts to halt the process of deterioration; then after a week in fresh water, the airframe was covered with a wax coating. It was the first time such a process had been tried on an aircraft. The Memorial's conservation team thanked fellow staff at the Mitchell annexe for their tolerance when the sodium bath 'started getting smelly'.

In its display in Aircraft Hall, the Memorial used the relic state of 5465 to advantage. As well as preserving battle damage, it graphically portrays an aspect of military aviation history that is not often depicted: the effects of a jungle environment on an aircraft abandoned for decades. Hundreds of other Second World War aircraft left in-situ throughout the Pacific are slowly corroding away. More so than a restored

aircraft, visitors can appreciate the toll taken by war, nature and mankind over the decades since this fragile little fighter was the most numerous weapon in the Japanese army's aerial arsenal.

Two Oscars already won

It is somewhat ironic that by the time the Memorial acquired 5465, it had already owned two Oscars. One was the Ki-43-II mentioned previously, sourced from RAAF Base Richmond around 1949, the mainplane of which had been disposed of in a way which the records do not make clear.

The other was an intact Ki-43-I with serial number 750, which had been received in 1949 but sold four years later; in the postwar years, former enemy aircraft were considered to be of little interest or value. Reportedly a veteran of the battles at Guadalcanal and Rabaul with the 11th *Sentai*, it had been found concealed in the jungle several kilometres from Vunakanau airstrip, New Britain, a month after the war ended. Three Japanese airmen were found still working on it. It was shipped to Australia and accepted by the Memorial, but a lack of storage or display space led to its sale for scrap value in 1953. It became widely known while displayed in the hangar of Sid Marshall (at the time, also the owner of the Memorial's Messerschmitt Bf 109) at Bankstown, New South Wales, and later joined the collection of the late Col Pay at Scone, New South Wales. In 1995, restored by the Alpine Fighter Collection in New Zealand, No. 750 returned to the air—albeit only a metre or so off the runway, lest the world's most complete Oscar should come to grief. At the time of writing it is in the Paul Allen collection in Seattle, Washington.

Top left: The Memorial's first *Hayabusa*, No. 750, at Rabaul in September 1945 with the Japanese servicemen who repaired it for despatch to Australia. AWM P00001.340

Above: The engine and rear fuselage of the Oscar in Aircraft Hall in 2000, conserved and displayed in the condition in which they were found in the New Guinea jungle. AWM PAIU2000/216.09

The Ki-43 in context

The Ki-43 made its operational debut when 40 Model 1a examples were sent to China just prior to the Pearl Harbor attack on 7 December 1941. Its appearance over Burma and the Malay peninsula over the following weeks came as a surprise to the Allies. The Japanese navy's A6M Zero had provided their first wake-up call at Pearl Harbor, and now the army, too, revealed itself to possess a modern fighter. Its development since 1937 as a replacement for the slower, fixed-undercarriage Type 97 (Ki-27), and even its first flight in January 1939, had been kept secret. Surprisingly, it was not well accepted at first by its pilots, as it proved less manoeuvrable than the Ki-27, but it had a speed advantage that they grew to like.

Often mistakenly referred to as Zeros in Australian records, Oscars of the 1st, 11th and 77th *Sentai* escorted the convoy which invaded the Malay peninsula on the first day of the Pacific war, and which was bombed by RAAF Hudsons. Over Malaya and Singapore, the 59th and 64th *Sentai* took a heavy toll of the obsolescent Buffalo fighters of 21 and 453 Squadrons RAAF. Later, in 1943, Ki-43-IIs of the 59th defended Timor against RAAF Hudson, Boston and Beaufighter attacks, and were also heavily involved in attacks on northern Australia. On 20 June they escorted Ki-21 Sally[54] bombers attacking Darwin and claimed nine of the defending Spitfires of 1 Fighter Wing RAAF under Group Captain Clive Caldwell, against a loss of one Ki-21 and one Ki-43 and their crewmen.[55] The Australian side of the story was quite different. The wing claimed its most successful encounter of the war: nine bombers and five fighters destroyed, for the loss of two Spitfires and pilots. Two days later, Captain Shigeo Nango led 20 Ki-43s of the 59th *Sentai* back to Darwin on a fighter sweep.

Overall, the Ki-43 was a good but not outstanding fighter. Like the Zero, its failings stemmed from insufficient engine power. To save weight the initial versions carried only two machine-guns and no armour protection for the pilot. While the resultant light weight was its primary asset, these measures made it more susceptible to combat damage and more difficult for its pilots, with such light armament, to shoot down the armoured Allied fighters. At low speed it was a good dogfighter with excellent agility and acceleration, and for this reason Allied pilots were instructed to use their superior speed, diving ability and armament to advantage. Heavier armament and armour plating were introduced with the Model 2 (Ki-43-II), the first major improvement, which entered production in November 1942. To compensate for the added weight and to improve performance, a new supercharged engine driving a three-bladed propeller provided 20 per cent more power. Other changes included a reduced wingspan for improved low-altitude performance, a heightened cockpit canopy, increased underwing bomb capacity, and self-sealing fuel tanks.

For much of the war the *Hayabusa* remained the army's most numerous fighter on every front, and developments up to the cannon-armed Ki-43-IIIb continued until war's end. By then, more advanced types such as the Ki-61 *Hien*, Ki-44 *Shoki* and Ki-84 *Hayate* had replaced the *Hayabusa* in many front-line units and it was largely relegated to suicide missions. However, Oscars were encountered by Australian airmen well into 1945—not only to Australia's north as we have seen, but by RAAF crews of the RAF in Burma and India. There, for example, the Rangoon-based 50th and 64th *Sentai* provided the main opposition to Australian Hurricane and P-47 Thunderbolt pilots during 1944. Overall, Australian airmen came up against the Oscar more frequently than any other Japanese Army fighter, and given its prevalence in New Guinea, possibly as frequently as the much better-known navy Zero.

TIMELINE—NO. 5465

1943	(May) Built as serial no. 465[56]
1944	Damaged and abandoned at Alexishafen, New Guinea
1944	(May) Evaluated with other aircraft by Allied Technical Air Intelligence Unit[57]
1962	Photographed by PNG Museum
1984	Recovered and transported to Canberra; stored at AWM store, Duntroon, ACT
1996	Chemically preserved at AWM Annexe, Mitchell, ACT
2000	Relic rear fuselage and engine displayed in Aircraft Hall

DATA

Type	Ki-43-IIb *Hayabusa* (Army fighter Type 1 Model 2b)
Design firm	Nakajima Hikoki KK, Japan
Manufacturer	Nakajima (city of Ota, Gumma Prefecture)
Role	Single-seat fighter
Used by	Imperial Japanese Army Air Force
No. built	5,178 (Ki-43-II). Ki-43 total 5,919
Type entered service	1941
Identity	465 (coded as 5465)
Powerplant	Nakajima Ha-115 Type 1 14-cylinder radial engine of 1,150 hp
Armament	Two nose-mounted 12.7-mm Type 1 machine-guns Provision for two 250 kg bombs
Wingspan	10.86 m
Length	8.9 m
Max. speed	530 km/h
Range	1,760 km on internal fuel
Max. takeoff weight	2,640 kg

NOTES ON COLOUR SCHEME

When recovered, the aircraft's original paint had largely weathered away, but traces of markings could be made out. The scheme was probably Japanese Army 'Type B' camouflage: bare metal with upper fuselage surfaces sporadically mottled with patches of Army A1 dark green. Red *hinomaru* national insignia in standard six positions, white-outlined except for those underwing. Blue-black anti-glare panels on upper fuselage fore and aft of cockpit. Service markings: yellow-orange strips on wing inner leading edges, and white combat band around rear fuselage. Unit tail marking: yellow arrow or chevron outlined in red. Serial no. 5465 on port side just below tailplane.

Korean War

1950–1953

METEOR A77-368

A77-368

16,000 ft, 16 km south of Anju, western North Korea
EARLY AFTERNOON, 3 NOVEMBER 1951

Twenty-five-year-old Pilot Officer Max 'Bluey' Colebrook of 77 Squadron RAAF knew the limitations of his Gloster Meteor jet fighter in combat with the faster, more nimble Soviet MiG-15. After the introduction of the MiG and the American F-86 Sabre over Korea a year earlier, the Meteor was considered by many to be obsolescent. Some even considered it outdated well before it had joined the war at the end of July 1951.

It did have some useful attributes, including a good initial rate of climb (better, in fact, than the Sabre), comparable service ceiling,[1] a higher thrust-to-weight ratio and four-cannon armament. It had the advantage of two engines, which left at least some power in the event of a 'flameout'. The Meteor was at its optimum height here in the denser air below 25,000 ft, while the Soviet fighters preferred a fight at high altitude where the performance of other aircraft diminished. However, at any height the Meteor could not turn with or keep up with the lighter MiG with its swept-back wing design— an innovation introduced on German jets during the Second World War to reduce

> *All I want for Christmas is my wings swept back.*
> *77 Squadron song*

At Kunsan, South Korea, in June 1954, pilots of 77 Squadron after a post-armistice operation. Left to right: Flight Lieutenant Keith Williamson RAF, Mike Ridgeway, and Sergeant Keith Cottee. AWM JK1025

Ivor Hele, *Return of the Meteor jets, Kimpo, Korea* (1953, oil on hardboard, 78.5 x 122 cm, AWM ART40304)

aerodynamic drag and improve control at speeds approaching that of sound.[2] Above about Mach 0.75 (three-quarters of the speed of sound) the forces on the Meteor's control surfaces, particularly the ailerons, increased dramatically. But from a tactical point of view, the Meteor's biggest disadvantage was that the pilots of 77 Squadron had not been properly trained in air-to-air combat since converting from piston-engined Mustangs. At most, their jet training had included just two air combat exercises.

Max Colebrook may have had some of these thoughts as he sat in the cockpit of Meteor A77-368, call sign 'Dog Four' in a formation of 16 Meteors out on a fighter sweep. Suddenly 40 MiGs appeared 10,000 ft above, and within seconds the first two came down for a rear attack. With the right tactics, at this lower height the Meteor could hold its own. Turn radius was all-important: those Meteors which did not turn tightly enough towards the attackers were immediately exposed to attack from above. In the melee, some pilots found themselves in a position to fire on the MiGs, but they could not close in on the faster Soviet fighters. Flight Sergeants Ernest Armit and Douglas Robertson had their aircraft badly damaged by the MiGs' powerful 37-mm cannon, and had to return to base.

The MiGs attacked in pairs. Dog Section was at the mercy of three pairs, and Colebrook called out 'Break!' over the radio to his four pilots as the first pair closed to 1,500 m. Now near Kunu-ri, he managed to haul his Meteor around in time to fire at one MiG from 300 m. No result. He barrel-rolled around them and fired long bursts at the other from 400 m. Its starboard wing started trailing smoke before it climbed to the north, out of range. With each subsequent pass of the enemy the Meteor pilots tried to turn into them, but they were too fast.

◄ ►

The Memorial's Meteor displayed in ANZAC Hall in 2001. Its forward section was incorporated into the *Conflicts 1945 to today* galleries in 2007. 'Rosemary' (painted beside the cockpit) is believed to have been the fiancé of Sergeant Bob Strawbridge DFM, who flew A77-368 in Korea before being killed in a mid-air collision off the coast of Williamtown, NSW, in 1953. AWM RELAWM31969

The scrap was soon over and all the Meteors returned to base at Kimpo in South Korea, though some were damaged, including Robertson's, which had a fire in a wheel well and belly-landed in with its hydraulics out. Luckily, the MiG pilots on this occasion appeared to have been poorly trained.[3] A few months later, on 13 April 1952, Max Colebrook went missing in another Meteor after being hit during a ground attack, his external fuel tank set aflame. Of the 101 missions he had tallied up in Korea, 39 were in A77-368. He was awarded the Distinguished Flying Medal and the US Air Medal. Another pilot of A77-368 to be decorated was Sergeant Ron Gilmour,[4] who flew it in June 1953 while leading a successful rocket strike on a radio transmitting station in North Korea, for which he was Mentioned in Despatches. A third frequent pilot of the aircraft was Pilot Officer Raymond Fox DFC and US Air Medal.

During its first few months in action with the Meteor, 77 Squadron had accounted well for itself, considering its mediocre aircraft. The Australians had been shocked by the MiG's agility, and its speed advantage of over 100 km/h, during their first major air-to-air combat on 29 August 1951, in which eight Meteors had fought off about 40 enemy jets for the loss of one of their own. A fight on 1 December, in which A77-368 flew as an airborne relay aircraft, had mixed results. Over Pyongyang a dozen Meteors were outnumbered more than four to one by MiGs; the Australian pilots made their first two victory claims, but lost three Meteors and their pilots (two of whom survived and were captured). The losses were instrumental in the decision to re-assign the squadron from fighter sweeps to airfield defence and ground attack, roles in which they were less likely to encounter the high-flying MiGs. It was the latter role in which 77 Squadron had excelled with the Mustang, and in which it was to excel again. Nevertheless, from May 1952 the Meteors began escorting fighter-bombers as well, and were once again thrown into air-to-air combat.

A77-368 finished the Korean War having flown 485 missions, covering all types of operations: patrols, escort for American B-26 and B-29 bombers, fighter sweeps, searches, and rocket strikes on all kinds of ground targets. MiG-15s were encountered on several of these flights. The squadron soldiered on with the 'Meatbox' until 1956, when it converted to Australian-built Sabres, finally getting its swept-back wings. The Meteors replaced Vampires in two of the RAAF's Citizen Air Force (CAF) squadrons, which kept them in the air a few years longer. A77-368 spent its last two years of service with one of these, 22 (City of Sydney) Squadron, its final claim to fame coming in 1959 when Air Vice Marshal Sir Valston Hancock CB CBE DFC (Chief of Air Staff from 1961 to 1965) made his first Meteor F.8 flight in it. The following year the CAF squadrons were re-organised into a non-flying role as auxiliary squadrons, and the Meteor was phased out of RAAF service.

The Meteor in context

The only Allied jet aircraft to see service during the Second World War, the Meteor began defending Britain against German V-1 flying bombs in July 1944. As one of a handful of aircraft types able to keep up with a V-1 at its low flying altitude, the jet accounted for 14 of these weapons before war's end.[5] The Allies' sole wartime jet unit, 616 Squadron RAF, moved its Meteor Mk Is and IIIs to Belgium and Holland during 1945 for ground attack and reconnaissance. In 1946 a Meteor F.4[6] broke the world record with a speed of 991 km/h; this was the version trialled by the RAAF at Darwin that year, although the first jet to join RAAF squadrons was the de Havilland Vampire three years later.

The Memorial's Meteor cockpit in 2008. AWM RELAWM31969.001.001

When China entered the Korean War in November 1950, United Nations forces were jolted from a position of near victory to retreat. That month, too, the MiG-15 made its appearance. Concerns were raised about how the piston-engined Mustangs of 77 Squadron would fare in an encounter with the enemy jet. Despite the Mustang's success in the ground attack role, the new jet threat made a replacement necessary. Sabres would not be forthcoming; the RAAF had requested them in 1950, but the Americans were reluctant to release any and the pro-British Menzies government did not press the point. The Australian-built Avon Sabre, which was superior in terms of engine and armament to the American F-86, would not come into service for another three years.

The only viable and available jet was the Meteor, which had by then evolved into its F.8 variant. With a redesigned tail and uprated Rolls-Royce Derwent engines, the F.8 had first flown in 1948 and entered British service in mid-1950. It was still Britain's most advanced fighter in production when, early the following year, the RAAF's first examples were shipped from Britain direct to 77 Squadron in Japan. Conversion training began there in April. After moving to the large and busy US base at Kimpo in South Korea, the squadron flew the RAAF's first jet operation on 29 July 1951 with a fighter sweep along the Yalu River, flying top cover for American Sabres.

Australians at Kimpo, South Korea, watch 77 Squadron Meteors heading out on an operation in April 1952. AWM JK0612

The squadron, in fact, shared Kimpo with Sabres, and both Australians and Americans had the extremes of the Korean weather to contend with. The hot, humid summers brought with them not only hazy conditions and uncomfortable working conditions for air and ground crews alike; there were also mechanical problems with the aircraft, which needed longer take-off runs owing to the thinner air, and suffered from molten bitumen covering their undersides. Dust could change to mud in minutes under a torrential downpour. The severe winters brought even more challenges, such as trying to keep the bitumen runway and pierced-steel plank (PSP) taxiways free of ice and snow. For crews on standby, waiting for a scramble, the freezing conditions were difficult to bear. While the pilot huddled in the cockpit, a ground crewmen might shelter from the wind in an engine nacelle.[7]

The squadron's commanding officer at the time of its jet conversion, Squadron Leader Dick Cresswell DFC, believed the Meteor to be up to the task of combating MiGs. His successor, Wing Commander Gordon Steege DSO DFC, disagreed, believing that the MiG had proven to be 'vastly superior'.[8] An impartial measure might put the Meteor somewhere between these two assessments. A lot depended on the relative skill and experience of the opposing pilots, and on the circumstances. Despite its design being years behind the MiG, the Meteor could, below 25,000 ft where it was more manoeuvrable, hold its own in combat.

The squadron's Meteors flew 15,000 sorties in Korea. Like the Mustangs they replaced, they excelled in the ground attack role, for which they were fitted with up to eight underwing 60-lb rockets. Most of the 3,700 buildings, 1,500 vehicles (including 150 in one day in March 1953), 16 bridges, 20 locomotives and 65 railway carriages destroyed by the squadron were achieved during its Meteor period. The majority of the 38 men from the squadron who were killed and the seven pilots who were captured were also flying Meteors.[9] For 'exceptionally meritorious service and heroism' in Korea, 77 Squadron received a Korean Presidential Unit Citation, and dozens of awards to individual pilots were made.

In its wider RAAF service, between 1951 and 1960 nearly a hundred Meteors served with five squadrons. About 60 more RAF Meteors were converted into radio controlled target drones for weapons trials at Woomera, South Australia. The aircraft's decade-long period of Australian service was relatively short, but it holds a place in history as the RAAF's first jet aircraft to go to war.

TIMELINE—A77-368

1951	(Feb) Delivered ex-UK to 77 Squadron RAAF, Japan aboard HMS *Warrior*. Operated in Korean War until truce signed in July 1953
1955	To 78 Wing, RAAF Williamtown, NSW
1958	To 22 (City of Sydney) Squadron, RAAF Richmond, NSW
1960	Transferred to AWM and stored at Duntroon, ACT
1982–83	Restored to approximate Korean War configuration and markings by RAAF apprentices at Wagga Wagga, NSW
2001	First display at the AWM (ANZAC Hall)
2007	Nose section displayed in *Conflicts 1945 to today* galleries

DATA

Type	Meteor F.8
Design firm	Gloster, UK
Manufacturer	Gloster, UK
Role	Single-seat fighter/ground attack aircraft
No. built	1,522 (Meteor total 3,550)
Type entered RAAF service	1951
Identity	A77-368 (RAAF) WA952 (UK)
Powerplant	Two Rolls-Royce Derwent Mk.8 centrifugal-flow turbojets, each of 3,600-lb static thrust
Armament	Four 20-mm Hispano cannon Up to eight 60-lb rockets under each wing
Wingspan	11.33 m
Length	13.59 m
Max. speed	962 km/h or Mach 0.81 at 30,000 ft
Range	1,234 km
Max. take-off weight	8,664 kg

NOTES ON COLOUR SCHEME

Overall silver. Red/white/blue roundels in six positions. Red/white/blue fin flashes. Serial number in black on rear fuselage sides. Name 'Rosemary' in red on port side of cockpit.

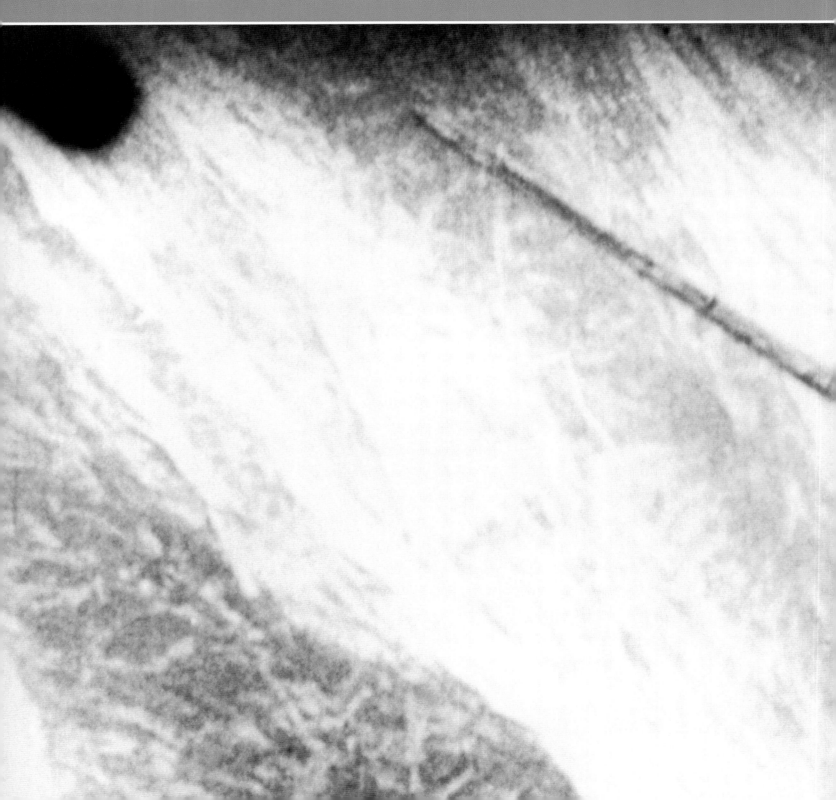

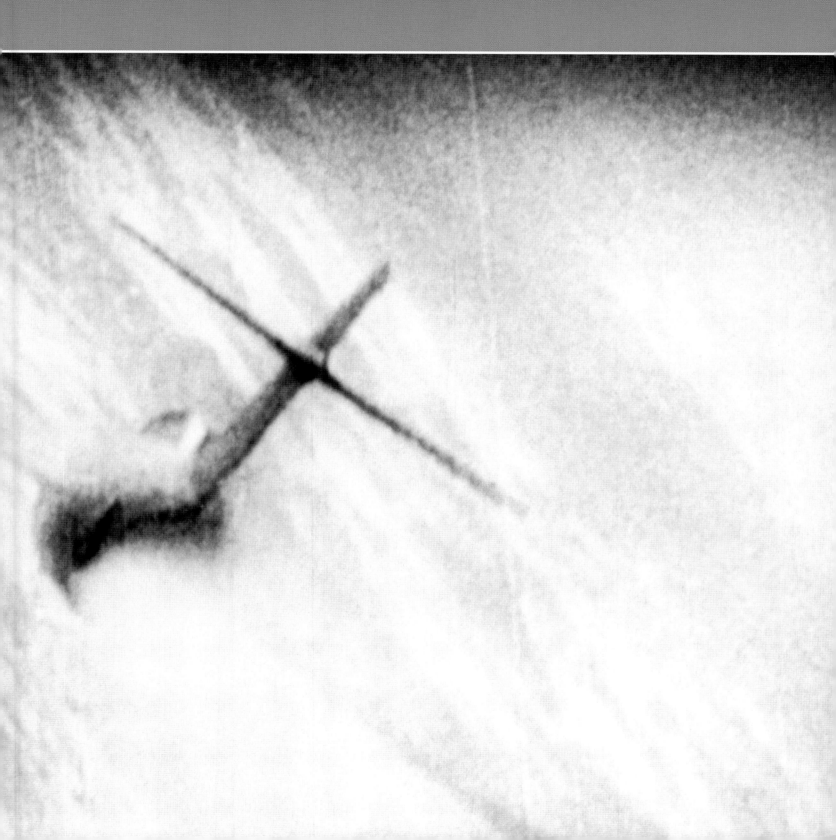

40,000 ft over Chongju area, North Korea
1140 HOURS, 29 AUGUST 1951

Kapitan Lev (or 'lion') Shchukin of the Russian 303rd Fighter Air Division had shot down three aircraft over Korea—an F-51 Mustang, an F-80 Shooting Star and an F-86 Sabre—and was now homing in on what would surely be an easy fourth. Below were two flights of four Meteor jets of 77 Squadron RAAF, which had moved to Korea the previous October and adopted the Korean temple lion for its badge. The Second World War-vintage Meteor and the modern MiG-15 had not yet seriously clashed; now, lion was about to meet lion squadron.

Shchukin and his five companions had a 5,000-ft height advantage. The lead Australian pilot, Squadron Leader 'Dick' Wilson in Meteor A77-616, turned left and

> *To put [the Meteor] into air-to-air operations against the MiG in Korea was just asking for an entire squadron to get knocked off.*
>
> *Wing Commander Gordon Steege DSO DFC*
> *Commanding Officer, 77 Squadron RAAF*

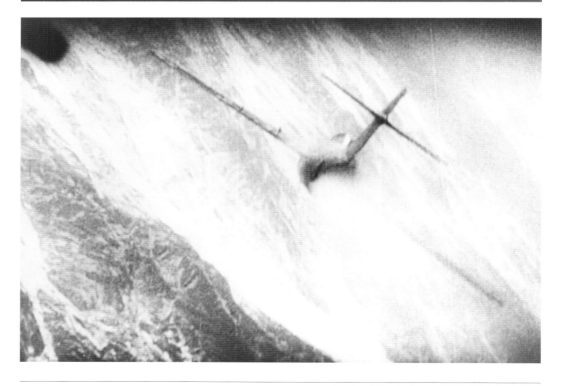

Still shot from the gun cine-camera of an American F-86 Sabre chasing a MiG-15 over Korea, c. 1953. AWM P02861.001

dived to follow a pair of decoy MiGs below. In the process he lost his wingman, who had to drop out after losing control in a spin. As Wilson fired, Shchukin came down for a head-on attack from the sun and his cannon rounds struck the aircraft, blasting a hole in one wing, putting an aileron out of action and holing the main fuel tank. Shchukin and his wingman, *Starshii Leytenant* Asanovski, then glanced behind to see two more Meteors giving chase. Flight Lieutenant Thomas and Flying Officer Blight followed the MiGs until the Russians throttled forward and climbed, leaving them far behind.

Although losing fuel, Wilson's Meteor was not critically damaged. However, with some 30 MiGs in the air, the Australian airmen's troubles were not yet over. *Kapitan* Babonin and *Starshii Leytenant* Svinititski, together with two other Russians, homed in on the second Meteor flight from behind and above. The flight broke left, but its number four, Warrant Officer Ron Guthrie in Meteor A77-721, lagged 50 m behind the others. Making his turn, he spotted the MiGs just as he was hit.

Before there was time to react a MiG came into Guthrie's sights, the red star of its national insignia clearly visible against a bare aluminium fuselage. He turned right and let off a long burst from his four 20-mm cannon. Simultaneously his Meteor shuddered as it was hit again. Watching pieces fly off the MiG, he thought he had been struck by the wreckage as the Russian jet rolled and dived; it was, in fact, cannon strikes from Babonin some 300 m behind. The Meteor flick-rolled uncontrollably and went nose down. Guthrie deployed his dive brakes, but his speed still built up. At a speed of Mach 0.84, the Meteor trailing smoke and shuddering as the transonic shockwave built up, he jettisoned his canopy and ejected at 38,000 ft.

For nearly half an hour Guthrie descended, the final minutes made harrowing by shots being fired at him from the ground. On landing, he came face to face with soldiers of the North Korean Home Guard. Soon his mother would be told that her son was missing, and then endure several months of uncertainty before finally receiving word that he was still alive, a prisoner of war.

◄   ►

While the rest of 77 Squadron RAAF escorted B-29 bombers through heavy flak over the railway yards at Maenjong Dong, the eight Meteors over Chongju had blooded the squadron with the RAAF's first combat in jets. Considering the potential outcome, they had not fared badly. The squadron had first encountered MiG-15s four days earlier, when shots were exchanged without result; but the Russian fighter had been active against US aircraft over Korea for ten months.

US reconnaissance photos had revealed MiGs on airfields in Antung province, Manchuria, and in North Korea, when the jet menace had first appeared in the air on 1 November 1950. It had single-handedly stolen United Nations supremacy in the air war, and forced an urgent response from the US Air Force, which was still flying Second World War designs. The next month the US introduced to Korea the F-86 Sabre, a roughly equivalent performer at low altitudes but a poorer climber and inferior at the heights at which the MiG preferred to operate. Australia's more delayed response was to replace 77 Squadron's piston-engined Mustangs with Meteors from Britain.

In 'MiG Alley', a region in the north-west of North Korea bordering China along the Yalu River, Sabre pilots were soon regularly encountering MiG-15s. From Antung the Russian and Chinese fighters would cross the border into North Korea, and soon that nation's air force had its own MiG units and trained pilots. Flying at up to 50,000 ft where they were in their element, they used their height advantage to dive on the enemy. The Meteor, meanwhile, struggled to get to 40,000 ft. The MiG took ten minutes less than the Meteor to climb to that height, was more manoeuvrable, and could fly over 100 km/h faster. On the other side of the coin, below 25,000 ft the Meteor was a good performer, out-turning and out-climbing the Sabre, though not the MiG. Also, the MiG did have weaknesses. For example, its slow-firing main 37-mm cannon was intended for downing bombers rather than fighters, making hits more difficult to obtain; and its pilots wore no g-suit until 1952 and were thus liable to black out in tight turns.

Dogfighting over Korea demanded all the tactics of Second World War combat, but at twice the speed. Quick thinking and a knowledge of the enemy's tactics were paramount. When MiGs and Sabres first met, it was evident that the former was marginally superior in climb rate, ceiling, and turn radius at high altitudes. US pilots made up for this with experience, and in statistical terms did better (MiGs shot down 102 Sabres, while Sabres shot down 379 MiGs[10]); but 77 Squadron RAAF entered combat with both an older aircraft and almost no training in air-to-air jet combat tactics. Worse, the Meteors were often outnumbered, sometimes dramatically. Thus, the best weapon at the Australian pilot's disposal was his piloting skills.

Following the 29 August encounter, a marked change in communist air tactics became evident. Pilot discipline in particular improved, and MiG formations grew in size. On 1 December, 14 Meteors were attacked by more than 40 MiGs in the Sunchon area. Considering their numerical disadvantage the RAAF pilots acquitted themselves well, claiming two MiGs shot down. In the confusion of battle the Russians claimed between nine and 16 Meteors; in fact, only three failed to return from the mission, but even this loss was considered unsustainable. The following day, 77 Squadron was taken off fighter sweep duties over North Korea and transferred to the supposedly safer role of ground attack and airfield defence, away from MiG Alley. Nevertheless, occasional encounters continued until 1953.

Many in 77 Squadron believed that the Meteors were withdrawn from air-to-air combat too hastily. Although the three losses on 1 December 1951 were significant, only two other Meteors were shot down by MiGs during the war. Against these, three MiGs were confirmed (with another two or three unconfirmed) shot down by Meteors, putting the two roughly on par with regard to air-to-air losses. Considering their disadvantages, the RAAF pilots did remarkably well.

77 Squadron over Korea: MiGs vs Meteors

MiG-15s claimed destroyed by Meteor pilots

1 Dec 1951	FO Bruce Gogerly DFC
1 Dec 1951	Squadron claim (probable)
4 May 1952	PO John Surman (probable)
8 May 1952	PO Bill Simmonds
27 Mar 1953	Sgt George Hale

Meteor pilots shot down by MiG-15s

Date	Meteor pilot	MiG-15 pilot
29 Aug 1951	WO Ron Guthrie (prisoner)	*Kapitan* Babonin and Shchukin shared (303rd IAD)
1 Dec 1951	Sgt Bruce Thomson (prisoner)	Serafim P. Subbotin (324th IAD)
1 Dec 1951	Sgt Ernest Armit (killed)	Sergei F. Vishnyakov (324th IAD)
1 Dec 1951	Sgt Vance Drummond (prisoner)	Sergei M. Kramarenko (324th IAD)

Data from Wilson, *Lion over Korea*, p. 196
In addition, nine Meteors and five MiGs were damaged in combat.

Russian MiG pilots who damaged Meteors

5 Sept 1951	Grigorii U. Ohay (2) (303rd IAD)
26 Sept 1951	Nikolai V. Sutyagin (303rd IAD)

Note: All these Soviet pilots were awarded the Hero of the Soviet Union medal. Overall, Soviet pilots claimed 28 Meteors downed, and Chinese and North Korean pilots seven. For many years, the Russian government denied involvement in the Korean War.

Data from www.acepilots.com/russian, www.wio.ru/korea and
www.acig.org/artman/publish/article_314.shtml

IAD = Fighter Air Division

The MiG-15 in context

During the Korean War, the MiG-15*bis* (*bis* meaning second in Latin) was the world's most potent high-altitude interceptor. As the sole Russian aircraft in the Memorial's collection, it offers an insight into the murky, oft-overlooked but hugely diverse subject of Soviet military aviation.

During the Second World War, Russia's Mikoyan-Gurevich, Yakovlev and Lavochkin design bureaus had already produced some of the world's best fighter aircraft. The first products of Mikoyan-Gurevich, the MiG-1 and MiG-3 piston-engined high-altitude interceptors, saw some success following the German invasion of Russia in 1941. After the war, with access to German jet fighter technology, Russia like America and Britain quickly moved on from piston-engined fighter design.

In 1946 the MiG-9 fighter, powered by a pair of locally-built German jet engines, won its designers the Stalin Prize. That year, in a gesture to improve diplomatic relations, Britain agreed to a Russian request for turbojet engines. It sent a consignment

The Memorial's MiG-15 fuselage in Aircraft Hall in 2007, showing the prominent nose air intake. AWM PAIU2007/021.05

of examples of the Derwent, the Meteor's powerplant, and the Nene, a larger and more powerful development of it. This proved to be a trump card for Russia, whose designers had been struggling to develop a powerful turbojet. Both engines were immediately reverse-engineered and put into unlicensed production as the Klimov RD-500 and RD-45, respectively. The RD-500 powered various Lavochkin and Yakovlev aircraft, while the RD-45 (later improved as the VK-1 with 20 per cent more power) went into the MiG-15. Thus, ironically, it was a development of the Meteor's engines that would power its enemy in Korea.

The MiG-15 began life as the I-310, first flown in December 1947, and went into production the following year. Intended as a bomber interceptor, it was trialled against the Soviet copy of the American B-29 Superfortress. Over Korea, it caused heavy enough losses to B-29 bomber formations that the American daylight raids were switched to night. Although theoretically capable of supersonic flight, its tailplane (which had elevators rather than an all-moving design) limited it to subsonic speed. The improved MiG-15*bis*, with the VK-1 engine and more sophisticated avionics, reached Soviet and Chinese service in 1950. It is reported that about 400 Russian MiG-15s, and another 400 serving with the Chinese and North Korean air forces, flew over Korea. The Memorial's example, although its service history is unknown, is of the same type and production batch as aircraft known to have flown in that conflict.

The aircraft's design reflects its intended role as a high-altitude interceptor. Primary factors included simplicity and light weight; hence there was little armour protection, no power assistance for the controls (until the MiG-15*bis*/SD appeared with hydraulic ailerons), no radar and no redundancy in its systems. It did have a number of innovations, however, which had appeared on German aircraft during the Second World War: a pressurised cockpit, an ejection seat and, perhaps most importantly, the swept-back wings which were a high-speed design feature developed by Germany for its jets. This feature alone made the MiG a more aerodynamically advanced aircraft than the Meteor. Combining such features with simplicity of manufacture was the key to its success.

Although superseded in Russian service by the MiG-17 after the Korean War, the MiG-15 remained the standard interceptor in service with Warsaw Pact nations and others for many more years. Chinese communist MiG-15s flew against Chinese nationalist aircraft, and in the Middle East, Arab nations flew them during the 1956 Suez Crisis and the 1967 Six Days War. In all, it has been flown by the air forces of over 40 countries. In addition to the USSR, China, Czechoslovakia and Poland licence-built the aircraft and its two-seat trainer version.

TIMELINE—MIG-15BIS NO. 2458

c. 1951	Built in USSR
1992	Discovered to be available in Russia
1993	Acquired by the AWM
1999	Forward fuselage displayed in Aircraft Hall
2000	Tail section displayed in *Out in the cold—Australia's involvement in the Korean War* temporary exhibition

DATA

Type	MiG-15*bis* (Type SD). NATO codename 'Fagot B'
Design firm	Mikoyan-Gurevich
Manufacturer	Mikoyan-Gurevich
Role	Single-seat interceptor fighter
No. built	12,000 (Russian-built, all subtypes)
Type entered service	1948 (MiG-15*bis* 1950)
Identity	No. 2458
Powerplant	Klimov VK-1 turbojet of 5,950-lb static thrust
Armament	37-mm N-37 cannon and two 23-mm NR-23 cannon
Wingspan	9.6 m
Length	11.36 m
Max. speed	1.075 km/h (Mach 0.9)
Range	1,860 km
Max. take-off weight	5,700 kg

NOTES ON COLOUR SCHEME

Overall bare aluminium with Soviet five-pointed red star in standard positions on fuselage sides and wings.

SEA FURY TF925 ('VX730')

Kojo region, east coast of North Korea
0630–0900 HOURS, 11 OCTOBER 1951

In perfect weather and against no opposition, ten Hawker Sea Fury FB.11 fighter-bombers from HMAS *Sydney*'s Carrier Air Group came in for an attack on ground installations and defences. Each aircraft was armed with eight 60-lb rockets and four 20-mm cannon, while another two Combat Air Patrol (CAP) aircraft covered them. Seven targeted a military encampment and destroyed several buildings, causing smoke that towered 1,500 m into the air. On each pass, the pilots looked for a 155-mm gun and a T-34 tank which had been reported in the area. There was no sign of them, but instead they found and strafed two new, unoccupied defensive positions. The remaining three rocket-armed Sea Furies air-spotted for a shell bombardment by the USS *New Jersey*, USS *Hansom* and HMS *Belfast*, reporting by radio the accuracy of their shell

> ## One of the finest piston-engined fighters ever built.
> Commodore Norman Lee, RAN

Ray Honisett, *HMAS* Sydney *in Korean waters* (1951–52, oil on canvas, 121.9 x 182.9 cm, AWM ART28077)

Sea Furies and Fireflies on the flight deck as HMAS *Sydney* rides out Typhoon Ruth, 14 October 1951. One aircraft was lost overboard, and others damaged. AWM 044819

strikes and launching rockets. *New Jersey*'s massive 16-in shells destroyed another ten houses.[11]

The attack over, the pilots returned to their aircraft carrier, HMAS *Sydney*. The carrier was sailing with Task Group 95.1, and was now a week into its first patrol of the Korean War. By sunset, *Sydney* would launch another six strike missions to the same region. On this one day 93 sorties were flown by mostly rocket-armed Sea Furies and dive-bombing Fairey Fireflies—a record number for a light fleet carrier. Together with the naval shelling, the attacks caused widespread destruction in the villages of Chonchon, Tongthow, Korim-ni and others. In the last mission of the day to Kojo, the enemy seemed to be expecting an invasion. Hundreds of troops were in the process of setting up stores dumps and digging trenches, when a dozen Sea Furies made repeated attacks that killed or wounded at least 200.

Three days later, *Sydney* itself was subjected to an attack. It came not from the North Koreans but from another great enemy on the Korean peninsula, the weather. On the night of 14 October, mother nature provided a particularly ferocious example of the namesake of the Sea Fury's antecedent, the Typhoon. For over seven hours, Typhoon Ruth lashed the ship's deck, sweeping a Firefly overboard and damaging others while *Sydney* listed alarmingly in the mountainous seas.

◄ ►

Although Australians in the Royal Navy's Fleet Air Arm (FAA) had flown from British aircraft carriers during the Second World War, it was only in 1947 that the

RAN committed itself to creating its own FAA. Accordingly, it received its first aircraft squadrons in the UK in August 1948. Based at Royal Naval Air Station Eglinton in Northern Ireland, 805 Squadron RAN equipped with what proved to be Britain's last piston-engined fighter, the powerful Sea Fury. Before RAN purchases were available, Sea Furies from the Royal Navy were issued to the new unit. The aircraft carrier to bring them to Australia, ordered in 1947, was the 15,000-t *Majestic* Class light fleet carrier HMAS *Sydney*, which had been laid down in 1943 as HMS *Terrible*. In June 1949 it arrived in Sydney carrying 805 Squadron with 27 Sea Furies, and 816 Squadron with 26 Fireflies aboard. The following year, *Sydney* returned to the UK and picked up 808 and 817 Squadrons with more of the same aircraft.

The *Sydney* was not only Australia's first aircraft carrier, but also the first carrier of a dominion nation to go to war. In the course of seven patrols over four months between October 1951 and January 1952, three squadrons flew 2,366 sorties and lost eight Sea Furies, three Fireflies and three Sea Fury pilots killed (Lieutenant Keith Clarkson DFM on 5 November, Sub-Lieutenant Richard Sinclair on 7 December and Sub-Lieutenant Ronald Coleman on 2 January). Their targets included anything that formed part of the enemy's war effort, particularly transport infrastructure and armaments: troops, vehicles, buildings, artillery, bridges, oxcarts, junks and sampans, stores and fuel dumps. Fitted with aerial cameras, they photographed the targets for assessment by intelligence staff. Close army support missions involved strafing enemy troops, guns and vehicles combating Commonwealth and American units.

Flying low, the aircraft often attracted anti-aircraft or small arms fire and many were hit. Also of concern was the MiG-15 jet, which could in theory easily out-perform the piston-engined fighter. Although no Australian Sea Fury combats with MiGs are recorded, one combat involving 802 Squadron, Royal Navy, in August 1952 ended in the Sea Fury's favour. Aircraft from HMS *Ocean* were returning from a mission to the Pyongyang area when they tangled with eight MiGs. By skilfully utilising the Sea Fury's advantage, its smaller turn radius, they destroyed one of the jets and damaged two more, without loss to themselves.

Flying from an aircraft carrier

Although unassisted take-offs were possible, HMAS *Sydney* was equipped with a hydraulic catapult for launching its aircraft in the short length of the flight deck. Aside from the violent kick of acceleration, take-offs were relatively straightforward.

Not so landings. Even in good conditions, successfully touching down on the deck of *Sydney*, a small, moving target in the vast ocean, required intense concentration, skilful judgment and quick reactions. Operational hazards added stress to the task: the ship's deck might be pitching in rough sea; fog might reduce visibility, and the aircraft or pilot might have been hit by enemy fire. For assistance a signalman, or 'batman' on the deck visually instructed him with hand bats on how to correct his landing approach. On 'short finals', much of the pilot's view of the deck disappeared beneath the Sea Fury's nose; the trick was to keep the batman in view while controlling speed, angle of descent and rate of turn. The batman signalled for the throttle to be cut; the pilot lowered the nose, and the aim was then for the aircraft's tail hook to catch one of the arrester wires stretched across the deck. Anything other than a three-point landing could result in a bounce and, possibly, a missed hook. In that case, the aircraft's next contact was with steel netting barriers.

With a dozen or more aircraft returning from an operation, the pilot had to keep strictly to the agreed landing procedure and circuit height of 400 ft in order to maintain the correct intervals between landings. A 'wave-off' by the batsman required immediate full power on the throttle so that a go-around could be made for another attempt.

Being a naval aircraft, the Sea Fury incorporated standard design features for carrier operations. Strong undercarriage for withstanding the force of landing (sometimes described, tongue-in-cheek, as a controlled crash) was one. Another was hydraulically folding wings to facilitate economical use of the limited stowage space.

The task of presenting the Memorial's Sea Fury to the public was an interesting case study in museum practice. Its identity, and therefore its history, have been confused by changes in serial number and amalgamations of components during its naval career. Official records have been of little use in cataloguing these changes, as the records are incomplete and at times contradictory. The major evidence, therefore, comes from the aircraft itself. Careful examination of the paintwork has shown that all three sections of its fuselage and its outer wings, at least, originate from Sea Fury TF925. Secondly, the serial VW232 has been painted on the rear fuselage, and applied a second time, indicating that the aircraft was repainted while it carried this second identity. Finally, the serial VX730 appears on the uppermost paint layer. These three serials represent three distinct Sea Furies, but it appears that the latter two numbers were appropriated. Briefly, the histories of each of the aircraft are as follows.[12]

TF925 started life as an F.X interceptor. It was delivered in the first production batch to the first Sea Fury unit, 807 Squadron, Royal Navy FAA, before transferring to 805 Squadron with its first Sea Furies. On 2 February 1949 it was damaged in a hard landing at Eglinton, and sent to Hawker for repairs. In the process, Hawker was instructed to convert it to FB.11 fighter-bomber standard, as the F.X interceptors were being replaced in favour of the ground attack variant. It received underwing bomb mounting points, updated radio equipment, and provision for Rocket Assisted Take Off (RATO) packs. It was sent to Australia as a ground training airframe aboard *Sydney*. It was re-serialled as VW232, perhaps because parts from that aircraft were combined with it (see page 270). Naval records, however, simply list TF925 as being authorised for reducing to spare parts in November 1949.

VW232 also served with 805 Squadron. Its service was broken by a four-month period with 802 Squadron (which had been the first unit to get the FB.11) from September 1948, flying from the aircraft carrier HMS *Vengeance*. On 24 February 1949 it was being flown by the senior pilot with 805 Squadron, Lieutenant Commander C.J. Cunningham, on a gunnery exercise over Moray Firth in north-east Scotland when it was hit by cannon fire from the number two Sea Fury (the patch over a bullet hole can still be seen near the wing radiator). Cunningham landed at Lossiemouth, but the damage must have been extensive; the aircraft was considered a write-off and did not fly again, instead being relegated to the status of a ground instructional airframe. The RAN purchased it in that capacity, and it arrived in Sydney aboard *Sydney* in June 1949. After arrival at the FAA base at Nowra, New South Wales, VW232 was authorised for conversion to spares.

VX730 arrived with *Sydney*'s second load of aircraft (Carrier Air Group 21) in December 1950, and served with both of *Sydney*'s Sea Fury squadrons, 805 and 808, including operations during the Korean War. In December 1951, in fact, it had battle damage repairs made at Iwakuni, Japan. Meanwhile VW232 had not, in fact, been converted to spares but survived intact, and a photograph shows it at Nowra in July 1953. The connection with VW232 comes in 1957. In June that year, VX730 made a forced landing on Currarong Beach on the New South Wales south coast, and was earmarked for the Department of Education as a ground training aid. Instead it was cut up for scrap by contractors. This appears to have been done in error, because VW232, which according to naval records had ceased to exist, was saved from the wreckers and given

VX730's serial number. The new VX730 was duly sold to Sydney Technical College in 1959 as a training aid for airframe apprentices, who practised their art by patching its aluminium skin.

Adding an element of intrigue, during restoration work in preparation for the display of the Memorial's Sea Fury in Aircraft Hall, faint traces of some 21 mission markings were found below the cockpit canopy. The markings may be spurious, part of an earlier attempt to dress up the aircraft in its VX730 identity; or they could indicate that the centre fuselage section does in fact come from another Sea Fury, identity unknown, which saw active service during the Korean War.

Although TF925 did not serve in Korea, some pilots who did serve in that conflict would earlier have trained and flown exercises in this aircraft. Also, it has been speculated that part of the original war veteran VX730 may now make it up. In any case, its display in Aircraft Hall, on a simulated section of *Sydney*'s flight deck, commemorates the service of those aboard Australia's only aircraft carrier to serve during hostilities.

The Sea Fury in context

Hawker's Typhoon and Tempest saw extensive Second World War service; both were designed by Sydney Camm, who had earlier designed the Hurricane. The Typhoon of 1941 made its name in the ground attack role, the Tempest of 1944 in defending Britain against V-1 flying bombs. The Tempest Mk II had been fitted with an 18-cylinder Bristol Centaurus radial engine, which gave a slight improvement in performance, and eventually better reliability, than the inline-engined variant. It was this engine which powered its offshoot, the Fury, designed in 1942 as a lighter version of the Tempest Mk II (although it actually evolved to be heavier). As it turned out, the impetus for the project came when Britain was presented with a German Focke-Wulf Fw 190A, after its pilot mistakenly landed at an RAF airfield. Changes to the Tempest included a fully monocoque fuselage and a higher cockpit for slightly improved visibility, and reduced-span wings. One of the prototypes was adapted for operation from an aircraft carrier with the addition of an arrester hook, and called the Sea Fury. It first flew in February 1945 and later gained a larger tail and five-bladed propeller to take advantage of the power of the Centaurus engine. Initially, equal numbers of the land-based and carrier-equipped variants were ordered for the RAF and Royal Navy, respectively, but the air force was more interested in jets and cancelled its order.

As it made its maiden flight only six months before the end of the Second World War, the Sea Fury came too late to see action during that conflict. The first production variant was the F.X interceptor of 1946. However, the Royal Navy decided early on that it wanted a ground attack aircraft, and that the Supermarine Seafire, a navalised Spitfire, would suffice as its fighter. By 1949, the Sea Fury F.X was largely replaced by

Cockpit of the Memorial's Sea Fury.
AWM PAIU2001/322.12

the FB.11[13] fighter-bomber, which was equipped for carrying bombs and rockets. During the Korean War, FB.11s flew in the fighter-bomber and CAP roles from the British carriers HMS *Glory*, *Ocean* and *Theseus*, as well as *Sydney*. The two RAN units to use them in action were 805 and 808 Squadrons; in addition, 850 Squadron went with the *Sydney* to Korea for a few months after the war in a peacekeeping role to help monitor the armistice. The Sea Fury was retired from RAN service in 1958 to make way for the de Havilland Sea Venom jet. However, the war service of *Sydney* was not yet over. Converted to a fast troop transport in 1962, it later became the 'Vung Tau ferry', taking troops, vehicles, aircraft and equipment to the war in Vietnam.

A number of other countries ordered Sea Furies between 1946 and 1957. They included Canada, Pakistan, Egypt, Burma, Germany, Cuba and Iraq, the latter's 'Baghdad Furies' being a source of vintage 'warbirds' in the 1980s. The Netherlands licence-built its own examples for carrier service. After Korea, the Royal Navy turned to jets for its fighters, beginning with the Sea Hawk in 1954. However, on the world stage Korea was not the Sea Fury's final battleground. Cuban *Fuerza Aerea Revolucionaria* Sea Furies saw action during America's unsuccessful 1961 Bay of Pigs invasion, against which aircraft played a vital role in attacking the amphibious invasion support ships.

A 2,500-hp wind generator

In 1986 the Memorial acquired a second Sea Fury from the Experimental Building Station at Ryde, Sydney. Its role there had certainly been one of the more unusual applications of a historic warplane: to generate wind, using its huge five-blade propeller, while the aircraft sat tethered on the ground. The aim was to test building structures and materials by subjecting them to gale-force winds. The aircraft, WG630, had served in the RAN Fleet Air Arm from 1952 until sold off in 1959. After the Memorial chose 'VX730' to conserve for display, WG630 was transferred to the Fleet Air Arm Museum at Nowra and was placed on display in time for the FAA's fiftieth anniversary in 1997.

NOTES ON COLOUR SCHEME

When acquired, the aircraft bore late 1950s RAN markings including kangaroo roundels, with both serials VW232 and VX730 on the rear fuselage. TF925 was found on the outer wings during rubbing back of overlying paint. During conservation for display in Aircraft Hall, in 2000, it was repainted in the markings of VX730, the Korean War veteran which had passed its serial number to TF925/VW232, as follows:

Sky (light grey-green) undersides, sides and tail; dark sea grey upper surfaces. Five-band black and white UN Forces stripes around rear fuselage and wings. Red/white/blue roundels in standard six positions; underside wing roundels are near wingtips. HMAS *Sydney* designator letter 'K' on fin sides. 'RAN' above 'VX730' in black on rear fuselage sides. Large aircraft number '109' in black and white on mid-fuselage sides, partially over fuselage stripes. Red spinner. Number '9' in black on forward edge of main landing gear covers. '109' in black under front of cowling.

TIMELINE—TF925 ('VX730')

1946	Built as Sea Fury F.X TF925
1948	Flew with 805 Squadron, RAN Fleet Air Arm. Damaged in service. Rebuilt as FB.11, re-serialled VW232
1959	Acquired, now identified as VX730, by Sydney Technical College as a training aid
1966	Acquired by Museum of Applied Arts & Sciences (MAAS), Sydney
1974–77	Displayed at Camden Museum of Aviation, NSW
1983	Acquired from MAAS (now Powerhouse Museum) by AWM in exchange for a DC-3
1984	To RAAF Fairbairn ACT for restoration which did not eventuate; returned to Duntroon store
1987	Loaned with Sea Fury WG630 to RAN Historic Flight, Nowra NSW
1993	Returned to Canberra (AWM Treloar Technology Centre)
1999–2000	Conserved using parts from WG630 and repainted, still as VX730, for display in Aircraft Hall

DATA

Type	Sea Fury FB.11
Design firm	Hawker Aircraft Ltd, UK
Manufacturer	Hawker, Kingston-on-Thames, UK
Role	Single seat carrier-based fighter-bomber
No. built	615 (FB.11); 726 (all Marks)
No. in RAN service	101
Type entered service	1948
Identity	TF925; reregistered VW232 Re-labelled as VX730
Powerplant	Bristol Centaurus XVIII supercharged 18-cylinder sleeve-valve radial engine of 2,480 hp (1,841 kW)
Armament	Four 20-mm Hispano Mk V cannon Twelve 60-lb rockets or up to 2,000 lb (908 kg) of bombs
Wingspan	11.7 m
Length	10.57 m
Max. speed	740 km/h
Range	1,127 km on internal fuel; 1,674 km with drop tanks
Max. take-off weight	6,645 kg

Vietnam War
1962–1975

BELL 47G SIOUX A1-404

Long Hai foothills, Phuoc Tuy province, South Vietnam
1415 HOURS, 21 FEBRUARY 1967

The scene was one of carnage. Lying on its side in a clearing of an old orchard was the remains of an M113A1 Armoured Personnel Carrier (APC), its machine-gun cupola and rear ramp lying nearby. One of its caterpillar tracks lay 25 m away. Around it were strewn dead and wounded Australian soldiers, some crushed under the vehicle, some having been blasted out the back of it. From Sioux helicopter A1-404, two Australian Army captains—direct support pilot Jim Campbell and battalion medical officer Tony White—took in the scene as they came in to land, and mentally pieced together what had happened minutes earlier.

The day had begun normally. Campbell had flown mail to the reconnaissance platoon, before taking three men to the fire support base. He returned with supplies of

> ### 'Dear Mum & Dad ... I have seen a bit of action lately.'
> Letter home from Captain Jim Campbell DFC

Sioux A1-404 in the background as Major Harry Smith briefs men of D Company, 6RAR, the day after the battle of Long Tan. AWM FOR/66/0676/VN

explosives, water and stores for the APC convoy that was transporting infantrymen of B Company of the 5th Battalion, Royal Australian Regiment (5RAR), for Operation Renmark. Transportation was a job that the larger RAAF Iroquois would have been more suited to, but none was available. On a further flight, Campbell had determined the position of C Company, which was to secure a new fire support base. While it was on the ground, bullets had been fired at the Sioux from the other side of the clearing, and Campbell had made a quick take-off and flown over their source. No one was there, although a ground party soon found footprints and 0.30-in cartridge cases.

Meanwhile, the column of APCs containing B Company had been rumbling along beside a track. While crossing over it, the 3 Troop lead vehicle (33 Bravo) of A Squadron, 3rd Cavalry Regiment, had triggered an enemy improvised mine, killing its two crewmen and three infantryman, and wounding nine. The blast had been enough to throw the APC 4 m backwards, and left a 3.5-m crater; it was later concluded that the explosive had probably been an unexploded American 5-in naval shell buried by the enemy. Soldiers from the following carrier ran forward to help the wounded, but set off an M16 'jumping jack' mine. Two more men were killed and 19 wounded. Now over 30 trapped survivors, most of them injured, warily stayed put in what was evidently a minefield, unsure if they would get out alive.

Campbell knew that he and White could be next if the landing skids of the Sioux came down on another mine; even the downblast from the rotor blades might do it. However, it was apparent that many other lives were at stake. When they landed in a clearing between trees, White jumped out and followed a narrow track that the engineers had now cleared of mines. 'The situation was out of control. The number of casualties was overwhelming. Horror was piled on horror,' he later wrote.[1] The APC driver's torso was lying nearby. White recognised some of the dead and wounded: there was the body of Private Mick Poole, a musician in the battalion band whose good humour had made him a favourite of the village kids back at Vung Tau.

Captain White assessed the situation. Some men, though still alive, were beyond any help. Others were not critical, so he concentrated on a third category of wounded, those in serious but survivable condition. He did what he could with dressings, splints and morphine. One by one, wounded men were brought back to the helicopter's cramped bubble cockpit, Campbell lifting them out to safety and returning to the minefield time and again. He flew a record eight and a half hours that day. He took four wounded to the battalion headquarters, before the first of five Iroquois helicopters of 9 Squadron RAAF arrived to transfer the rest of the casualties to the 2nd Field Ambulance at Vung Tau.[2] Between them, the Sioux and Iroquois crews helped save many lives. The hospital staff would do the rest.

The following day, Second Lieutenant Blair Weaver took the Sioux to A Company carrying several mine detectors, with which a path was cleared for the APC convoy to the headquarters. More mines and booby traps were discovered. Weaver flew the remains of the APC driver to the hospital, then directed an air strike into the Long Hais.

Captain Jim Campbell (right) with Major Harry Smith, before a Sioux of 161 (Indep) Recce Flt in Vietnam, 1966–67. AWM P03625.001

Some days later, the commander of B Company and a platoon commander died of wounds, raising to nine the death toll of the ill-fated Operation Renmark.

◄ ►

Captain Campbell's Distinguished Flying Cross, awarded for the 'complete disregard for his own safety' he showed that day, was the first of 12 DFCs[5] made to Australian pilots of 161 (Independent) Reconnaissance Flight (161 [Indep] Recce Flt) in Vietnam. To the men of the flight, codenamed Possum, it was all in a day's work.

During their six years in Vietnam from 1965 to 1971, the flight's 37 Sioux helicopters flew a remarkable 66,000 sorties, providing direct support to all major Australian ground operations. A1-404 flew around 1,200 of these over two and a half years in-country. The Sioux were often flown into dangerous areas, attracting small arms fire from the unseen enemy as pilot and observer skimmed the treetops in an effort to make themselves a harder target. More than half of the Sioux were, at one time or another, hit by ground fire. Using ad hoc fitments of M60 machine-guns borrowed from the US Army, some could fire back. Two of the weapons were mounted on the side litters and fired by the pilot, aimed with the help of a circle marked in chinagraph pencil on the acryllic glass bubble. Other armaments included a single M60 mounted in the open doorway. Crewmen also carried their own small arms, normally an M16 rifle or M79 grenade launcher, and a 9-mm pistol. Armament was restricted by the Sioux's limited load carrying capacity, which was further reduced by the thin tropical air on hot days. Normally they flew with no mounted weapons. Eight of the helicopters were brought down in action, though in all these cases the crewmen survived.

161 (Indep) Recce Flt Sioux helicopter crashes in Vietnam[4]

Date	Aircraft	Crew, details
10 Oct 1966	A1-395	2nd Lt Bill Davies (seriously injured) Shot down on Route 15 during Operation Canberra
26 May 1967	A1-409	2nd Lt Blair Weaver Shot down in Xuyen Moc area. Destroyed by air strike
2 Jun 1967	A1-403	Lt Ross Hutchinson and passenger (injured) Engine failure, Horseshoe area. Aircraft rebuilt
20 Nov 1967	A1-401	Lt Paddy O'Brien, WO Brian Quee (injured) Lost power, Thua Tich area. Destroyed by air strike
22 Nov 1967	A1-400	2nd Lt Roger Colclough, Pte Stephen Moore (minor injuries). Brought down by booby trap near Dat Do
19 Feb 1969	A1-639	Capt Ted Brooker (NZ) (injured), Signalman Robert Vallance. Shot down in Courtney rubber plantation
23 Mar 1970	A1-635	Capt Bob Hills, Capt John Digweed Crashed near Nui Dat
9 Nov 1970	A1-637	2nd Lt Terry Hayes, Lt Col John Church (injured) Shot down during Operation Cung Chung III in mangrove in south-west Phuoc Tuy

The fitment of weapons to the helicopters was, in fact, against stated policy. Army aircraft were to support ground forces in ways other than by fire, as the RAAF had claimed this role. This caused some resentment within 161 (Indep) Recce Flt, as Sioux crews often saw Viet Cong or found targets of opportunity without the ability to effectively bring fire to bear on them. Of course, policy was ignored as opportunity allowed.

The flight's main tasks, visual reconnaissance and artillery direction for the 1st Australian Task Force (1ATF), were reminiscent of the role of First World War tactical reconnaissance units, such as 3 Squadron AFC, which had also been an army unit. The Sioux flew at a similar speed to those aircraft of 50 years earlier, but generally much lower. Reconnaissance in Vietnam included searching for signs of Viet Cong and North Vietnamese Army activity, and assessing proposed areas for troop insertion. Based on their observations, the task force was able to better plan operations in response to situational changes and enemy activities, and then direct troop movements or attacks, both air and artillery, as needed. A helicopter from 161 (Indep) Recce Flt was always available for direct support to the battalion. During Operation Forrest, second-in-command Major Alf Garland observed and directed the battle from a Sioux throughout the day, and then hovered over a jungle clearing while Iroquois dust-off helicopters winched out wounded. In Operation Concrete I the commanding officer directing the operation had his Sioux hit by ground fire, but returned to base.

The Sioux displayed in the Memorial's Vietnam gallery in 1999. AWM PAIU1999/152.16

Much work was done with 'trackies'—soldiers of the APCs and Centurion tanks—flying as convoy cover ahead of the vehicles to search for routes and signs of ambush up ahead. Often a vehicle commander, in radio contact with his section, flew in the right-hand seat. For artillery ranging flights, an artillery officer would take the seat. These and other tasks were also carried out with the flight's Cessnas, and later its Porters and Kiowa helicopters. One task was forward air control for air strikes, in which white phosphorous grenades were dropped to mark targets, and for the subsequent bomb damage assessment following a strike. Another was 'psy ops' (psychological operations), which included leaflet drops and more direct communication: an amplifier and a bank of downward-pointing speakers was fitted to a Sioux, and tapes played over enemy positions in an attempt to entice them to surrender. These 'voice'-equipped Sioux were also used to alert villagers of impending cordon and search operations. On a few occasions medical evacuation ('medevac') or 'dust-off' flights, carrying wounded on the helicopter's side litters as pioneered during the Korean War, augmented the missions of the specialist 'dust-off' Iroquois of 9 Squadron RAAF. In addition to all these roles came the more routine tasks of liaison, courier runs and administrative support.

In September 1971, the last Sioux left the flight and returned to Australia. By then, eight examples of the gas-turbine powered, four-seat Bell OH-58 Kiowa helicopter on loan from the US Army had replaced them. This lead was followed three years later when Australian Kiowas replaced the Sioux in Australian Army service. In 1979, when the decision was made by the army to transfer a Sioux to the Memorial, A1-404 was a natural choice. As eight years had passed since the aircraft had left South Vietnam, some work had to be done to present it in Vietnam-period configuration. On 14 June 1979, A1-404—by then the only Sioux flying with the army—completed its final journey from the army aviation centre at Oakey, Queensland, to the grounds of the Memorial for its official handover. Major Campbell and Colonel Raymond Harding, the army's first helicopter pilot in 1960, were at the controls. The aircraft was presented by the Chief of General Staff, Lieutenant General Donald Dunstan, to the Memorial's Chairman of Council, Lieutenant General Sir Thomas Daly. After a short hop to the rear car park, the engine was run one last time for inhibiting,[5] and a crane lifted the little Sioux into Aeroplane Hall for the Memorial's first display of a helicopter.

With the opening of the Vietnam gallery in the early 1980s, it was decided to suspend the Sioux in a dramatic flight pose over the eastern internal stairwell. It hung there for some 15 years, until the stairwell was removed during the Memorial's major gallery redevelopment of the late 1990s. The Sioux was then lowered to the ground floor for display, together with an M113A1 Fire Support Vehicle, on simulated mud groundwork in the relocated Vietnam gallery. Space did not allow for its inclusion in the revitalised *Conflicts 1945 to today* galleries, which opened in February 2008.

Away from the Memorial too, the name of Possum Flight lived on after Vietnam. Its work was recognised in 1991 when, together with the six other units of 1RAR Battalion Group, it received the US Army Meritorious Unit Commendation for service during 1965–66.[6] Then in 1995, the reincarnated 161 (Indep) Recce Flt moved from Holsworthy, near Sydney, to Darwin. In 1999 a detachment of three of its Kiowas deployed to East Timor with INTERFET, later UNTAET, flying nearly 11,000 hours on border reconnaissance patrols until the detachment was withdrawn in July 2003.

The Sioux in context

Flown in December 1945, just months after the end of the Second World War, the Bell 47 was the world's first helicopter in wide-scale use. Between then and the 1970s, it was probably built in larger numbers than any other helicopter. The military H-13 variant revolutionised battlefield medical evacuation for United Nations forces during the Korean War, when it airlifted Australian casualties to Mobile Army Surgical Hospitals, popularised in the 1970s television series *MASH*. The Model 47G of 1953 featured a three-seat cabin configuration, and the 47G-3B subtype (represented by the Memorial's example) used a more powerful 270-hp turbocharged engine.

Instrument panel and control pedals of the Memorial's Sioux in 2008.
AWM REL/04248

Australians first encountered American Bell 47Ds during the Korean War as aero-medical evacuation patients. AWM P01479.019

Known as the Sioux, the military version of the Model 47G became the first helicopter in Australian Army service in 1960. The first unit to equip with it, 16 Army Light Aircraft Squadron at RAAF Amberley, Queensland, was in fact a joint Army–RAAF unit. Subsequent army units to operate it were the Army School of Aviation and 161, 162, 163, 173, 182 and 183 Flights/Squadrons. The basic Bell 47 design was over 20 years old by the time of its service in Vietnam with 161 (Indep) Recce Flt. Its small size and agility suited it well to new roles in jungle warfare, but its drawbacks—lack of load carrying ability and speed—eventually led to its replacement by the Kiowa.

The Sioux's Vietnam service was its most significant period of Australian war service. However, other Australian soldiers were encountering the type at the same time. For example, Britain licence-built the Bell 47G-3B-1 and deployed some to Sarawak during the Indonesian Confrontation (1963–66), where soldiers of 4RAR were stationed. The Australian Army itself flew the Sioux in a number of overseas locations other than Vietnam, including Papua New Guinea, Indonesia, Malaysia and Singapore.

NOTES ON COLOUR SCHEME

Repainted in 1979 to Vietnam early-period scheme of overall olive drab nitro acrylic lacquer, with matt black markings as follows: 'A1-404' on fin sides, kangaroo national insignia on rear of cabin sides, 'ARMY' on fuel tank sides, '404' on front of cabin bubble. Main rotor blades black with yellow tips, rear rotor white with single red stripe mid-blade. Forward section of skids black. Red/white/blue flash on horizontal stabiliser fin tips.

TIMELINE—A1-404

1965	(Sep) Delivered ex-USA to Australian Army at RAAF Amberley, Qld
1966	(Jun) Deployed to 161 (later Independent) Reconnaissance Flight at Vung Tau, South Vietnam
1967	(Mar) Relocated with unit to Luscombe Field, Nui Dat (Apr) Returned to Australia; (Nov) redeployed to Vietnam for second tour of duty
1968	(Sep) Returned to Australia (1 Aviation Regiment, Amberley)
1971	(Dec) Placed in storage at 2 Base Ordnance Depot, Melbourne
1979	Refurbished and repainted in Vietnam period markings. Flown from Army School of Aviation, Oakey, Qld, to AWM for presentation, and displayed in Aeroplane Hall
c. 1985	Displayed in Vietnam gallery
1996	Relocated with Vietnam gallery to lower ground floor
2007	Stored at AWM Treloar Technology Centre after Vietnam gallery redeveloped

DATA

Type	Bell 47G-3B-1 (US military designation OH-13)
Design firm	Bell Helicopter Company, Texas, USA
Manufacturer	As above
Role	Three-seat light utility helicopter
No. built	Over 5,600, including approx 3,900 in USA (Bell 47 total)
Used by	Australian Army
Type entered service	1960 (Bell 47G)
No. in Aust Army service	51 (Bell 47G total 65)
Identity	A1-404 (previously A1-207) US Constructor's no. 3404
Crew	2 (pilot and observer)
Powerplant	Turbocharged Lycoming TVO-435-D1B horizontally-opposed 6-cylinder piston engine of 270 hp (209 kW)
Armament	Limited 'unofficial' use of US Army armament kit: two remotely controlled M60 machine-guns mounted on side litters, or a single door-mounted M60 or M79 grenade launcher. Various small arms carried by crew
Rotor diameter	11.32 m
Fuselage length	9.63 m
Max. speed	169 km/h
Range/endurance	340 km/2.5 hours
Loaded weight	1,340 kg

Phuoc Tuy province, South Vietnam
13 APRIL 1967

A Special Air Service (SAS) patrol ran towards their 'slick' troop transport, a UH-1B Iroquois helicopter, and scrambled in through its side doorway. With the ever-present threat of enemy gunfire from the surrounding foliage, it was not a time for sightseeing. Iroquois A2-1019 lifted off quickly, and Flight Lieutenants David Champion and Geoffrey Banfield lowered its nose to move out. Suddenly, a loud bang came from the engine compartment behind them. With power lost, the Huey[7] came down heavily, splaying its skids, and the flexing rotor blades chopped into the tail. With American helicopter gunships orbiting the landing zone, the lead 'slick' picked up the crew while the SAS men moved out into the trees to form a defensive perimeter.

> ### The rotor blades were useless when we got back.
> Flight Lieutenant Les Morris, 9 Squadron RAAF

Australian soldiers wounded in the fighting during Operation Beaumaris, in Phuoc Tuy province, South Vietnam, on 14 February 1967 were 30 minutes by air from hospital. Iroquois A2-1019 is about to fly a wounded soldier of C Company, 5th Battalion, Royal Australian Regiment (5RAR), to hospital at Vung Tau. AWM COL/67/0140/VN

In short order an American CH-47 Chinook heavy lift helicopter came in, and with the badly damaged Iroquois slung below, flew back to the 9 Squadron RAAF base at Vung Tau. The maintenance men removed the engine cowlings to piece together what had happened. It was evident that there had been a compressor failure, and the men speculated about its cause: perhaps a bullet from an unseen Viet Cong sniper? A mechanical cause was more likely, as several 9 Squadron Hueys were to suffer engine failure.

A replacement tailboom is attached to Iroquois A2-1019 in the 9 Squadron hangar at Vung Tau in mid-1967. AWM P04984.002

◄ ►

Engine changes were routine, but replacing the broken tailboom was not. Iroquois A2-1019 sat at Vung Tau awaiting its fate. Eventually a replacement arrived courtesy of the US Army, but as the Australians looked over the forlorn wreck of 1019 at the workshop, an idea formed in the mind of Squadron Leader Clive Cotter, the engineering officer. Cotter planned to graft the rear fuselage of another Iroquois onto 1019. It had never been tried before, and the Americans scoffed. They could afford to; they had many thousands of Iroquois in Vietnam, and it was not worth the effort. The Australians, with just eight, did not have that luxury.

In June another 9 Squadron Iroquois, A2-1024, crashed and its intact tailboom was removed. Another unofficial source of parts was the nearby American 'helicopter graveyard' compound, a pile growing weekly as damaged helicopters airlifted from the battlefield were literally dropped onto it. Iroquois A2-1019 was given the status 'repairable stock'. During August and September 1967, between more routine maintenance and without the luxury of sophisticated jigs and other proper equipment,

Leading Aircraftmen Brian Taylor (left) and Brian (Ron) Hill, gunners aboard A2-1019 during Operation Bribie on 17 February 1967. Their pilot was Flight Lieutenant Les Morris. AWM VN/67/0022/02

the operation was completed as a spare-time project. On 22 September the hybrid 1019 flew again, with no ill effects from its Frankenstein surgery. Cotter's team had saved the Australian taxpayer $330,000, the price of a new Huey. The initially dubious Americans were impressed enough to embark on their own rebuilding program, but not before they had relieved Clive Cotter of the key to their compound.[8]

Soon back in the hot seat was a veteran pilot with some 3,800 flying hours even before he had come to Vietnam. Flight Lieutenant Les Morris, who had joined the squadron the previous Remembrance Day on 11 November 1966, had since flown 1019 more than most. His second last operation, a few days before going home on 25 October, was one of his hottest and earned him a Mention in Despatches. Morris in 1019 was controlling the operation. Just after the insertion helicopter had landed an SAS reconnaissance patrol, the men came under enemy fire. Four of the five-man patrol re-boarded and were lifted off, but in the confusion the fifth was left behind. Morris's lead helicopter had no load, so he swapped duties and went down to pick up the man. 'They were laying down very heavy rocket and bomb fire immediately adjoining the clearing,' he recalls, 'so it was pretty hectic in there, but we got the fellow out.'[9]

At the time, A2-1019 was halfway through two years of service in Vietnam. Its list of battle honours reads like a who's who of Australian service in that war: Operations Sydney, Hobart, Vaucluse, Canberra, Hayman, Ingham, Canary, Renmark, Leeton, Forrest, Pinnaroo and more. On 17 February 1967 it inserted troops of the 6th Battalion, Royal Australian Regiment (6RAR), into the landing zone for Operation Bribie, 'one of the most difficult battles fought by Australians in Vietnam'.[10]

The previous year, during the famous battle of Long Tan on 18 August 1966, 9 Squadron delivered critical ammunition supplies to D Company of 6RAR as they fought some 2,500 Viet Cong. Two Iroquois (A2-1020 and A2-1022) brought half a tonne of ammunition from nearby Nui Dat to the troops, overflying the rubber plantation battlefield at treetop height to stay under the cloud base. In the torrential rain, a smoke signal from the ground was needed to mark the drop zone. With replenished ammunition, the Australian artillery and APCs were able to continue the battle.

Top: In 2001 the Memorial's Iroquois was displayed on a support pole in ANZAC Hall. AWM REL/12323

Above: In 2007 A2-1019 was incorporated into this dramatic set-piece for the *Conflicts 1945 to today* galleries. AWM PAIU2008/010.05

Left: Cockpit of the Memorial's Iroquois in 1967. AWM P01597.012

The enemy retreated, suffering 245 killed and hundreds wounded; 18 Australians were killed and 24 wounded.

That night, A2-1019 was among the Iroquois flown in to evacuate the dead and wounded, guided only by the dim light provided by APCs as the helicopters cautiously came in to land in a clearing.

An Iroquois crew was a close-knit team. The co-pilot in the left seat assisted the pilot in the task of keeping the aircraft flying, and handled much of the navigation. A crewman and a gunner in the rear compartment sat ready at M60 machine-guns, eyes peeled for signs of the enemy below. Rear crewmen also took care of any load being carried. In picking up wounded from the jungle, one crewman typically operated the side winch while the second was lowered into jungle taking with him a rescue harness, a 'Stokes litter' man-carrier or a collapsible stretcher, while the pilot kept the helicopter hovering.

Morris's flights in A2-1019 included operations such as 'rice shifts', in which caches of Viet Cong rice discovered by army troops were picked up to deny the enemy access to supplies. His logbook also records a number of medical evacuation ('medevac') flights, also known as 'dust-offs', a role for which the Iroquois became renowned. A helicopter was always on standby at Vung Tau or the hospital at Nui Dat, or at one of the battalion helipads. Rain, hail or shine, day or night, the Iroquois were called in to evacuate wounded, and sometimes dead, in the aftermath of an action. Many men owe their lives to the quick response time of medevac helicopters and their crews.

With enemy forces often in the vicinity, 9 Squadron's operations were rarely routine. Les Morris recalls another occasion:

> I'd gone out in 1019 which was a smaller helicopter.[11] The patrol on the ground had casualties and were under fire, and we went in to get them out. The D-model was too big to get to the pad, so I elected to go in with the B-model, but I found the pad was too small even for it. I made a decision to chop away [the trees] into the pad, working on the basis that I'd probably be able to get the patrol out before we'd suffered too much damage. That's exactly what I did, and we got out ... the rotor blades were useless when we got back. I got a pat on the back for doing it—and a kick in the bum.

A2-1019 flew 489 sorties in Vietnam, and survived enemy encounters on at least half a dozen occasions. After returning to Australia in a C-130 Hercules in 1968, its subsequent service consisted of more sedate training and search-and-rescue duties around Australia.

In 1981, representations were made to the Memorial, asking it to request Iroquois A2-1021 from the RAAF in 1981. Three years later Clive Cotter wrote in with his story. This, with the rest of 1019's Vietnam history, was compelling enough for it to be chosen for preservation. The UH-1B 'Bravo' was phased out of service at the end of 1984, leaving the UH-1H 'Hotel' model in service.[12] The last official flight of a Bravo came on 21 May the following year when, with some 6,000 flying hours logged, 1019 was landed on the grounds of the Memorial by one of its Vietnam pilots, Wing Commander Mick Haxell DFC, before returning to RAAF Fairbairn for an official handover to the Memorial by Air Marshal David Evans AC DSO AFC.

The Iroquois in context

Bell's Model 204 was designed to military specification as a general utility helicopter capable of front-line casualty evacuation, a capability pioneered during the Korean war, and first flew in 1956. Its military designation became UH-1. The first UH-1Bs joined the RAAF six years later when the RAAF's first helicopter squadrons, numbers 5 and 9, were formed. In March 1966, with an increased Australian commitment to the Vietnam War, it was announced that a helicopter squadron would be sent as transport support for the army. The eight Iroquois of 9 Squadron, including A2-1019, made a farewell flypast over Sydney before flying onto the transport carrier HMAS *Sydney* (the former aircraft carrier) for the sea journey, arriving at Vung Tau, South Vietnam, in June. From their base there, the helicopters were flown daily in and out of the Australian task force base at Nui Dat.

A primary role of 9 Squadron was to insert troops into combat areas, and extract them after completing their task. Often, these troop movements were made en masse with dozens of US Iroquois. The other primary role was medevac. The value of the Iroquois in fast casualty evacuation is well known: the morbidity figures of hospitalised casualties in Vietnam were a third of those for the Second World War. Still other roles carried out by the squadron were leaflet drops in support of 'psy ops' (psychological operations); 'olfactory reconnaissance'[13] missions to detect enemy base camps in the jungle; the spraying of insecticides and defoliants; and, from April 1969, the use of later-model Iroquois converted to gunships as firepower support for the 'slicks'. During 1966–68, when A2-1019 was with the squadron, the role of firepower support was undertaken by the Americans.

During the squadron's first few months in Vietnam, conflict arose between the Australian Army and the RAAF over the control and operational procedures of the helicopters, and relations were later described as bitter and antagonistic.[14] Thereafter they improved somewhat, and overall it can be said that 9 Squadron provided indispensable support to the army during its six years in Vietnam.

With an increase in late 1967 of the Australian Army's commitment to three battalions, 9 Squadron's helicopter establishment was doubled. The UH-1B Iroquois were gradually replaced by the UH-1H, which could carry more troops; over the next year the earlier models, including A2-1019, returned to Australia in the training and search-and-rescue roles. In addition to 9 Squadron, another group of Australian air and ground crews operated the Iroquois during the war; this was the RAN's Helicopter Flight Vietnam, attached to a US Army unit. After Vietnam, the Iroquois also saw service in the white United Nations paint scheme for peacekeeping operations in the Sinai during the 1970s and 1980s.

The Iroquois is still probably the most recognised symbol of the Vietnam War. It is also a commemorative link to the 520 Australians, some of whom had been flown to their last action in a Huey, who died during the war in Vietnam.

TIMELINE—A2-1019

1964	(9 Oct) Received ex-USA by 9 Squadron, RAAF Fairbairn, ACT
1966	(May) To South Vietnam with first RAAF helicopter contingent
1968	(Oct) To 5 Squadron, RAAF Fairbairn
1974	(Jun) To 2 Flying Training School (2 FTS), RAAF Pearce, WA
1975–85	To 5 Squadron, RAAF Fairbairn; based also at RAAF Williamtown, NSW and with 2 FTS. Duties included search & rescue
1985	(21 May) Flown to AWM and stored at RAAF Fairbairn
1986	(20 Jul) Struck off RAAF charge
1988	Trucked to AWM annexe, Mitchell, ACT
2001	Displayed in ANZAC Hall
2007	(Dec) Displayed in *Conflicts 1945 to today* galleries following a major conservation project and repaint

DATA

Type	UH-1B Iroquois
Design firm	Bell, USA
Manufacturer	Bell
Role	Utility helicopter
No. built	1,014 (UH-1B) Over 13,000 (UH-1 total)
Type entered service	1961
Identity	A2-1019 (RAAF) 63-13587 (US military) Constructor's no. 1019
Accommodation	4 crewmen (pilot, co-pilot, crewman, gunner) Five troops or 1,360 kg of freight. Many more passengers were carried on occasion.
Powerplant	Lycoming T53-L-11 turboshaft engine of 820 kW
Armament	One M60 machine-gun in each doorway
Rotor diameter	13.41 m
Length	11.7 m
Max. speed	222 km/h
Range	460 km
Max. take-off weight	4,309 kg

NOTES ON COLOUR SCHEME

1967-period Vietnam service: RAAF dark green overall with black anti-glare section forward of windscreen. 'RAAF' followed by kangaroo in black on boom sides. '19' and kangaroo in black on nose. Sealing tape strips were commonly applied around nose radio hatch. Cherry insignia on door. Tail fin: serial number in black above red/white/blue fin flash on both sides. Red warning arrow on rear of boom. Main rotor: dark green (upper) and black (underside) with one red tip and one yellow and red tip. Tail rotor: black with red/white/red tips.

CANBERRA A84-247

80 km west of Hue, northern South Vietnam
1445 HOURS, 14 MARCH 1971

'Magpie 41' was 14,000 ft above the jungle canopy. The Canberra bomber, A84-228 of 2 Squadron RAAF, was on a Combat Skyspot bombing mission to strike an enemy target. A thick cloud covering, common in this region bordering Laos, was not a major problem as the mission was being voice-directed by a radar controller on the ground. During the bomber's southerly run, navigator Flight Lieutenant Allan Pinches mentioned a pertinent piece of information to his pilot and commanding officer, Wing Commander John Downing: enemy surface-to-air missiles (SAM) were possibly active in the region. Neither crewman was particularly concerned.

Had this been a visual bombing mission, the Canberra would have descended under the cloud and Pinches, sitting behind the cockpit, would have unstrapped himself and crawled into the aircraft's nose to man the bomb sight. However, on Combat Skyspot missions the crew were told when and where to release their bombs, and the bomb sight was not used. The Canberra had just made a steep turn onto its southerly attack run, Downing recalls:

A beautiful, viceless aeroplane.

Air Marshal David Evans AC DSO AFC
Commanding Officer 2 Squadron RAAF, Vietnam
Chief of Air Staff, 1982–85

Canberra A84-247 in service. AWM P03654.017

There was an almighty crash, and the whole aircraft shook. The first thing I noticed was that my canopy was shattered … About that stage I saw a missile go past; it was ballistic and was outside proximity [detonation] range, so it just went past. That's the only reason I knew what had hit us. I thought, if we've been hit with a missile that smashed the canopy, it's probably done a lot of damage I can't see; so I said, 'Eject, eject, eject …'

It was like I was watching myself reach down to pull the control column snatch release to explode the detonators around the elevator control … Reaching for my helmet and situating myself properly, I pulled the blind.[15]

Pinches followed suit and ejected out through his escape hatch. Floating down under parachutes, the two watched A84-228 go down, its starboard wing enveloped in flame, and disappear through a blanket of cloud. After emerging beneath the cloud a few thousand feet up, the two men came down in trees on the steep side of a valley. They were about 400 m apart, and both suffered injuries—Downing a fractured kneecap, Pinches fractured vertebrae from the force of ejection—but with difficulty they were able to walk.

Back at Phan Rang base, anxiety rose when the two became overdue. The squadron chaplain held a service to offer prayers for their safe return.

Although not able to meet up on the ground and enduring a cold, wet and painful night in the jungle, they made radio contact with each other the next day. Their transmissions were picked up by a C-130 rescue coordinator, and 24 hours after ejecting, they were being winched to the safety of an Iroquois helicopter.

◄ ►

Thus ended only the second, and the last, mission in which a Canberra bomber of 2 Squadron RAAF was lost.[16] It was also the first occasion on which a crew had successfully ejected out of an Australian Canberra, and it earned the men membership of both the Irvin Air Chute company's Caterpillar Club and the Martin-Baker company's Ejection Tie Club. The enemy SAM site commander earned a bottle of champagne for his victory. Considering the intensity of operations over a four-year period from April 1967 to May 1971, and the USAF casualties suffered over that period, the squadron could have expected a greater loss rate.

The Australian squadron in Vietnam was unique in flying Canberras on level bombing strikes. In this role they filled a gap between the massed bomb drops of the B-52s and dive bomber/fighter-bomber strikes. In the lead-up to a typical day mission from Phan Rang, the pilot sat in his perspex-bubbled hothouse under a tropical sun that scorched the tarmac, his navigator behind him not much cooler. Sweat built up in their flying suits. It could be hours before a radio call crackled in their headphones: time to go. Taxiing from their concrete revetments to a 12,000-ft (3.6-km) runway, they took off and headed skyward. Just minutes later, at 40,000 ft, sweat turned to ice.

Nearing the target, the Canberra might come down to 14,000 ft if on a Combat Skyspot mission, or to 3,000 or even below 1,000 ft for close air support missions. The lower the bombing height, the more accurate the result, but at 1,000 ft came the added danger of being struck by shrapnel from one's own bomb.

The squadron was integrated into the 35th Tactical Fighter Wing (TFW), US Seventh Air Force, which included several squadrons flying F-100 fighter-bombers and the American version of the Canberra, the Martin B-57. To the American wing and other friendly forces, the RAAF Canberras were known as Magpies. To the Viet Cong, they were 'screaming birds' which never ran out of bombs.

The thousands of attacks made by 2 Squadron are often overshadowed by a better-known RAAF role in Vietnam, the helicopter operations of 9 Squadron. Yet the bombers' service was no less important. The squadron was recognised by the Americans with a USAF Outstanding Unit Award for exceptionally meritorious service, while its parent wing received a Cross of Gallantry with Palm from the Republic of Vietnam. Brigadier General W.T. Galligan, former commander of the wing, said of 2 Squadron, 'I only wish that all USAF units could do as well.'[17]

The Canberra's *modus operandi* in Vietnam was quite different from that of the B-57. In RAAF hands the Canberra was a level bomber, while the B-57 had no bombardier crewman and was primarily used as a dive-bomber. The Canberra's bomb sight was fed information on drift and ground speed determined by radar. Higher accuracy was possible, although it required very accurate flying. Also, the Canberras had the advantage of a longer endurance than the US fighter-bomber types. Wing Commander Downing speaks of this aspect which gave the squadron much greater operational flexibility:

> The other close air support 'in country' was all fighter attack and dive bombing. With their ordnance stores, they had at the most 20 minutes on target. Our endurance even with a full bomb load could be up to five hours ... if we went down to IV Corps in the Delta and a mission was called off, you could hawk your bombs up and down the country and finish up bombing in I Corps. But we didn't tell them that, because they'd put us on the end of the queue every time.[18]

The crew of Canberra A84-247 made use of the Canberra's endurance on 24 March 1968, nine months into this aircraft's period in Vietnam. Pilot Officer Richard Strudwick and navigator Flight Lieutenant John Gazley were on a visual bombing attack in hilly country near the demilitarised zone to flight check a newly arrived navigator. Cloud obscured the target, so Gazley contacted a Forward Air Controller (FAC) of the US Marines for an alternative. Flying to within 20 km of the North Vietnamese border, they made a successful attack. Such close approaches could be worrying, as the aircraft carried no missile warning system.[19]

During its first six months in Vietnam, 2 Squadron's operations were primarily Combat Skyspot missions at night, for which accurate altitude, heading and speed were critical to success. The squadron considered them 'milk runs', although the men rarely knew the nature of the target or received much feedback concerning bomb damage assessment. They were bombing blind without known results.

Bombing effectiveness went up in September 1967 with the start of daytime low-level visual strikes, controlled by an airborne FAC who marked the target with smoke bombs. Wing Commander Tony Powell had argued for this method, against American fears that level bombing would put the relatively slow Canberra in danger from enemy ground fire.

Initial results under forward air control were mixed, as many controllers were unfamiliar with the squadron's methods and the Canberra's capabilities. However, after several FACs were invited along on missions in the jump seat to see just how a Canberra mission was conducted, their understanding improved and cooperation was consistently good. Powell was vindicated when, by 1969, the squadron was responsible for 16 per cent of bomb damage to the targets hit by the 35th TFW while flying just 6 per cent of its missions.[20] Using the yardstick of assessed target damage per sortie, it was nearly three times as effective as the other squadrons, and no Canberras had yet been lost. Apparently, the Viet Cong did not expect a level-flying aircraft to pose a threat until it was too late.

By 1970, 2 Squadron was dropping more bomb tonnage than any other unit in South-east Asia. Nevertheless, the squadron's prime concern was not tonnage but accuracy. Targets were photographed for damage assessment, particularly on close air support missions, and the conversations between crew and FAC were recorded on tape for later analysis. After each mission the crews were anxious to read the bomb damage assessment reports; if a bomb landed much more than 20 m from its target, the crew were debriefed in detail after the mission to find out why. The aircraft's bombing system may even have been examined to establish any faults. One problem was the varying ballistics of the Second World War-vintage British bombs used—the Mk 4 and Mk 13 500-lb, and the Mk I medium capacity and general purpose 1,000-lb. When stocks of these ran out, American M117 750-lb bombs were used. When compared with 1940s level-bombing accuracy, which was often measured in hundreds or even thousands of metres, 2 Squadron's accuracy was remarkable.

As the Americans came to recognise the capabilities of the RAAF Canberras and their crews, they allowed the squadron to attack higher priority but potentially more dangerous targets in close air support missions. In 1968–69 most targets were concentrated in the southern III Corps military region and in the flat Mekong Delta region of IV Corps, the regions more conducive to a level bombing run. The Canberra's 'stick' bombing method was considered to be most effective against the 'line targets' (linear formations such as canals and tree lines where enemy positions were known to be) common in those areas. In 1970, however, they began striking north into the

Canberra A84-247 over
South Vietnam, c. 1971.
AWM P04845.001

mountainous I Corps region towards the North Vietnamese border, though by strict instruction all targets were to remain within the borders of South Vietnam. The targets were many and varied: troop concentrations, Viet Cong base camps and bunkers, caves, river sampans, vehicles, anti-aircraft sites, troop lines. Bombs could be fused to explode on, below or above the ground, depending on the target type. Some missions were in support of Australian troops, but as the squadron was attached to a US wing, it more often supported US and South Vietnamese army operations. One such was under way when A84-228 was shot down: the ill-fated Operation Lam Son 719 offensive against the Ho Chi Minh Trail in Laos.

◄ ►

Canberra A84-247 had spent two years and nine months in South Vietnam by the time it flew its last mission on 6 February 1971 and returned to RAAF Amberley, Queensland. The records of 2 Squadron show that it flew a remarkable 670 bombing sorties. With only eight Canberras at Phan Rang on line at a time, each aircraft averaged more than one mission per day. With such a high use rate, the squadron's section of the huge base at Phan Rang was active around the clock. Bombs, nearly 80,000 of them by war's end, had to be assembled, prepared and loaded by a team of armourers. A reliable parts delivery service by C-130 Hercules had to be kept up to maintain the Canberras, with routine work being done in the hangars in three eight-hour shifts. For 250-hourly inspections they were flown to 478 Maintenance Squadron at Butterworth, Malaysia, while for 2,000-hourly major overhauls the aircraft went back to Amberley.

To fly the squadron's Canberras, just eight two-man crews were available at any time. During their year-long tour of duty in Vietnam, crewmen could easily rack up over

The Memorial's Canberra in storage at the Treloar Technology Centre in 1994. AWM PAIU1994/168.18

200 missions. Despite (or perhaps because of) this high rate of operations, morale was exceptionally high. In their spare time, the personnel would typically help with work around the base to enhance living conditions, such as building a swimming pool. Great initiative and energy went into such projects as soapbox derbies, Australia Day sports carnivals, and even the construction of a miniature Sydney Harbour Bridge over a monsoon drain.

In addition to the two Canberras lost, a few squadron aircraft were hit by ground fire or by shrapnel from their own bombs. A84-247 received minor damage from ground fire on 26 August 1969, during a mission flown by Flight Lieutenant Merv Lewis and Flying Officer Bob Molony. In 1970, Flying Officer Richard O'Ferrall flying 247 in the IV Corps area made a very difficult low level attack on a 0.50-in anti-aircraft machine-gun that a 'very excited FAC had just seen rolled out of the jungle'.[21] Evidently the aircraft escaped being hit on that occasion.

A decade earlier, however, it had been hit by what could be called a variation of friendly fire. At the time, 2 Squadron was in Malaya as part of Australia's commitment to the Malayan Emergency (1950–60), attacking communist insurgents. Sitting in dispersal at 2 Squadron's base at Butterworth, Malaya, in July 1959, not long before the squadron's last bombing strikes in Malaya, another Canberra was having a test run of its engines. Suddenly the starboard engine starter came away, and the ensuing explosion threw fragments of a disintegrating Avon engine up to 80 m away. One piece of turbine found its mark in the port side of A84-247, piercing the navigator's station. The small hole was quickly repaired, and 247 remained with 2 Squadron at Butterworth to contribute to Australia's security force throughout another period of conflict, the Indonesian Confrontation (1963-66).

The Canberra in context

In addition to its Vietnam service, there is a technological aspect to the historical significance of A84-247: it was the second last of 48 Canberra Mk 20s licence-built in Australia. Produced by the Government Aircraft Factory at Fisherman's Bend, Melbourne, between 1953 and 1958, the Canberra replaced the piston-engined Lincoln to take Australia into the age of the jet bomber.

A British design first flown in 1949, the Canberra was named after the Australian capital by Australian Prime Minister Robert Menzies in 1951. The English Electric company had produced a jet-age extension of the concept exemplified by the earlier de Havilland Mosquito: a bomber that could carry a useful load at the expense of all defensive armament, but fly fast and high enough to render such defences unnecessary.

It was a cutting-edge design during its heyday in the early 1950s, breaking record after record in speed, distance and altitude. The flight of the RAAF's first Canberra from London to Canberra in 1951, in fact, set a new record of 26 hours, averaging 900 km/h. Parer and Macintosh in their lumbering DH.9, 30 years earlier, would have been amazed. By the time of the Vietnam War the Canberra was aging—some said 'ancient'— but it was still reliable, and suited to its role.

The Canberra served as Australia's strike bomber for nearly two decades, equipping 82 Wing's 1 and 6 Squadrons at Amberley in addition to 2 Squadron. It was temporarily replaced in that role by the F-4E Phantom and, two years later, by the long-awaited F-111C. In the cartographic survey role it soldiered on until retiring from service in 1982, some 30 years after its first Australian flight.

Cockpit of the Memorial's Canberra in storage at the Treloar Technology Centre in 2008. AWM REL/08295

TIMELINE—A84-247	
1958	(Jun) Built and delivered to RAAF
1958–68	Served in Malaya with 2 Squadron RAAF; major servicing in Australia
1959	(7 May) Flown from Butterworth, Malaya, to Tengah by Air Vice Marshal Sir Valston Hancock CBE DFC (later Chief of Air Staff, 1961–65)
1960	(23 Nov) Flown in Manila Air Display
1961	(31 Oct) Flown on weather reconnaissance mission by Sqn Ldr David Evans AFC (Chief of Air Staff, 1982–85)
1967	(Jul) To Vietnam with 2 Squadron RAAF; major servicing at Butterworth, Malaysia
1968	(Sep) To 1 (Bomber) Operational Conversion Unit, RAAF Amberley
1969	(Jul) Returned to 2 Squadron, Vietnam
1971	(Feb) Left Vietnam. Request by AWM for a Canberra with a Vietnam War history
1974	Wings replaced at 3 Aircraft Depot
1979	Last flight in RAAF service (total flying hours: 5,144)
1981	Transferred by RAAF to AWM
1982	Refurbished to Vietnam configuration by 3 Aircraft Depot. Transferred to AWM on cessation of RAAF service, trucked to AWM store at Duntroon, ACT, and partially assembled
1995	Disassembled by RAAF Museum team, and road-transported from Duntroon to AWM Treloar Technology Centre, Mitchell, ACT

DATA

Type	Canberra Mk 20 (modified B.2)
Design firm	English Electric, UK
Manufacturer	Government Aircraft Factory, Melbourne
Role	Two-seat tactical bomber
No. built	48 (Australia) 926 (UK) 403 B-57s (USA)
Type entered RAAF service	1953
Identity	A84-247
Crew	2 (pilot, navigator/bomb aimer)
Powerplant	Two Rolls Royce RA.7 Avon Mk 109 jet turbine engines, each of 7,500 lb static thrust
Wingspan	19.50 m
Length	19.96 m
Max. speed	933 km/h
Range	5,841
Max. take-off weight	23,134 kg
Max. bomb load	3,629 kg. Max. load in Vietnam: eight 500-lb, or six 1,000-lb GP plus two 500-lb, or (later) six US M117 750-lb bombs, mounted internally and on wingtip racks

NOTES ON COLOUR SCHEME

The 1982 refurbishment by the RAAF included a repaint in the Vietnam period scheme of dark grey overall with disruptive olive drab camouflage on the upper surfaces, 18-in (46-cm) kangaroo roundels on rear fuselage sides, red/white/blue fin flashes on tail, and Australian flag on each side of nose. A red lightning bolt signifying 2 Squadron is on both sides of tail. Serial number in black on nosewheel doors; larger '247' in black on rear fuselage sides.

Low over Binh Ba rubber plantation, South Vietnam
APPROX. 2330 HOURS, 3 DECEMBER 1969

Captain Barry Donald and Second Lieutenant Alan Jellie sat side by side in the cockpit of Turbo Porter A14-686. Donald commanded the fixed-wing section of 161 (Independent) Reconnaissance Flight (161 [Indep] Recce Flt), Australian Army. Like the civilian Cessna 180 it was replacing, the Porter had not been designed specifically for military use and was somewhat vulnerable, but it performed better and could carry more. The unit's three Porters were still a novelty, having arrived in country from Australia only five days earlier aboard the 'Vung Tau ferry'—the former aircraft carrier HMAS *Sydney*. They had just been flown from Vung Tau to Luscombe Field at Nui Dat, Headquarters 1ATF.

That morning Jellie had been busy flying a target-marking mission for an air strike, a successful mission which resulted in two enemy bunkers being destroyed and four more exposed. Recent activity was detected around two other bunkers. At 2230 hours, Donald and Jellie took off from Luscombe on the first night training flight in the new Porter. They were now following Route 2 on the southward approach back to base and overflying the rubber plantation at Binh Ba, the site of a hotly-fought Australian battle

> *The exploitation of its full capabilities brought new dimensions to fixed-wing operations.*
>
> Peter Nolan, Possums and Bird Dogs

Porter A14-690 over Vietnam. Courtesy of Colin Pugh

six months earlier. The pilots knew that it was not unusual for a low-flying 'Possum' (the callsign for the flight's aircraft) to be struck by ground fire. Both pilots had been shot at numerous times, particularly Donald, a veteran pilot and instructor with over ten years' army service and two tours of duty in Vietnam. He had recently been recommended for a Distinguished Service Medal. Jellie, a Sioux helicopter pilot, had once been hit by a bullet that was miraculously deflected by his pen holder. So far, though, only one Possum pilot[22] had been killed in action, and the men of 161 (Indep) Recce Flt quietly wondered how long it would be before their luck changed.

The Porter took several hits. Small arms fire had come up from the plantation as it over-flew a firefight in progress.[23] South Vietnamese soldiers at nearby Duc Thanh watched as the aircraft descended on fire, clipped some rubber trees, and exploded at the plantation's edge.

First on the scene was the Australian liaison officer at Duc Thanh, Sergeant James 'Blue' Twomey of B Squadron, 1st Armoured Regiment. It was a sight that would stay with him.[24] The explosion had not been survivable, and at 2350 hours Twomey radioed back to base that both pilots were dead and recovered the aircraft's secret radio codes. Meanwhile, New Zealand pilot Captain Bill Flanagan DFC took a flare-equipped Sioux to locate the crash site, and a ground party headed by Warrant Officer Don Collins arrived from Nui Dat. The bodies of Donald and Jellie, two of the flight's most respected airmen, were removed for burial and a guard posted at the site overnight.

The burned-out wreckage of the Porter was trucked the few kilometres to Nui Dat, where it was buried. It was a bad start to a new era in the flight's Vietnam service, but as it turned out this was the sole loss of an Australian Porter and crew in Vietnam. Its replacement, A14-690, flew into Luscombe Field shortly afterwards, and Donald was posthumously awarded his DSM.

◄ ►

Ruggedness and versatility were the hallmarks of the Pilatus PC-6 Turbo Porter. In particular, few other military aircraft could take off in a 150-m run; its landing run was less than half that, thanks to a reversible-pitch propeller. It was this STOL (short take-off and landing) capability, combined with agility, low-speed performance and a stall speed of under 100 km/h, which made the Porter the natural choice for a visual reconnaissance and liaison aircraft for the Australian Army. It had an excellent climb rate for clearing obstacles or for leaving a hostile environment, one of several advantages over the Cessna 180. Apart from performance characteristics, its physical attributes also attracted the army: simple, strong construction with all-terrain undercarriage, and adaptability for cargo carrying. Removable rear seats created a spacious freight compartment accessed by sliding doors, and this, combined with the Porter's powerful turboprop engine and large, high-lift wing, allowed it to carry twice the load of the Cessna.

The flight's initial complement of fixed-wing aircraft consisted of four Cessna 180s, later joined by a couple of borrowed Cessna O-1 Bird Dogs. When the three Porters arrived, one Cessna 180 was retained; it departed in February 1971, and an additional Porter raised the type's complement to four. Eight Sioux helicopters, replaced with Kiowas from July that year, made up the flight's rotary-wing section. Owing to a scarcity of proper servicing equipment, only routine ground maintenance and minor repairs could be done at the airfield in Luscombe Field's purpose-built hangar. The tireless ground crews maintained a 97 per cent serviceability rate among the aircraft. For major overhauls they were flown to Saigon's Tan Son Nhut airport, where the CIA's airline, Air America, operated and serviced Porters.

During their two years in South Vietnam, the flight's six Porters (including two replacements) flew nearly 7,000 sorties on many and varied tasks.[25] The majority were daily visual reconnaissance flights, with command and control, air observation post (AOP), liaison, courier, resupply, VIP flights, training, test flights and occasionally 'dust-offs' (medical evacuations) adding to the list of roles they fulfilled. A few other specialised duties particularly illustrate the nature of the war in Vietnam. Porters were, for example, flown in the role of forward air control (see Bronco chapter). Target marking was done by firing white phosphorous rockets from under-wing stores hardpoints. It was performed for both ground artillery and air strikes by US and, on occasion, RAAF Canberra bombers—as on 28 May 1969, when two Viet Cong bunkers were destroyed. Even naval gunfire was target-marked. In April 1971, A14-690 ranged for the guided missile destroyer HMAS *Brisbane*,[26] enabling its 5-in guns to shell enemy bunkers. Rockets of the lethal variety, high-explosive or containing flechette anti-personnel steel darts, were carried by Porters flying top cover for helicopters on visual reconnaissance, resupply or troop extraction sorties. Launched in a 45-degree dive to ensure accuracy, a devastating 14 or even 38 rockets could be delivered to target.[27]

Each night, two 161 (Indep) Recce Flt Porters were on standby in case of enemy attack, loaded with flares for illumination and marker rockets. Parachute flares were used for lighting up battlefields at night. Up to 28 were carried and thrown out the floor hatch at intervals by a third crewman (being careful not to fall out with them), thus providing 75 minutes of illumination if the aircraft could remain circling that long.[28] One example of their use came during Operation Cung Chung II, which was aimed at cutting off enemy supply routes into villages. In the early hours of 12 August 1970, the men of 8 Platoon, C Company, 8th Battalion, Royal Australian Regiment (8RAR), ambushed some 50 Chau Duc guerrillas leaving the village of Hoa Long, and killed 19. In the face of the opposition, the enemy retreated. With the help of Porter-dropped flares, Second Lieutenant Peter Bysouth in a Sioux located several of the enemy hiding in bushes. He directed an APC ready-reaction force (1 Troop, B Squadron, 3rd Cavalry Regiment) to them, where six surrendered. For their actions, Bysouth was awarded a Distinguished Flying Cross and Sergeant Chad Sherrin, 8 Platoon leader, a Military Medal.

Shush flights: spying on the air waves

One important role for the Porters of 161 (Indep) Recce Flt was daily signals intelligence gathering (SIGINT) from enemy radio traffic. Secret 'shush' flights involved the electronic surveillance of enemy high frequency radio transmissions, with specially trained crewmen triangulating on the signals using Aerial Direction Finding Equipment (ADFE) to home in on their source. Radio specialists of the army's 547th Signal Troop provided the airborne operator and equipment which played a crucial role in the planning of ground operations. A battery of high frequency receivers and transmitters could be carried, enabling the Porter not only to eavesdrop on transmissions but to determine their bandwidths and frequencies. With these sets, the aircraft also became an airborne radio relay station for base and command centres. A reel-to-reel tape recorder was available for recording transmissions and for playing through speakers (the 'voice' missions described below). An AN/PRC 25 set, the standard man-portable radio, enabled communication with ground forces. A lookdown/side-scan radar set could detect enemy activity at night.

Porters were involved in some unusual types of operation. One was top cover for 'sniffer' flights in which a helicopter dangled a sensitive chemical instrument, an Automatic Personnel Detector (APD), to sample the air for ammonia—a possible sign of human activity. The helicopter, initially a Sioux and later a 9 Squadron RAAF Iroquois, flew straight, low and slow while the Porter navigated and relayed the results to 1ATF by radio. Another role was 'psy-ops' (psychological operations), flown with an 1,800-watt sound system wired to a microphone, a radio and a tape recorder for broadcasting to the enemy below—the so-called voice flights. Broadcasts included Vietnamese music which was blared out across the jungle with the aim of driving the enemy to distraction. It seems that the idea had a similar effect on 'friendlies', namely 9 Squadron at Vung Tau, whence the equipment originated. When the voice Porter was flown over the base playing carols during Christmas 1969, 'weapons opened up from everywhere … Vung Tau went mad that night and we got out of the place' reported a crewman.[29] It was during one voice flight in August 1971, with Major Neil Harden, the commanding officer of 161 (Indep) Recce Flt, at the controls over the Long Hai mountains, that A14-690 received its

Some of the electronic surveillance equipment fitted to a Porter in Vietnam. AWM P03057.001

only recorded battle damage when three rounds of ground fire hit the engine bay, rear fuselage and wing.

Aerial photography was yet another task of the Porter. The 1st Topographic Survey Unit based at Nui Dat used downward-pointing cartographic cameras mounted in the aircraft's floor hatch for photographic surveys of Phuoc Tuy province. The photographs were used to produce maps of the province which were then screen-printed and distributed among the soldiers.

At the start of October 1971, 161 (Indep) Recce Flt moved back to Vung Tau after four and a half years at Nui Dat. It was welcomed with three enemy 122-mm rockets which exploded at the north-east corner of the airfield, killing a Vietnamese civilian. More rocket and mortar attacks were to come, but the tent lines of 161 (Indep) Recce Flt escaped being hit.

By then many believed that Vietnam was an unwinnable war. On 6 October three Kiowa helicopters made a formation flypast over HMAS *Sydney* to see off the 3rd Battalion, Royal Australian Regiment (3RAR). It was a farewell to remember, as the Kiowas were accompanied by a 'voice' Porter which serenaded the troops. However, as Australian Army presence in Vietnam was wound down to 2,300 personnel by year's end, Porter operations continued. On 15 October, A14-701 was hit by a 7.62-mm round which embedded itself in a wing-mounted high-explosive rocket motor. On the 26th the same aircraft was hit again, this time from M16 ground fire which almost severed the main fuel line but did not prevent a safe landing at Dong Tam.

Porters took over the mail and courier deliveries to Vung Tau and Nui Dat that had been flown by the hard-pressed Wallaby Airlines, the RAAF Caribou transport squadron. They also carried another essential cargo—beer—to the two bases. The four aircraft flew their final missions in December. On 1 January 1972 they were towed to the local pier for shipping to Australia, and loaded aboard the Japanese freighter *Harima Maru*—the only vessel on which space could be found, after the approval to fly the aircraft to Australia had been withdrawn. On arrival in Australia, the flight relocated to Oakey, Queensland.

Because of its small numbers and the secrecy of some of its roles, the Porter did not achieve the fame of its contemporaries in Vietnam, such as the Iroquois helicopter. Nevertheless, its two-year presence there expanded the capabilities of 161 (Indep) Recce Flt and made a considerable contribution to Australia's war effort. A14-690 soldiered on with the rest of the army Porter fleet until the type was retired in 1992. Apparently, 690 was not favoured among air and ground crews because of an inexplicable refusal to fly straight, despite efforts to correct the problem—possibly an explanation for two crashes it sustained at Oakey during 1978–80.[30]

Australian Army Turbo Porters in Vietnam

Serial number	Period operational	Replaced by
Original deliveries:		
A14-680	(Nov 1969 – May 1970)	A14-701
A14-681	(Nov 1969 – Jan 1972)	
A14-686	(Nov 1969 – Dec 1969)	A14-690
Replacements, additions:		
A14-690	(Dec 1969 – Jan 1972)	
A14-701	(May 1970 – Jan 1972)	
A14-692	(Jan 1971 – Jan 1972)	

Aircraft flown by 161 (Indep) Recce Flt in Vietnam

Type	Period operational	Number of aircraft
Cessna 180	(Sep 1965 – Feb 1971)	7 (3 destroyed)
Bell 47G Sioux	(Sep 1965 – Sep 1971)	37 (8 destroyed)
Pilatus PC-6 Porter	(Nov 1969 – Jan 1972)	6 (1 destroyed)
Bell OH-58A Kiowa	(Jul 1971 – Feb 1972)	8 (loaned from US Army)
Cessna O-1 Bird Dog	(Sep 1967 – 1971)	3 (1 destroyed)

The Turbo Porter in context

The Porter was designed in Switzerland for the civilian market. It first flew as a piston-engined aircraft in 1959, the turboprop version (powered by a gas turbine engine driving a propeller) following two years later. It soon became widely used by civilian organisations, police and military forces around the world, with some 20 nations placing orders. The first four for the Australian Army were delivered in February 1968, and a further ten (including A14-690) at the end of the year. The final five came in May 1971, bringing to 19 the total supplied. In addition to 161 (Indep) Recce Flt, the Porter served with several other units of the Australian Army Aviation Corps (AAAVN): 163 (Indep) Recce Flt, 171 Air Cavalry Flight, 173 General Support Squadron, and the Army Aviation School.

Instrument panel of the Memorial's Turbo Porter. AWM REL27881

There is a diplomatic aspect to the Porter story that is unique in the Memorial's aircraft collection. Neutral Switzerland allowed the type to be sold on the basis that it would not be used offensively. With their deployment from Australia to Vietnam, sales were halted while the respective governments discussed the aircraft's intended roles. Once the Australian government had made assurances that the Porters would not be armed or used in combat, deliveries were resumed. The unofficial use of explosive rockets, however, clearly stretched the definition of non-combat use.

The Porter has wider relevance to the Memorial's charter than its service in Vietnam alone. The army has sent examples to Papua New Guinea, Vanuatu and elsewhere, and the type has been used extensively around the world in United Nations peacekeeping operations in which Australians have been involved. An example is the UN Mission for the Referendum in Western Sahara (Minurso), during which Australian medical officer Major Susan Felsche was killed in a Porter crash in June 1993. In Australian Army service, the Porter had been replaced the previous year by new deliveries of the Australian Nomad. However, new versions of the Porter were still being sold some 40 years after 161 (Indep) Recce Flt flew it in Vietnam, and it continues to be used world-wide in a variety of roles including passenger and freight transport, rescue, water bombing, parachuting and crop spraying. It was also built in America under licence, as the Fairchild AU-23A Peacemaker, for counter-insurgency (COIN) operations.

TIMELINE—A14-690

1968	Flown to Australia from Switzerland
1969	(Jan) Accepted by 1st Aviation Regiment, Australian Army, Amberley, Qld
	(Dec) Delivered to Vietnam aboard HMAS *Melbourne*. Served with 161 (Indep) Recce Flt in South Vietnam
1971	(Mar) Major servicing by Air America at Tan Son Nhut, Saigon
1972	(Jan) Returned to Australia by Japanese freighter
1989	Type requested from Army by AWM
1992	(Nov) Withdrawn from service. Allocated to AWM but held by Museum of Australian Army Flying at Army Aviation Centre, Oakey, Qld
2000	Transferred to AWM and trucked to Treloar Technology Centre

NOTES ON COLOUR SCHEME

When delivered to the Memorial, the aircraft retained its 1992 army camouflage (tan, green and black disruptive pattern) and markings. Rear fuselage markings (both sides) consist of 'ARMY', black kangaroo national insignia and 'A14-690' stencilled over the camouflage in opposite colours. A black shark mouth is painted on the nose.

Its Vietnam period paint scheme was: overall dark olive with black anti-glare panel forward of windscreen, spinner bare metal. Red/white/blue kangaroo roundels on fuselage sides and wing upper (starboard only) and lower surfaces; red/white/blue tail fin flash; 'ARMY' forward of fuselage roundels and full serial number aft, both in white; larger 'ARMY' in white on port wing upper surface and starboard wing lower surface; dayglo yellow-orange wingtips and fin tip; '690' in black on fin tip.

DATA

Type	PC-6/B1-H2 Turbo Porter
Design firm	Pilatus Flugzeugwerke, Switzerland
Manufacturer	Pilatus Flugzeugwerke, Switzerland
Role	Eight-seat STOL (short take-off and landing) utility transport; reconnaissance and liaison
No. built	Over 500 (total PC-6)
Type entered service	1968
Identity	A14-690 (Australian Army Aviation Corps)
Crew	2 (pilot, observer)
Powerplant	Pratt & Whitney Canada PT6A-20 turboprop engine of 550 shaft hp
Armament	Cluster of 7 rocket tubes or 19-rocket pod under each wing
Wingspan	15.14 m
Length	10.91 m
Max speed	262 km/h
Endurance	3 hours
Max. load	6 passengers or 2 stretchers, or 1,000 kg freight (limited to 360 kg in hot conditions)
Max. take-off weight	2,767 kg

BRONCO 67-14639

Near Trai Bai base camp, Tay Ninh province, South Vietnam
6 JUNE 1970

Squadron Leader Graham Neil and Flight Lieutenant Ken Semmler were airborne after taking off in an OV-10A Bronco of the US 19th Tactical Air Support Squadron (TASS). This was to be a routine visual reconnaissance mission, supporting the 3rd Brigade of the US 25th Infantry Division. Just ten minutes into the flight, two 'hot spots' developed simultaneously: a US armoured road convoy returning from Cambodia was ambushed by Viet Cong, and 4 km away another VC attack was concentrating mortar and small arms fire on Trai Bai base camp.

The convoy was the first priority, as the enemy were just 75 m from it in the treeline. While Semmler (a pilot himself but occupying the back seat on this mission) radioed for an air strike on the forces attacking Trai Bai, Neil brought the Bronco down and fired a salvo of 2.75-in high-explosive rockets from its underslung pods. Meanwhile, a US Army Cessna O-1 Bird Dog pilot spotted a dozen of the enemy running away, and marked them with smoke rockets for Neil to make another rocket attack.

> *A magnificent flying machine, a real sports car ... How I would love to have a Bronco in the backyard!*
>
> Flight Lieutenant Ken Semmler RAAF

Bronco 67-14639 at Vung Tau, South Vietnam, on 13 July 1970 with RAAF Caribou transports.
AWM P05114.002

Squadron Leader (later Air Vice Marshal) Graham Neil and Flight Lieutenant Kenneth Semmler climb into a 19th TASS Bronco at Cu Chi, South Vietnam. AWM P05581.010

Next, aiming into the treelines on both sides of the road, he made strafing runs with the Bronco's four M60C machine-guns and the last of his rockets. For the time being, the enemy fire ceased.

As an American 'dust-off' helicopter came in to extract wounded, Neil flew in to cover for it before turning his attention to Trai Bai. At the ground commander's request he fired into enemy positions in a treeline west of the camp. Now out of ammunition, he called in two more OV-10As and directed them onto the targets. The fighter-bombers arrived just 20 minutes after Semmler had called them in, and they too were directed onto the targets. First, a pair of A-37 Dragonflies coordinated their attacks with US helicopter gunships, dropping napalm and Mk 82 bombs right onto a cluster of enemy bunkers. Three minutes later, Semmler directed two F-100 Super Sabres to drop their Mk 117 bombs on five more bunkers. With friendly emplacements just 250 m away, accuracy was critical. Their Bronco now running low on fuel, Neil and Semmler called in another Bronco to take over, and headed for the nearest airfield at Tay Ninh West.

◄ ►

The action was a classic example of the effectiveness of Forward Air Control (FAC[31]) in coordinating precision tactical attacks on enemy positions. For his part in it, Squadron Leader (later Air Vice Marshal) Neil was awarded the Distinguished Flying Cross.[32] During the preceding four months, Neil had been in command of the US Air Force Tactical Air Control Party (TACP) based at Cu Chi near Saigon. Serving as Air Liaison Officer to the US 25th Infantry Division's 2nd Brigade, he was also air adviser to the colonel in command of the brigade. Under Neil's command were eight Australian, American and New Zealand pilots, their eight Broncos, and a US Air Force ground staff and maintenance detachment. During his time in the Bronco, Neil controlled 113 air strikes,[33] including 20 in the Memorial's Bronco, 67-14639, which was one of the workhorses of the 19th TASS between 1968 and 1971. In this very mobile war, it flew out of numerous bases including Bien Hoa, Tay Ninh, Di An, Cu Chi, Long Thanh, Lai Khe, Phan Tiet, and Vung Tau, where the Australian task force was based.

Semmler, too, flew regularly in 639, and one flight in it was particularly memorable. Returning at night to base at Cu Chi with New Zealander, Flight Lieutenant John Denton, in the back seat, the runway lights could not be turned on. To make matters worse, the aircraft's intercom system failed and they could not communicate. With the aid of the headlights of some jeeps and their own landing light, the two managed to locate the runway and make a safe landing.

In a broad sense, the airborne control of attacks from the air or from ground artillery has a long history. The artillery spotting or 'ranging' activities of 3 Squadron AFC during the First World War were aimed at improving accuracy of fire. During the Second World War, aerial controllers were used on a wide variety of Australian operations. Artillery spotting was one of the tasks of the Wirraways and Boomerangs of 4 and 5 (Army Cooperation) Squadrons RAAF in New Guinea, and the first operations which could be called forward air control were flown by these units (see Wirraway chapter). The naval bombardment and amphibious assault of Borneo were observed from RAAF B-24 Liberators by army liaison officers in radio contact with the command ships. In the strategic bombing of Germany, Bomber Command's Pathfinder Force under Australian Air Vice Marshal Don Bennett CB CBE DSO marked targets at night for the main force to attack. These operations were coordinated by a 'master bomber' circling the area as a command and control post, in much the same role of the later FACs.

The technique of forward air control was more specifically developed during the Korean War, using light aircraft such as the Cessna O-1 Bird Dog (L-19). Mobile or hidden targets such as gun emplacements often required low and slow flying to locate, followed by precision marking for air strikes. RAN Sea Furies and Fireflies from HMAS *Sydney* often 'ranged' for the naval bombardment of North Korean positions (see Sea Fury chapter). At the same time in Malaya, attacks by Lincoln bombers of 1 Squadron RAAF against communist terrorist base camps in the jungle were often directed by smoke canisters dropped from an Auster light aircraft.

In the early 1960s the RAAF began FAC training courses for experienced fighter pilots, so that in Vietnam the Australian FAC pilots generally had far more relevant experience than their American counterparts.[34] The method proved almost indispensable in attacks on tactical targets, many of which were hidden or required accurate visual identification. Initially they flew conventional light aircraft converted for military use, primarily the Cessna O-1 and the O-2A Super Skymaster, but in July 1968 a purpose-built aircraft, the turboprop-powered Bronco, arrived in Vietnam. It was faster, while still retaining low-speed capability, manoeuvrability and a short take-off and landing run of 230 m. It was armed with underslung weapons sponsons mounting a battery of four

M60C machine-guns and pods of target-marking and high explosive rockets. The O-1 and O-2 had also carried rocket pods, but the Bronco introduced machine-guns for fire support and for its own defence. Its crew had excellent visibility through its generous cockpit canopy. Equally importantly, an array of VHF, UHF, longer-range HF, and FM radios allowed the Bronco crew to communicate with headquarters, ground forces, other FACs and the strike aircraft they were controlling[35].The variety of attack aircraft controlled ranged from A-37, F-100 and F-5 strike aircraft to AC-47 'Spooky' gunships, RAAF Canberra bombers, and even B-52 Stratofortress bombers on 'arc light' missions in which each B-52 could carry a formidable 30-t bomb load.

Controlling an air attack required precise coordination. After identifying a target, the controller requested clearance to call in an attack and make radio contact with the friendly ground force. He then formulated an attack plan and fire coordination line, considering such factors as the location of friendly forces and the trajectories of artillery fire. Arranging a rendezvous point for the attacking aircraft, the FAC briefed their pilots on where and how they were to attack, and then marked the target by firing phosphorous smoke rockets at it. During the ensuing attack, the FAC maintained a position above or off to the side of the strike aircraft. Meanwhile, friendly troops marked their own positions with coloured smoke grenades. After each aircraft dropped its ordnance, the FAC assessed their accuracy and adjusted the next pilot's instructions as needed. Finally, he made a bomb damage assessment.[36]

Forward Air Control greatly assisted in strike accuracy and target identification. However, communication with the ground commander, and a strict sequence of clearances when an air strike was ordered, were often vital. A couple of years prior to Neil's tour in Vietnam, an incident occurred in which an American FAC's instructions were not made directly to the commander, but were instead relayed through an artillery radio network. The resulting air strike hit friendly troops, with several casualties among the 2nd Battalion, Royal Australian Regiment (2RAR).[37]

In another incident in February 1970, an Australian FAC was shot down by enemy ground fire. Flight Lieutenant Chris Langton and a US Army observer, flying out of Dau Tieng in a notoriously dangerous region, were controlling an artillery and fighter-bomber strike near the Cambodian border when their Bronco went into an uncontrollable spin. The two ejected. Although the Bronco was under 1,000 ft and rolling upside down, its ejection seats were designed for this eventuality, and both landed unharmed among trees. Langton survived a dramatic rescue attempt in which his rescue helicopter was shot down, before both men and the helicopter crew were winched out by UH-1 helicopters.[38]

The RAAF FACs, all highly experienced fighter pilots, were sent to Vietnam in batches of three or four. They first went through the 'theatre indoctrination school' which, during the period that Broncos were operational, was at Phan Rang (home also of the Canberra bombers of 2 Squadron RAAF) and was later replaced with in-squadron training. They were attached to one of two squadrons of the 504th Tactical Air Support

Pilot's and observer's cockpits of the Memorial's Bronco, while stored at the Treloar Technology Centre in 2008. AWM REL35907

Group (TASG), US 7th Air Force: the 19th Tactical Air Support Squadron (TASS), based at Bien Hoa near Saigon (covering the III Corps area bordering Cambodia) and the 20th TASS at Da Nang (covering I Corps which bordered North Vietnam and Laos).

The Australians were under instruction not to violate a buffer zone along each border; this was an unpopular order with many, as it restricted their area of operations considerably, while the American crews had no such restriction. In this respect and by their uniforms they stood apart from the Americans, but in all other matters including chain of command, they were integrated into the US Air Force for the duration of their tour of duty in Vietnam. In all, 36 RAAF fighter pilots were seconded to fly as FACs in Vietnam between 1966 and 1971, and of these, 23 flew Broncos. As the only aircraft in the Memorial's collection which has seen American service, Bronco 67-14639 commemorates the close working relationship between US and Australian forces in Vietnam. At the end of 1971 the aircraft transferred to the 23rd TASS and, flown by US crews, flew nearly two more intensive years of missions over Cambodia and Laos, including the Ho Chi Minh Trail, before the ceasefire and the aircraft's departure from the South-East Asian conflict.

Australians who flew Bronco 67-14639 in Vietnam with 19th TASS

Pilot	No. of missions	Period
Flt Lt Peter Condon	41	Jul–Dec 1969
Flt Lt Ron Slater	38	Oct 1969–Feb 1970
Sqn Ldr Graham Neil	20	1970
Flt Lt Ken Semmler	18	Apr–Jul 1970
Flt Lt Richard Gregory	5	May 1970
Flt Lt Bruce Searle	1	May 1970
Flt Lt Ray Butler	10	Jul 1970
Wing Cdr Colin Ackland	1	Jul 1970

The Bronco in context

The North American Rockwell OV-10 Bronco was the result of a 1963 US tri-service (air force, navy and marines) Light Armed Reconnaissance Aircraft (LARA) specification to replace the Cessna O-1 and O-2. Starting life as the NA-300, it first flew in 1965. The OV-10A two years later was the first production variant, and the only one flown by the US Air Force. The company's original idea had been for a much lighter and simpler aircraft capable of operating from confined spaces including roads, and with the jungle fighting environment in mind. The US Department of Defense, however, insisted on a larger and more complex aircraft than the designers first envisaged, and from those specifications the Bronco evolved. Nevertheless, its nimbleness and a substantial speed

Another Bronco of the 19th TASS over South Vietnam, c. 1970. The four pods under the fuselage each hold seven 2.75-in rockets. AWM P05581.002

advantage over the Cessnas, combined with its armament, made it popular with its crews, to whom it felt like a fighter in comparison.

Indicative of the risks of FAC work are the statistics which reveal that, between the three US services flying Broncos, 81 aircraft were lost during five years of flying over North and South Vietnam, Laos and Cambodia. These losses involved 61 fatalities, including several from the 19th TASS.[39] However, losses were still lighter than those suffered by Cessna O-1 and O-2 crews, partly because the faster Bronco was a more difficult target.

The Bronco served in the US Air Force until 1991 and in the Marines until three years later, by which time the type had also seen action in Operation Desert Storm against Iraq. In 1991–92 the Philippine Air Force's 15th Strike Wing acquired 27 ex-US Air Force OV-10As to replace its T-28 Trojans in the fight against local rebel and terrorist forces. Following its retirement from service, the Memorial's aircraft came from this source. The remaining aircraft, together with some ex-Thai examples, were flown well into the first decade of the 21st century.

TIMELINE—67-14639

1968	(Mid-year) Built and accepted by US Air Force (Aug); test flown by Al Saduski
1968	(Sep) To 19th Tactical Air Support Squadron (TASS) of 504th Tactical Air Support Group, US 7th Air Force at Bien Hoa, South Vietnam
1971	(Nov) Transferred to 23rd TASS at Da Nang, Tan Son Nhut (Saigon) etc. Flew operations over Laos and Cambodia
1973	(Aug) Ceased operations in South-East Asia
1974	To 20th TASS, 601st Tactical Air Control Wing (TACW) at Wiesbaden, West Germany, (NATO support)
1977–83	To Sembach US Air Force Base (AFB), West Germany, and on detachment to Spain
1984	To 27th TASS at George AFB, Victorville, California, USA (stored)
1985	To 19th TASS, 51st Tactical Fighter Wing at Osan AFB, South Korea (attached 5th Tactical Air Control Group, US 7th Air Force)
1988	To 20th TASS, 507th TACW at Shaw AFB, South Carolina
1992	To 15th Strike Wing, Philippine Air Force, at Danilo Atienza Air Base, Sangley Point, Philippines
1993	(Oct) Total flying time logged: 10,790 hours
2001	Identified for acquisition by AWM
2003	(Jul) Transferred to AWM ownership
2005	(Feb) Official handover to RAAF Chief of Air Force
2007	Shipped from Philippines aboard HMAS *Tobruk* and arrived at AWM Treloar Technology Centre for storage

Source: US Air Force Historical Research Agency, Maxwell AFB, Alabama, USA, via Darryl Whitcomb

NOTES ON COLOUR SCHEME

Scheme in service with 19th TASS: Overall satin gull-grey, with white wing upper surface. Grey walk strip on wing upper surface. Black rectangular area behind engine exhausts. 'USAF' above '14639' in black on fin sides. Small US national insignia on both fuselage sides (below rear canopy) and on upper left and lower right wing surfaces. Propeller blades bare metal, and spinners red with yellow central band. Standard warning insignia include triangular ejector seat signs below forward canopy and red propeller stripes.

DATA

Type	OV-10A Bronco
Design firm	North American Rockwell Corporation
Manufacturer	North American Rockwell, Columbus, Ohio, USA
Role	Counter insurgency, forward air control, light attack
No. built	157 (total OV-10 production 271)
Type entered service	1968
Identity	67-14639 (US Air Force) 74639 (Philippine Air Force) 305-47 (construction no.)
Crew	2 (pilot and observer)
Powerplant	Two 715 shaft hp (533 kW) Garrett-AiResearch T76-G turboprop engines
Armament	Up to 1,630 kg weapons load: four rocket pods each mounting seven phosphorous target-marking or high explosive 2.75-in rockets; alternative load of bombs; four 7.62-mm M60C machine-guns. Provision for two underwing AIM-9 Sidewinder missiles
Wingspan	12.2 m
Length	12.7 m
Max. speed	450 km/h at sea level
Range	367 km (combat radius with load); 2,224 km with auxiliary fuel tank
Max. take-off weight	6,560 kg

Glossary of terms

Ranks referred to in this book

1. RAAF/RAF

Traditional usage	Present day usage	
Officers		
ACM	ACM	Air Chief Marshal
Air Mshl	AIRMSHL	Air Marshal
AVM	AVM	Air Vice Marshal
Air Cdre	AIRCDRE	Air Commodore
Gp Capt	GPCAPT	Group Captain
Wing Cdr	WGCDR	Wing Commander
Sqn Ldr	SQNLDR	Squadron Leader
Flt Lt	FLTLT	Flight Lieutenant
FO	FLGOFF	Flying Officer
PO	PLTOFF	Pilot Officer
Other ranks		
WO	WOFF	Warrant Officer
Flt Sgt	FSGT	Flight Sergeant
Sgt	SGT	Sergeant
Cpl	CPL	Corporal
LAC	LAC/LACW	Leading Aircraftman/woman
AC	AC/ACW	Aircraftman/woman

2. Navy (including foreign)

Lt Cdr	Lieutenant Commander
Sub-Lt	Sub-Lieutenant
Lt(jg)	Lieutenant Junior Grade
CPO	Chief Petty Officer
PO1	Petty Officer Class 1

3. Army

Gen	General
Lt Gen	Lieutenant General
Maj Gen	Major General
Brig Gen	Brigadier General
Col	Colonel
Lt Col	Lieutenant Colonel
Maj	Major
Capt	Captain
Lt	Lieutenant
2nd Lt	Second Lieutenant
WO1	Warrant Officer Class 1
WO2	Warrant Officer Class 2
Sgt	Sergeant
Cpl	Corporal
Pte	Private

4. German *Luftwaffe* (1939-45)

Genobst	*Generaloberst*
Obstlt	*Oberstleutnant*
Maj	*Major*
Hptm	*Hauptmann*
Olt	*Oberleutnant*
Lt	*Leutnant*
Fw	*Feldwebel*
Uffz	*Unteroffizier*

AFC

Australian Flying Corps

AIF

Australian Imperial Force

aileron

A moveable control surface for banking (laterally tilting) an aircraft. Two opposing ailerons are generally fitted, one on each outer trailing edge of the wings.

airframe

The main structure of an aircraft.

air ace

An airman with five or more enemy aircraft confirmed destroyed.

Australian War Museum

Original name of the Australian War Memorial; it evolved out of the activities of the AWRS. While located in Sydney in the 1920s the museum was called the Australian War Memorial Museum.

AWRS

Australian War Records Section (formed in May 1917)

biplane

An aircraft with two wing planes or four wings.

CAC

Commonwealth Aircraft Corporation

canopy

A transparent enclosure over a cockpit or crew compartment

covering

The outer skin of a fabric-covered aircraft.

DAP

Department of Aircraft Production

dust-off

A term originating during the Vietnam War for an aeromedical evacuation ('medevac') helicopter or mission

EATS

Empire Air Training Scheme

elevator

A moveable control surface for climbing or diving an aircraft. Normally fitted to the trailing edge of a tailplane.

elevon

An aircraft control surface, normally mounted on the wing trailing edge on a tailless aircraft (lacking a horizontal stabiliser), which combines the functions of elevators and ailerons.

empennage

An aircraft tail section.

FAA

Fleet Air Arm

fin flash

A rectangular national marking on an aircraft's tail surfaces.

fixed-wing aircraft

An aeroplane, as opposed to a helicopter.

flak

Anti-aircraft artillery fire from the ground (from the German *Flugabwehrkanone*, aircraft defence cannon). Rounds were normally fused to explode at a predetermined height.

flaps

The moveable surfaces on inner trailing edges of wings, lowered to increase lift on landing and/or take-off.

flight

A part of a squadron (three or four flights per squadron was standard).

former

An internal vertical member of an aircraft's structure giving it form and joined by stringers.

FAC

Forward Air Control/Forward Air Controller

fuselage

The aircraft body, excluding wings and empennage.

GAF

Government Aircraft Factory

g-force

The simulated force of gravity exerted on an aircraft and its crew during high-speed manoeuvres or aerobatics.

German Air Service

The air arm of the German military during the first World War (full title: Imperial German Army Air Service, or *Deutsche Luftstreitkräfte*).

ground effect

An aircraft's buoyancy just before landing, caused by the aerodynamic effects of proximity to the ground.

JAAF

Japanese Army Air Force

Jasta

Short for *Jagdstaffel*, a German fighter squadron.

JNAF

Japanese Naval Air Force

lift

The aerodynamic force generated by a wing or rotor which keeps an aircraft aloft.

longeron

See **stringer**

Luftwaffe

The German air force (Second World War and after)

mainplane

A wing or pair of wings.

mission

See **operation**

monoplane

An aircraft with a single mainplane.

nacelle

An aerodynamically shaped part of an aircraft that houses an engine, undercarriage, crew compartment, etc.

NEIAF

Netherlands East Indies Air Force

oleo

A hydraulic/pneumatic shock-absorbing undercarriage leg or strut

on the deck

Flying close to the ground.

operation

An operational flight, normally by a number of aircraft, against the enemy (US term: mission).

PAF

Philippine Air Force

photo-reconnaissance

Aerial photography, normally for gaining intelligence on enemy locations or activities.

powerplant

The source of power for an aircraft; an engine.

pusher-type aircraft

An aircraft with propeller(s) at the back or behind the engine(s).

RAAC

Royal Australian Armoured Corps

RAAF

Royal Australian Air Force

RAF

Royal Air Force

RAN

Royal Australian Navy

RASC

Royal Australian Service Corps

RCAF

Royal Canadian Air Force

RFC

Royal Flying Corps

RGA

Royal Garrison Artillery

RN

Royal Navy

RNAS

Royal Naval Air Service (which merged with the Royal Flying Corps in 1918 to form the Royal Air Force).

rotary-wing aircraft

A helicopter, as opposed to an aeroplane; an aircraft kept aloft by means of a rotor.

roundel

A round national insignia (e.g., blue and white disc used by the RAAF).

slick

A helicopter configured for troop transport; a standard Iroquois during the Vietnam War was a 'Huey slick'.

sortie

An individual aircraft's operational flight. An operation flown by ten aircraft would consist of ten sorties.

sternframe

The rearmost section of aircraft fuselage.

strafe

To attack ground or water targets from the air using gunfire.

stringer

An internal longitudinal member of an aircraft's structure, joining formers.

tractor-type aircraft

An aircraft with propeller(s) at the front (rather than the back) or forward of the engine(s).

trim

To adjust control surfaces to regulate the force required to keep the aircraft straight and level.

type example

An example of an aircraft which is representative of its type. The few aircraft in the Memorial's collection which have little or no known individual histories are significant primarily as type examples.

undercarriage

Aircraft landing gear

unit

A discrete military formation. Examples include a RAAF squadron or a German *Staffel*.

USAAF

United States Army Air Force

USAF

United States Air Force

wing rib

An internal longitudinal structural former of a wing.

spinner

An aerodynamically shaped cover for a propeller hub

squadron

The basic operational formation of an air arm, typically operating 12 to 24 aircraft.

Appendices

APPENDIX 1

Storage and display milestones for the Memorial's aircraft collection

A number of captured German First World War aircraft were exhibited at Australia House in London from November 1918 until the following August. About 70 in total were ceded to Australia under the terms of the armistice, and their packing and dispatch from Fienvillers in France was overseen by Lieutenant MacKinolty MC of the AFC. Once in Britain, they were administered by the Trophy Store of the Australian War Records Section (from which the Australian War Museum, later the Australian War Memorial, evolved). Seven examples of each type were requested (one for each state and one for the Commonwealth), but in the event it is believed that less than half the requested number were sent and that four states (Queensland, Western Australia, South Australia and Tasmania) were actually allotted aircraft by the Australian War Museum Committee.

Fifteen German and five British First World War aircraft are recorded as having been preserved, and most were included in the museum's first display at the Exhibition Building in Melbourne from 1920. Complementing them were a number of contemporary Australian Air Corps service aircraft and civil types, which were not taken on charge by the museum.

In 1925 some of the aircraft were transported to Sydney with the museum's relocation there (a move undertaken partly because of the fire hazard in Melbourne). They remained in Sydney until the exhibition's closure in 1935 for the ultimate move to Canberra. The remaining aircraft were held in the museum's main store in Melbourne. This store was retained into the 1940s, and replaced by a new fibro shed at Duntroon, ACT, in 1955. Owing to the difficulty of storing and displaying the aircraft in the available space, disposals took place in 1936 and 1942 and between 1950 and 1963.

TIMELINE	
1918–19	Captured German aircraft displayed at Australia House, London
1920	Temporary display in Adelaide for Motor Traders' Association of South Australia
1922	Australian War Museum opens at Exhibition Building in Carlton, Melbourne
1925	Relocation to Exhibition Building in Prince Alfred Park, Sydney, as the Australian War Memorial Museum, after fire destroys some crated German aircraft
1935	Sydney exhibition closes
1941	Australian War Memorial opens in Canberra, with First World War aircraft display in Aeroplane Hall
1945–51	Second World War aircraft hangared at RAAF Base Canberra (later renamed RAAF Fairbairn), and subsequently parked outside
1955	Second World War aircraft installed in Aeroplane Hall
	Storage shed at Duntroon, ACT, opens
1988	Newly restored DH.9, Avro 504K and Zero displayed at Bicentennial Airshow, RAAF Richmond, NSW
1994	Duntroon store closes. Aircraft relocated to Mitchell B store and later to adjacent Treloar Technology Centre in Mitchell, ACT
1996	Aircraft Hall temporarily renamed Bradbury Aircraft Hall
1999	Aircraft Hall temporarily closes for installation of *Air power in the Pacific 1941–53*
2001	ANZAC Hall opens
2007	Qantas sponsorship; collection named Qantas Aircraft Collection
2008	*Over the front: The Great War in the air* opens in ANZAC Hall

APPENDIX 2

Aircraft type designation and numbering systems

Throughout the history of aviation, and around the world, numerous systems of naming aircraft types have been applied. They follow a complex array of schemes, which have varied with country of origin, armed service, and period. The Memorial's aircraft, arranged by country of manufacture, are listed here with brief notes. As aircraft designation systems is such a large topic, these notes will be confined to the types referred to.

Australia

➤ de Havilland Australia DH.82A Tiger Moth
➤ CAC CA-5 Wirraway II
➤ DAP Beaufort Mk VIII
➤ de Havilland DH.98 Mosquito PR.40
➤ GAF Canberra B.20

Australia followed British designation systems, which were applied also to US-built aircraft in RAAF service. See Great Britain, 1939–45 below. RAAF and Army aircraft were and are still allocated individual serial numbers in the form A17-704 ('A' denoting aircraft, '17' the aircraft type, in this case Tiger Moth, and '704' the individual aircraft, normally but not always a sequential number in order of receipt).

Great Britain, pre-1919

- ➤ Deperdussin school-type monoplane
- ➤ Avro 504K
- ➤ Airco (de Havilland) DH.9
- ➤ Royal Aircraft Factory SE5a

Generally the design firm was followed by a design number, and this was often preceded by letters denoting the aircraft's role. DH.9 was the ninth type designed by Geoffrey de Havilland for Airco. SE5a was the first modified subtype (a) of the fifth 'scout experimental' type designed for the Royal Aircraft Factory. Avro 504K was the 11th subtype of A.V. Roe's Model 504. Individual aircraft serial numbers allocated in Britain consisted of a letter followed by a number of up to four digits, as in H2174. In Australia from 1921, these were replaced in RAAF service by a serial number in the 'A' numbering scheme referred to above, as in A3-4. The Deperdussin predates these schemes, and was serialled simply CFS.5 as the fifth aircraft of the Central Flying School at Point Cook, Victoria.

Great Britain, 1939–45

- ➤ Avro 683 Lancaster B.1 (or Mk I)
- ➤ Supermarine Spitfire Mk IIa
- ➤ Gloster Meteor F.8
- ➤ Hawker Sea Fury FB.11

The full title included the design firm and often its design number (the latter was normally left out in general reference), its name, and its mark number preceded by a letter or letters indicating its role ('B' for bomber, 'F' for fighter, 'FB' for fighter-bomber, 'NF' for night fighter, etc). Mark numbers were originally in Roman numerals, and changed to Arabic numerals later in the war. Where applicable, subtypes of marks were indicated with a lower case letter (a, b, etc.) Schemes for aircraft names varied with design firm, e.g., Avro bombers were named after British cities. Individual aircraft serial numbers followed the alphanumeric scheme referred to above but could include two letters, as in TF925. In RAAF service, these were replaced by a serial number in the 'A' numbering scheme referred to above, as in A77-368.

USA

- ➤ Douglas C-47B-20-DK (Dakota Mk IV)
- ➤ Lockheed A-28 (Hudson Mk IVA)
- ➤ North American P-51D-20-NT Mustang
- ➤ Curtiss P-40E-1 (Kittyhawk Mk IA)
- ➤ Bell 47G-3B-1 Sioux

- ➤ Bell UH-1B Iroquois
- ➤ North American Rockwell OV-10A Bronco

For aircraft built to US Army Air Force (USAAF, later US Air Force) contracts, the design firm was followed by a role designation letter ('A' for attack, 'B' for bomber, 'C' for cargo or transport, 'P' for pursuit, 'T' for trainer, 'UH' for utility helicopter, etc.), an air force type designation number (e.g., P-51 was the 51st pursuit type contracted by the USAAF), a subtype or model designation letter running alphabetically, a production block number (1, 5, 10, 15, etc.) identifying minor variations within a subtype, a two-letter code identifying the manufacturer and factory (e.g., 'NT' for North American Aviation's plant at Dallas, Texas), and a popular name. As with British aircraft these names often followed a theme, such as the hawk series of Curtiss fighters and the native American tribal names for Bell helicopters. Names of US-built aircraft were often changed in RAF and RAAF service. The US Warhawk became Tomahawk (P-40B and C) and Kittyhawk (P-40D and subsequent models), and the A-20 Havoc became Boston, in RAF and RAAF service. US-built aircraft in RAF and RAAF service were referred to by this name and a mark number corresponding to the US subtype or model designation letter; thus the P-40E was the Kittyhawk Mk IA, P-40K and M were Mk III, and P-40N was Mk IV. US-allocated individual aircraft serial numbers were in the form 44-13106, the first two digits being the year in which the aircraft's construction was contracted for the USAAF (the first digit and hyphen were deleted in the painted serial). In Australian service, this was replaced by a serial number in the 'A' numbering scheme referred to above, as in A1-404.

Germany, 1914-18

- ➤ Albatros D.Va
- ➤ Pfalz D.XII

For the German Air Service, the *Idflieg* (*Inspektion der Fliegertruppen*, the aviation bureau of Germany's War Office) introduced a system in which a letter denoting the aircraft's role was followed by a sequential Roman numeral. 'D' referred to a single-seat armed aircraft. Thus, the Pfalz D.XII was the Pfalz company's 12th design of the D type. As with other national systems, a lower-case letter suffix (as in Albatros D.Va) indicated a minor variation or modification to the design. Individual aircraft serial numbers consisted of a sequential number followed by the last two digits of its year of entry into service, for example, 2600/18.

Germany, 1939-45

- ➤ Messerschmitt Bf 109G-6
- ➤ Messerschmitt Me 163B *Komet*
- ➤ Messerschmitt Me 262A-1a *Jabo*

The *Luftwaffe* (Germany's air force) used the RLM designation system devised by the *Reichsluftfahrtministerium* (Reich Aviation Ministry) which designated aircraft by their design firm and project number. 'Me' indicated Messerschmitt, except for designs prior to mid-1938 which used 'Bf' for *Bayerische Flugzeugwerke* (Bavarian Aircraft Factory) such as the Bf 109. Alphanumeric suffixes indicate a descending sequence of subtypes or variants, hence in Me 262A-1a, 'A' is a major variant, '1' a minor variant of A, and 'a' a sub-variant of A-1. Conversions of these subtypes were indicated by '/R' (*Rüststand*) or '/U' (*Umrüstsatz*) followed by a number (e.g., Bf 109G-6/U3). Some aircraft also gained an official or unofficial name, hence *Jabo* (for *Jagdbomber*, fighter-bomber) or *Sturmvogel* (stormbird) for the fighter-bomber version of the Me 262, and *Komet* (comet) for the Me 163. Some types were identified primarily by their subtype, hence the Bf 109E became known as *Emil*, the G as *Gustav*, etc. Individual aircraft serial numbers, called *Werknummern*, were (in the case of the Memorial's aircraft) of six digits, as in 191907.

Japan

➤ Navy Type 0 Carrier Fighter, Model 21 (Mitsubishi A6M2 *Reisen*, Zero-sen or Zeke)
➤ Army Type 1 Fighter, Model 2b (Nakajima Ki-43-IIb *Hayabusa*, or Oscar)

Japan designated its aircraft by service (army or navy), type (indicating the Japanese year it entered service), role and model. For the Zero, Type 0 (or 00) refers to the aircraft's entry into service in the Japanese year 2600, or 1940 in the Western calendar. Its common name was *Reisen* (for *Rei-shiki sentoki* meaning Zero fighter) or Zero-sen. Side by side with this designation scheme were separate schemes for navy and army. The Japanese Naval Air Force (JNAF) used a shortened scheme to identify an aircraft's role and manufacturer: a letter to designate the role (e.g., 'A' for carrier-borne fighter), a sequential number to identify the aircraft type within that role, a second letter designating the manufacturer (e.g., 'M' for Mitsubishi), and a second number designating the subtype. Hence, A6M2 equates to the Zero Model 21. The Japanese Army Air Force (JAAF) used the *Kitai* (Ki) system of sequential airframe design numbers, with the number often followed by a Roman numeral model number, and 'a', 'b', 'c', etc. designating a subtype. Hence, Ki-43-IIb *Hayabusa* (peregrine falcon) was the Army Type 1 Fighter, Model 2b. A fourth scheme also needs to be mentioned. The Allies used a codename system for Japanese aircraft, devised by US intelligence staff in Melbourne from July 1942. Male names were used for fighters (hence Zeke, a 'hillbilly' name chosen by Captain Frank McCoy, and Oscar). Individual aircraft serial numbers were short numbers, as in 5784.

Soviet Union

➤ MiG-15*bis*

Soviet aircraft were named by their design firm followed by a sequential design number. MiG-15 was aircraft no. 15 (though the 9th, not 15th, design) of the Mikoyan-Gurevich design bureau. The suffix *bis* (second) indicated modifications to the original production model. Individual aircraft serial numbers were short numbers, as in 2458.

➤ Pilatus PC-6-B1/H2 Turbo Porter

The PC-6 was the third Pilatus production aircraft (following the P-2 and P-3 trainers). Subtypes were designated sequentially A1, A2, B1, B2, H2, etc., mostly indicating different engines. In Australian Army service, individual aircraft were numbered according to the 'A' scheme referred to above, as in A14-690.

APPENDIX 3

Military aviation organisation: some relevant notes

Australia and Great Britain: During the First World War, the AFC (the only flying corps operated by a dominion nation) had eight squadrons in Britain, Europe and the Middle East, four for training and four operational, which came under the control of British wings and brigades. In the RFC (later RAF) structure about six squadrons – scout, reconnaissance and bombing – were assigned to each wing, three wings to a brigade, and one brigade to an army. Attached to the Australian Corps was 3 Squadron AFC, consisting of three flights each with a different role. During the Second World War the RAF and RAAF were both structured according to the following hierarchy, in ascending order: flight, squadron, wing, group, command (Bomber, Fighter, Coastal, Training and Transport Commands). The basic unit was the squadron, typically operating between a dozen and 24 aircraft, depending on role. Flying training schools were also divided into flights. During the Korean War, the RAN embarked its aircraft aboard HMAS *Sydney* in two Carrier Air Groups, with two squadrons per group. In Vietnam, Australian Army aviation was conducted by a flight of the 1st Aviation Regiment.

United States: The US Army Air Corps (USAAC) became the US Army Air Force in 1942 and the US Air Force (USAF) in 1947. During the Second World War the organisational hierarchy was, in ascending order: squadron, group, wing, division, air force. Unit abbreviations were in the form 319th BS (Bombardment Squadron), 90th BG (Bombardment Group). The component squadrons (normally three or four) of a group may or may not have been stationed at the same base. An air force operated in a particular area within a theatre of war at any one time; the Fifth Air Force, for example, operated in the South-West Pacific Area (SWPA), including Australia. With the formation of the USAF, existing groups were renamed wings. During both the Korean and Vietnam Wars, an RAAF squadron was assigned as a fourth squadron to a US fighter interceptor wing (in Korea) and a tactical fighter wing (in Vietnam). In Vietnam, Australians also flew with tactical air support squadrons (within a tactical air support group), and with tactical fighter squadrons (within a tactical fighter wing).

Japan: The Imperial Japanese Navy and Imperial Japanese Army operated separate air services during the Second World War. Higher formations within the services are not included here.

Japanese Army Air Force (JAAF) hierarchy, in ascending order:
- *shotai* (flight of three aircraft)
- *chutai* (squadron of nine to 12 aircraft)
- *sentai* (air group of three *chutai* and a *sentai honbu* headquarters section, plus reserves. This was the basic operational unit.)
- *hikodan* (wing or air brigade)

Japanese Naval Air Force (JNAF) hierarchy, in ascending order:
Carrier-based:
- *shotai* (flight of three aircraft)
- *hikotai* (squadron of nine to 16 aircraft)
- *kokutai* (air corps of up to 150 aircraft)
- *koku sentai* (air flotilla)

Land-based:
- *homen kantai* (area fleet)
- *kokutai* (air corps of up to 150 aircraft)

Germany: During the First World War, the basic German Air Service unit was the *Jasta* (*Jagdstaffel*). During the Second World War, *Luftwaffe* units were organised as follows:
- *Staffel* (equivalent to a flight)
- *Gruppe* (equivalent to a squadron, normally containing three *Staffeln*)
- *Geschwader* (equivalent to a wing, containing three or four *Gruppen*. The two *Geschwader* types applicable to the Memorial's aircraft were *Jagdgeschwader* (fighter wing) and *Kampfgeschwader* (bomber wing)

Above these were divisional and corps organisations. Abbreviations were in the form 2/JG53 (2nd *Staffel* of *Jagdgeschwader* 53) and II/KG51 (2nd *Gruppe* of *Kampfgeschwader* 51).

Selected sources

1. Australian War Memorial

The curatorial aircraft folders maintained by the Memorial's Military Heraldry and Technology Section, together with Memorial registry files, contain the majority of the records and correspondence upon which this book is based. As these are not generally publicly available, they are not specifically cited as sources.

Additional references include the Memorial's official records holdings listed below, and the Memorial's Photographs, Film and Sound collections, including interviews with relevant personnel. Specific one-off references are given in the endnotes.

Official Records

AWM64: RAAF Operations Record Books (A50) and Detail of Operations (A51)

AWM4, Class 8: Australian Flying Corps war diaries
AWM99: Technical documentation and log books
AWM289: Records of Australian Army: 161 (Indep) Recce Flt – Vietnam

Private Records

PR87/014: Flt Lt T.E. Osborn DFC, 460 and 33 Squadrons RAAF
PR MSS1512: R.N. Levy manuscript

Reports and papers held by Military Heraldry and Technology Section

Owers, C., Unpublished manuscript 'The Deperdussin Monoplane Type A' (1985)
Owers, C., Unpublished manuscript 'Pfalz D.XII 2600/18' (1986)
Owers, C., Unpublished manuscript 'Royal Aircraft Factory SE5a A2-4' (c. 1986)
Owers, C., Unpublished manuscript 'The first Australian aeronautical collection' (1988)
Owers, C. and Waugh, R., Plans and notes on Pfalz and Albatros
Swan, J.M., Unpublished manuscript 'Tiger tails, kat-tails and some digressions' (1997)
US HQ PACAF report *The RAAF in SEA* [South-East Asia] (Sept 1970)
Whitcomb, D., Unpublished history of OV-10A Bronco 67-14639 (2007)

2. National Archives of Australia

Series A9186: RAAF Operations Record Books and Details of Operations (Forms A50 and A51)
Series A9845 and A705: aircraft crash files

3. Office of Air Force History

Aircraft record cards (RAAF Form E/E.88)
RAAF unit records

4. Royal Australian Navy Fleet Air Arm Museum

Operational diaries: 805 and 808 Squadrons
Debriefing Report – HMAS *Sydney*, 11 October 1951

5. Articles

Argent, A., 'The Army, its men and its flying machines', *Australian Army Journal*, No. 28, May 1968, pp. 3–21
Claringbould, M.J., 'Hudsons vs the first New Guinea Oscars', **www.aerothentic.com/historical/articles/HudsonsVsOscars.htm**
Crotty, D., 'One Wirraway's war', *Wartime* No. 11, p. 20
Heaton, J., 'The last Stormbird', *Journal of the Australian War Memorial*, No. 2, 1983, pp. 24–33
Kilduff, P., 'Albatros of *Jasta* 29', *Cross and Cockade (Great Britain) journal*, Vol. 20 No. 2, 1979, pp. 176–78
Owers, C. 'The Avro 504K in the RAAF', *The '14–'18 Journal*, 1989, pp. 20–29
Owers, C. 'Three two one zero', *FlyPast*, March 1985, p. 16
'Figure smash of Croesus of aviation' (career of Armand Deperdussin), *New York Times*, 7 August 1913
Royal Air Force, 'Pfalz D.XII technical report', *Cross and Cockade (Great Britain) journal*, Vol. 6 No. 1, 1975, pp. 16–27

6. Books

Anderson, P.N., *Mustangs of the RAAF and RNZAF* (Terrey Hills, NSW: Reed, 1975)
Bennett, J., *Highest traditions: the history of No. 2 Squadron RAAF* (Canberra, ACT: AGPS, 1995)
Bennett, J., *The Imperial Gift: British aeroplanes which formed the RAAF in 1921* (Maryborough, Qld: Banner Books, 1996)
Boehme, M., *JG7: the world's first jet fighter unit* (Atglen, PA, USA: Schiffer, 1992)
Boyne, W.J., *Messerschmitt Me 262: Arrow to the future* (Washington, DC: Smithsonian Institution Press, 1980)
Brown, E., *Wings of the Luftwaffe* (Shrewsbury, UK: Airlife, 1987)

Bullard, S. (trans.), *Japanese army operations in the South Pacific Area: New Britain and Papua campaigns, 1942–43* (Canberra, ACT: Australian War Memorial, 2007)

Cobby, A.H., *High adventure*, (Melbourne, Vic: Kookaburra, 1981)

Coulthard-Clark, C., *The RAAF in Vietnam*, Official History of Australia's Involvement in Southeast Asian Conflicts 1948–75, Vol. IV (Sydney, NSW: Allen & Unwin, 1995)

Coulthard-Clark, C., *Hit my smoke: targeting the enemy in Vietnam* (St Leonards, NSW: Allen & Unwin, 1997)

Chorley, W.R., *Royal Air Force Bomber Command losses of the Second World War* (Leicester, UK: Midland Counties Publications, 1992)

Cutlack, F.M., *The Australian Flying Corps*, Official History of Australia in the War of 1914–18, Vol. VIII (Sydney: Angus & Robertson, 1923)

Dierich, W., *Kampfgeschwader 'Edelweiss'* [History of KG51] (London: Ian Allen, 1973)

Emmerling, M. and Dressel, J., *Messerschmit Me 163 Komet* (West Chester, PA, USA: Schiffer, 1992)

Eather, S., *Target Charlie* (Canberra, ACT: Aerospace Publications, 1993)

Ethell, J., *Komet: the Messerschmitt 163* (Shepperton, Surrey, UK: Ian Allan Ltd, 1978)

Ethell, J., *Mustang: a documentary history* (London: Jane's, 1981)

Foreman, J and Harvey, S.E., *The Messerschmitt Me 262 combat diary* (London: Air Research Publications, 1990)

Francillon, R.J., *Japanese aircraft of the Pacific War* (London: Putnam, 1979)

Gillison, D., *Royal Australian Air Force 1939–42*, Australia in the War of 1939–45, Series 3 (Air), Vol. I (Canberra, ACT: Australian War Memorial, 1962)

Gray, P. and Thetford, O., *German aircraft of the First World War* (London: Putnam, 1970)

Green, B., *Augsburg's last eagles: colors, markings and variants of the Messerschmitt Bf 109 from June 1944 to May 1945* (Hamilton, Montana, USA: Eagle Editions, 2000)

Green, B. and Evans, B., *Stormbird colors: construction, camouflage and markings of the Me 262*, EagleFiles No. 5 (Hamilton, Montana, USA: Eagle Editions, 2003)

Grosz, P.M., *The Pfalz D.XII*, No.199 (Windsor, UK: Profile Publications, 1967)

Hobson, C., *Vietnam air losses: United States Air Force, Navy and Marine Corps fixed-wing aircraft losses in Southeast Asia 1961–1973* (Earl Shilton, Leicester, UK: Midland Publishing, 2001)

Hata, I., Izawa, Y. and Shores, C., *Japanese Army Air Force fighter units and their aces 1931–1945* (London: Grub Street, 2002)

Isaacs, K., *Military aircraft of Australia 1909–1918* (Canberra, ACT: Australian War Memorial, 1971)

Jackson, A.J. and R.T., *De Havilland aircraft since 1909* (London: Putnam, 1987)

Jane's, *All the world's aircraft* (London: Jane's, 1914–69 editions)

King, C.G., *Luck is no accident: flying in war and peace 1946–1986* (Loftus, NSW: AMHP, 2001)

Lewis, C., *Sagittarius rising* (Harmondsworth, UK: Penguin, 1977)

McAulay, L., *Six aces* (Melbourne, Vic.: Banner Books, 1991)

McKernan, M., *Here is their spirit: a history of the Australian War Memorial 1917–1990* (St Lucia, Qld: University of Queensland press, 1991)

McNeill, I. and Ekins, A., *On the offensive: the Australian Army in the Vietnam war 1967–1968*, Official History of Australia's Involvement in Southeast Asian Conflicts 1948–1975 (Crows Nest, NSW: Allen & Unwin, 2003)

Middlebrook, M. and Everitt, C., *The Bomber Command war diaries* (Harmondsworth, UK: Viking/Penguin, 1985)

Middlebrook, M., *The Peenemünde raid* (London: Allen Lane, 1982)

Mikesh, R.C., *Albatros D.Va: German fighter of World War I* (Washington, DC: Smithsonian Institution Press, 1980)

Mikesh, R.C., *Zero fighter* (London: Jane's, 1981)

Morgan, H. and Weal, J., *German jet aces of World War 2*, Osprey 17 (Botley, Oxford, UK: Osprey, 1998)

Nolan, P., *Possums and Bird Dogs: Australian Army Aviation's 161 Reconnaissance Flight in South Vietnam* (Sydney, NSW: Allen & Unwin, 2006)

Nowarra, H.J., *Messerschmitt Bf 109* (Sparkford, UK: Haynes Publishing, 1989)

O'Connell, D., *Messerschmitt Me 262: the production log 1941–1945* (Leicestershire, UK: Classic Publications, 2005)

Odgers, G., *Air war against Japan 1943–45*, Australia in the War of 1939–45, Series 3 (Air), Vol. II (Canberra, ACT: Australian War Memorial, 1957)

Odgers, G., *Royal Australian Air Force: an illustrated history* (Brookvale, NSW: Child and Henry, 1984)

Office of Air Force History, *Pathfinder collection*, Vol. 1 (Canberra, ACT: Air Power Development Centre RAAF, 2006)

Parer, R., *Flight and adventures of Parer and McIntosh* (Melbourne, Vic.: J. Roy Stevens, 1921)

Parer, R. and McIntosh, J., *The record flight from London to Calcutta* (Calcutta, India: Development Ltd, 1920)

Parnell, N. and Lynch, C., *Australian Air Force since 1911* (Sydney, NSW: Reed, 1976)

Parry, S.W. and Foreman, J., *Luftwaffe night fighter victory claims, 1939–1945*, (Walton on Thames, Surrey, UK: Air Research, 2003)

RAAF Historical Section, *Units of the Royal Australian Air Force: a concise history*, Vols. 1–10 (Canberra, ACT: AGPS, 1995)

Ransom, S. and Cammann, H., *The Me 163 rocket interceptor* (Crowborough, Sussex, UK: Classic Publications, 2002)

Robinson, A. (ed), *In the cockpit* (London: Orbis, 1979)

Sakai, S. and Caidin, M., *Samurai!* (New York: Doubleday, 1957)

Scott, P., *Emblems of the rising sun: Imperial Japanese Army Air Force unit markings* (Aldershot, UK: Hikoki, 1999)

Shores, C., *Fighter aces* (London: Hamlyn, 1975)

Southall, I., *Bluey Truscott* (Sydney, NSW: Angus & Roberton, 1958)

Späte, W., *Top secret bird: the Luftwaffe's Me 163 Komet* (Missoula, Montana, USA: Pictorial Histories, 1989)

Tallman, F., *Flying the old planes* (New York: Doubleday, 1973)

Thetford, O., *Aircraft of the Royal Air Force since 1918* (London: Putnam, 1979)

Thorpe, D.W., *Japanese Army Air Force camouflage and markings, World War II* (Fallbrook, California, USA: Aero Publishers, 1968)

Van Wyngarden, G., *Pfalz scout aces of World War 1* (Botley, UK: Osprey, 2006)

Vincent, D., *Mosquito monograph* (Highbury, SA: David Vincent, 1982)

Vincent, D., *The RAAF Hudson story (Book One)* (Highbury, SA: David Vincent, 1999)

Williams, Air Marshal Sir Richard, *These are facts* (Canberra, ACT: Australian War Memorial, 1977)

Willmott, H.P., *Zero A6M* (London: Bison, 1980)

Wilson, D., *Lion over Korea: 77 Fighter Squadron RAAF 1950–53* (Canberra, ACT: Banner Books, 1994)

Wilson, S., *Military aircraft of Australia* (Canberra, ACT: Aerospace Publications, 1994)

Wilson, S., *Aircraft of WWII* (Canberra, ACT: Aerospace Publications, 1998)

Wilson, S., *In Australian service* Australian airpower collection [many volumes] (Canberra, ACT: Aerospace Publications, 1988+)

Windrow, M.C. (ed), *Aircraft in profile* (Windsor, UK: Profile Publications, 1965–70)

Wright, K.M., *The sky was their battlefield* (Mildura, Vic.: self-published, 2002)

Ziegler, M and H.E., *Rocket fighter: the story of the Me 163* (London: Macdonald, 1963)

7. Internet websites

Government sites

Australian War Memorial **www.awm.gov.au**
National Archives of Australia **www.naa.gov.au**
World War 2 nominal roll (Department of Veterans' Affairs) **www.ww2roll.gov.au**
Royal Australian Air Force Museum **www.defence.gov.au/RAAF/raafmuseum**

Non-government sites

Australia at war (Second World War) **www.ozatwar.com**
Australian military aircraft serial numbers and histories **www.adf-serials.com**
Warbirds forum (military aviation) **www.warbirdforum.com**
Pacific aircraft wreck database **www.pacificwrecks.com**
Aces and aircraft of the First World War **www.theaerodrome.com**
History of Australian aviation 1914–1919 **www.australianflyingcorps.org**

8. Talks

Clark, C., 'The Malayan Emergency', 55th anniversary talk at AWM, 16 June 2003
Londey, P., 'Remembering 1942: Milne Bay', talk at AWM, 5 September 2002

9. Interviews

Transcripts and recordings from the sound collection of the Australian War Memorial, including the Keith Murdoch Sound Archive, have been consulted for general reference. Specific quotations have been used from the following interviews:

Wing Cdr F.J. Downing DFC (by Col David Chinn) at AWM, Sep 2005 (AWM S03826)
Flt Lt L. Morris (by Michael Nelmes) at AWM, Dec 2000 (AWM S02274)
LAC Keith Hayden (by Michael Nelmes) at Narromine Aviation Museum, Oct 2004

Notes

First World War (1914–1918)

1 The impetus for the formation of a military aviation corps dates back still earlier, to 1911, when Charles Campbell of the Australian Air League proposed to the Department of Defence that it purchase four Blériot XI monoplanes and two training gliders.

2 The two Deperdussins, although very similar, were intended for different training purposes: one for ground handling, the other for flying.

3 The same problem would re-emerge in 1919 with the arrival of Avro 504Ks.

4 Tallman, *Flying the old planes*, p. 27.

5 *New York Times*, 7 August 1913 (Career of Armand Deperdussin).

6 Renumbered 3 Squadron AFC in January 1918.

7 Knight's Cross 2nd Class with Swords (Orders of Albrecht and Saxon Merit).

8 Letter from Maj Alf Reed to Australian War Museum, 4 July 1920.

9 Information from International Committee of the Red Cross Central Tracing Agency, Geneva.

10 Clauss's biographical details and *Jasta* 29 documents courtesy of Dieter Groeschel MD, Manfred Thiemeyer via Hans Trauner (on www.theaerodrome.com forum), Yvonne Ahsman, and Richard Duiven (USA) via Chris Goddard. His name is also occasionally spelt Clausz, but appears in the above documents as Clauss.

11 Report by Neville Hewitt in *WW1 Aero*, May 1989.

12 Owers, 'The Pfalz D.XII 2600/18' (unpublished manuscript), p. 9.

13 R. Stark, *Der Jagdstaffel, unsere Heimat*, quoted in Van Wyngarden, *Pfalz scout aces of World War 1*, p. 86.

14 Bavarian Jagdstaffeln 23, 32b, 34, 35, 76, 77 and 78; other Jagdstaffeln 3, 17, 36, 37, 43, 49, 61, 64w, 65, 71, 73 and 81 (from Van Wyngarden, *Pfalz scout aces of World War 1*, p. 88).

15 Owers, 'The Pfalz D.XII 2600/18' (unpublished manuscript), p. 26.

16 Bennett, *The Imperial Gift*, pp. 40–41, citing National Archives (Victoria) file MP367/1 524/10/196.

17 An exception was a single Bristol Scout 'D' at Point Cook; however, it was rarely flown.

18 Cobby, *High adventure*, p. 29

19 The RFC became the Royal Air Force in April 1918.

20 Details of these differences are at the end of this chapter. It is no longer the Memorial's policy to repaint aircraft in markings other than their own.

21 Lewis, *Sagittarius rising*, pp. 181–82.

22 www.australianflyingcorps.org

23 Compiled from Garrison, *Australian fighter aces* 1914–1953; www.theaerodrome.com; and www.australianflyingcorps.org

24 Alberry had lost a leg in action with the army in July 1916.

25 Capt Jones reportedly survived 28 crash landings.

26 Parer, *Flight and adventures of Parer and McIntosh*, p. 213.

War in Europe (1939–1945)

1 Southall, *Bluey Truscott*, p. 82; based closely on Truscott's report to the squadron intelligence officer, PO Denys Lane Walters.

2 Wing Cdr B.E. Finucane DSO DFC and 2 Bars, had shot down 32 enemy aircraft by the time he was killed in July 1942.

3 www.adb.online.anu.edu.au.

4 National Archives of Australia, 400213 Truscott, K.W. personal file, p 36.

5 National Archives of Australia, 400213 Truscott, K.W. casualty file, p. 44

6 Fajtl, *I flew with the 313rd*; the author was the squadron commander.

7 National Archives of Australia, 257414 Bungey, R.W. casualty file, p. 10.

8 The 'a' refers to the wing design, which accommodated eight .303-in machine-guns.

9 O'Byrne's logbook records a different Spitfire on this and the following day.

10 Unidentified newspaper cutting included in papers of Warrant Officer T.E. Osborn DFC, AWM PR87/014.

11 Middlebrook, *The Peenemünde raid*, p.172.

12 Parry and Foreman, *Luftwaffe night fighter victory claims 1939–1945*, p. 104.

13 Pathfinder units were responsible for marking a target to make it visible to the main bombing force. The master bomber tactic was first used three months earlier by Wing Commander Guy Gibson during the most famous precision night attack, the 'Dambusters' raid.

14 'V' stood for *Vergeltungswaffe* or vengeance weapon. The V-1 and V-2 were Germany's retaliation for Britain's 'terror attacks' on German cities.

15 Von Braun went to America after the war and designed the Saturn V rocket, which took men to the Moon.

16 There was also a tragic downside to this, as some 20,000 slave labourers were to die there from malnutrition and overwork.

17 McKernan, *Here is their spirit*, p. 253.

18 Information from John Beaman via Matt Thompson-Moltzen.

19 Information from Matt Thompson-Moltzen.

20 The G-6 in the collection of the US National Air and Space Museum, for example, had been stripped of paint so that no clues of its service history remained.

21 Numerous variations are published; this figure is from Nowarra, *Messerschmitt Bf 109*, p. 297.

22 The American P-47M Thunderbolt, with a level speed of 750 km/h. No Me 262s met with British Meteor jet fighters.

23 Foreman and Harvey, *The Messerschmitt Me 262 combat diary*, p. 179.

24 Dierich, *Kampfgeschwader 'Edelweiss'*, p. 100.

25 Research into 500200's UK period courtesy of Ken Merrick and Phil Butler, c. 1981.

26 *Werknummer* 112372 is now displayed at RAF Museum Cosford, UK.

27 O'Connell, *Messerschmitt Me 262: the production log 1941–1945*, p. 156. Me 262s built under Regensburg administration were codenamed Me 609.

28 Undated letter from P. Dale to Military Heraldry and Technology Section, AWM, early 1990s. A detailed account is recorded in Foreman and Harvey, *The Messerschmitt Me 262 combat diary*, pp. 152–55.

29 Later Squadron Leader with DFC and 2 Bars. Gaze was a former wingman of Group Captain Douglas 'Tin Legs' Bader.

30 Correspondence from Tony Gaze to AWM, quoted in Heaton, 'The Last Stormbird', *Journal of the Australian War Memorial*, No. 2, 1983, p. 29.

31 Foreman and Harvey, *The Messerschmitt Me 262 combat diary*, Appendix VI.

32 Boyne, *Messerschmitt Me 262*, p. 55.

33 Foreman and Harvey, *The Messerschmitt Me 262 combat diary*, Appendix I.

34 Brown, *Wings of the Luftwaffe*, p. 68.

35 Boehme, *JG7: the world's first jet fighter unit*, p. 44.

36 Boehme, *JG7: the world's first jet fighter unit*, p. 42.

37 Account adapted from report by FO Haslope in Ransom and Cammann, *The Me 163 rocket interceptor*, p. 277.

38 The plan, instigated by *Major* Wolfgang Späte, who headed the Me 163 experimental unit at Peenemünde-West, was for airfields to line the primary Allied bomber routes through Germany.

39 Reinhard Opitz quoted in Ransom and Cammann, *The Me 163 rocket interceptor*, p. 312.

40 Ziegler, *Rocket fighter*, p. 126.

41 Totalled from production table in Ransom and Cammann, *The Me 163 rocket interceptor*, p. 426.

War in the Pacific (1941–1945)

1 AWM Private Records manuscript MSS1512.

2 Gillison, *Royal Australian Air Force 1939–1942*, p. 91.

3 Unpublished manuscript: Swan, 'Tiger tails, kat-tails and some digressions' (1997).

4 These squadrons, numbered in the range 450 to 467, were formed in accordance with Article XV of the EATS agreement, which allowed the dominions to operate squadrons of their own national air forces. In practice, each had a mix of British and Commonwealth nationals in their personnel.

5 The remainder of Australian production went to South Africa, Rhodesia, the Netherlands East Indies, India, New Zealand, America, and Burma.

6 Reports vary considerably regarding Archer's height and the enemy's bearing. He initially reported that he was at treetop height, and that the enemy had been flying at the same height and overtook him on his left. Subsequent reports give Archer's height as between 200 and 1,000 ft.

7 'Zeke' was the Allied codename for the Zero (see Zero chapter).

8 Bullard (trans.), *Japanese Army operations in the South Pacific Area: New Britain and Papua campaigns, 1942–43*, p. 190.

9 Gillison, *Royal Australian Air Force 1939–42*, p. 665.

10 Gillison, *Royal Australian Air Force 1939–42*, p. 672.

11 Office of Air Force History, *Pathfinder collection*, Vol. 1, p. 109: 'Airborne forward air control – a first for the RAAF'.

12 Nancarrow later recalled that a man in one of the jeeps was injured and possibly killed, although his identity has not been established.

13 Named 12 Repair and Salvage Unit prior to January 1945.

14 RAAF Beaufort fatalities made up of 467 in RAAF units and 38 in RAF units. Some 122 were with 100 Squadron. Figures researched by AWM volunteers Alan Storr and Derek Fowler.

15 Elevator trim tabs regulate the force needed to be exerted by the pilot to hold the aircraft in level flight, in response to different load conditions.

16 Odgers, *Royal Australian Air Force*, p. 100.

17 RAAF Historical Section, *Units of the Royal Australian Air Force*, Vol. 2, p. 41.

18 Londey, 'Remembering 1942: Milne Bay' (AWM talk, 5 September 2002).

19 Gillison, *Royal Australian Air Force 1939–1942*, p. 617.

20 Letter from Wilson to Military Heraldry and Technology Section, 1992.

21 Claringbould, 'Hudsons vs the first New Guinea Oscars', www.aerothentic.com/historical/articles/HudsonsVsOscars.htm .

22 Shindo, 'Japanese air operations in New Guinea', *Journal of the Australian War Memorial*, 34, June 2001.

23 Vincent, *The RAAF Hudson story*, ch. 6.

24 Parnell and Lynch, *Australian Air Force since 1911*, p. 67.

25 Clark, 'The Malayan Emergency', 55th anniversary talk at AWM, 16 June 2003.

26 Quoted in Robinson (ed.) *In the cockpit*, p. 95.

27 King, *Luck is no accident*, p. 129.

28 More than half a century later, in 2005, 87 Squadron was re-formed as part of the RAAF Aerospace Operational Support Group to provide intelligence and combat targeting expertise to the operational and tactical levels of the air force.

29 Vincent, *Mosquito monograph*, pp. 219–20.

30 Plus numerous examples in European War service with 456 and 464 Squadrons RAAF; the former also flew various night fighter (NF) marks.

31 Added to this number are numerous of the other Australian marks converted from FB.40s.

32 Commanding Officer monthly report, 2 OTU, Feb 1945 (Office of Air Force History).

33 Wright, *The sky was their battlefield*, p. 17.

34 RAAF Historical Section, *Units of the Royal Australian Air Force*, Vol. 8, p. 63.

35 Ethell, *Mustang: a documentary history*, pp. 10–11.

36 Some Mustangs had the N-9 gunsight fitted, replaced by the Mk IIL in late 1945.

37 Arguably the best four to reach production were the Kawanishi N1K-J *Shiden-Kai*, the Mitsubishi J2M *Raiden*, the Nakajima Ki-84 *Hayate* and the Kawasaki Ki-100.

38 The link between Sakai's account and the loss of Cowan's Hudson was made as a result of research by David Vincent (Adelaide), Bob Piper (Canberra) and Sakai's biographer, Henry Sakaida (USA).

39 Sakai and Caidin, *Samurai!*, p. 164. Similar accounts are recorded by Henry Sakaida in *Imperial Japanese Navy aces 1937–45*, p. 28, and by Bob Piper et al in *Australian Story*, ABC-TV, 1 July 2002.

40 The group was named after its earlier base of Tainan in Formosa (Taiwan).

41 http://forum.axishistory.com.

42 Sakai and Caidin, *Samurai!*, p. 164.

43 www.pacificwrecks.com.

44 Although designed to fly from aircraft carriers, the Zero was equally a land-based fighter.

45 Owers, in *FlyPast*, March 1985, p. 16.

46 One report states that the fin marked V-173 is a replacement, fitted in 1972 in lieu of the damaged original. Interestingly, two Tainan Zeros numbered V-172 and V-174 had been captured by the Chinese in November 1941. (www.j-aircraft.com/research/WarPrizes).

47 Associated Press, 10 August 2000.

48 Mikesh, *Zero fighter*, p. 3.

49 Only in 1944 did Japanese aircraft production figures surpass America's 1941 figures.

50 Shindo, *Japanese air operations in New Guinea*, ch. 3, at http://ajrp.awm.gov.au/ajrp.

51 Richard L. Dunn, *Double lucky?* at www.warbirdforum.com/lucky11.htm, citing ATIS (Allied Translator and Interpreter Service) documents.

52 www.pacificwrecks.com/airfields/png/alexishafen.

53 www.pacificwrecks.com/airfields/png/alexishafen.

54 Until 1957 a K-21 Sally, which had reportedly bombed Darwin five times, was stored at RAAF Base Canberra.

55 The remains of the 523 known Japanese who died in Australia during the war are now buried at Cowra, NSW.

56 Source: James Long, USA.

57 www.pacificwrecks.com/aircraft/ki-43/5465.html.

Korean War (1950–1953)

1 The maximum height at which a climb rate of 30 m per minute can be maintained.

2 Compressibility problems (mentioned in the Mustang chapter) are substantially less severe with a swept-wing design, and higher speeds can be achieved without buffeting and loss of control.

3 On this occasion the MiGs may have been manned not by Russians but by less experienced Chinese or North Korean pilots.

4 Gilmour also flew the Memorial's Wirraway while at Point Cook in 1952.

5 Fighter aircraft – mainly Tempests, Spitfires, Mosquitos and Mustangs – accounted for 1,759 (40 per cent) of the 4,261 V-1s brought down.

6 Postwar RAF nomenclature: 'F' (for fighter) in place of 'Mk' (mark), and Arabic numerals in place of Roman numerals.

7 Wilson, *Lion over Korea*, pp. 159–60.

8 Wilson, *Lion over Korea*, p. 97.

9 RAAF Historical Section, *Units of the RAAF: a concise history*, Vol . 2, p. 59.

10 Wilson, *In Australian service* (vol. entitled *The Meteor, Sabre and Mirage*), p. 25. MiG loss figures are uncertain, as some aircraft claimed as shot down but not observed to crash may have survived.

11 Information from Debriefing Report – HMAS *Sydney*, 11 October 1951.

12 Information courtesy of Memorial staff John White and John Kemister.

13 At the same time, Roman numerals gave way to Arabic numerals in aircraft model designations.

Vietnam War (1962–1975)

1 McNeill and Ekins, *On the offensive*, p. 119

2 Among them was Iroquois A2-1019, which would join the Memorial's collection shortly after the Sioux.

3 Two DFCs also went to New Zealanders serving in the unit; one of the Australians also received an American DFC.

4 Sources include Nolan, *Possums and Bird Dogs*, and www.161recceflt.org.au.

5 The circulation of an anti-corrosive preservative fluid in the engine.

6 Nolan, *Possums and Bird Dogs*, pp. 211–13.

7 The nickname Huey came from the original designation of the Iroquois, HU-1.

8 Details from letter to AWM from Clive Cotter, 10 May 1984.

9 Source of quotations: interview with Les Morris by Michael Nelmes at AWM, 15 Dec 2000 (AWM S02274) with confirmations from his log book.

10 Minister for Veterans' Affairs, the Hon. Bruce Billson MP, media release 16 Feb 2007.

11 The UH-1B model of the Iroquois had a shorter cabin than the UH-1D and H which replaced it.

12 In 1986 the UH-1Hs were transferred to the army, and the last were retired in 2007.

13 A process of chemically detecting traces of human activity from the air.

14 Coulthard-Clark, *The RAAF in Vietnam*, p. 144.

15 Releasing the spring-loaded control column projects it out of the way of the pilot's legs before ejection. Interview by Col David Chinn with Wing Cdr F.J. Downing DFC, 15 Sep 2005, AWM S03826.

16 On a night-time Combat Skyspot mission four months earlier on 3 November 1970, A84-231 and its crew had gone missing in the Da Nang region and were never found.

17 From US HQ PACAF report *The RAAF in SEA* [South-East Asia] 30 September 1970.

18 Interview by Col David Chinn with Wing Cdr F.J. Downing DFC, 15 Sep 2005, AWM S03826.

19 Correspondence from Gp Capt J.G. Gazely to Col David Chinn (AWM), April 2005.

20 Coulthard-Clark, *The RAAF in Vietnam*, p. 195.

21 Correspondence from Richard O'Ferrall to Col David Chinn (AWM), April 2005.

22 Major George Constable, the officer commanding, shot down in a Cessna Bird Dog in May 1968.

23 G. Hill-Smith in Nolan, *Possums and Bird Dogs*, p. 157.

24 Information courtesy of Bruce Cameron.

25 Nolan, *Possums and Bird Dogs*, p. 198.

26 In 2008 the Memorial put on display the bridge from HMAS *Brisbane*; it joined a 5-in gun mount from *Brisbane* already in place at the rear of the main Memorial building.

27 Nolan, *Possums and Bird Dogs*, p. 164.

28 Nolan, *Possums and Bird Dogs*, p. 163.

29 G. Hill-Smith in Nolan, *Possums and Bird Dogs*, p. 164.

30 www.adf-serials.com.

31 The abbreviation FAC is also used for a pilot who is a forward air controller.

32 Coulthard-Clark, *The RAAF in Vietnam*, pp. 273–74.

33 Coulthard-Clark, *Hit my smoke*, p. 143.

34 Coulthard-Clark, *Hit my smoke*, p. xvii.

35 Coulthard-Clark, *Hit my smoke*, p. xiv.

36 Coulthard-Clark, *Hit my smoke*, pp. xviii–xix.

37 Coulthard-Clark, *Hit my smoke*, p. 145.

38 Coulthard-Clark, *Hit my smoke*, pp. 133–34.

39 Hobson, *Vietnam air losses: United States Air Force, Navy and Marine Corps fixed-wing aircraft losses in Southeast Asia 1961–1973*, App. 4.
With thanks to Darrel Whitcomb and Peter Condon (FAC Association) for their assistance with the Bronco chapter.

Index